IMAGES
of America

Fort Worth's Oakhurst Neighborhood

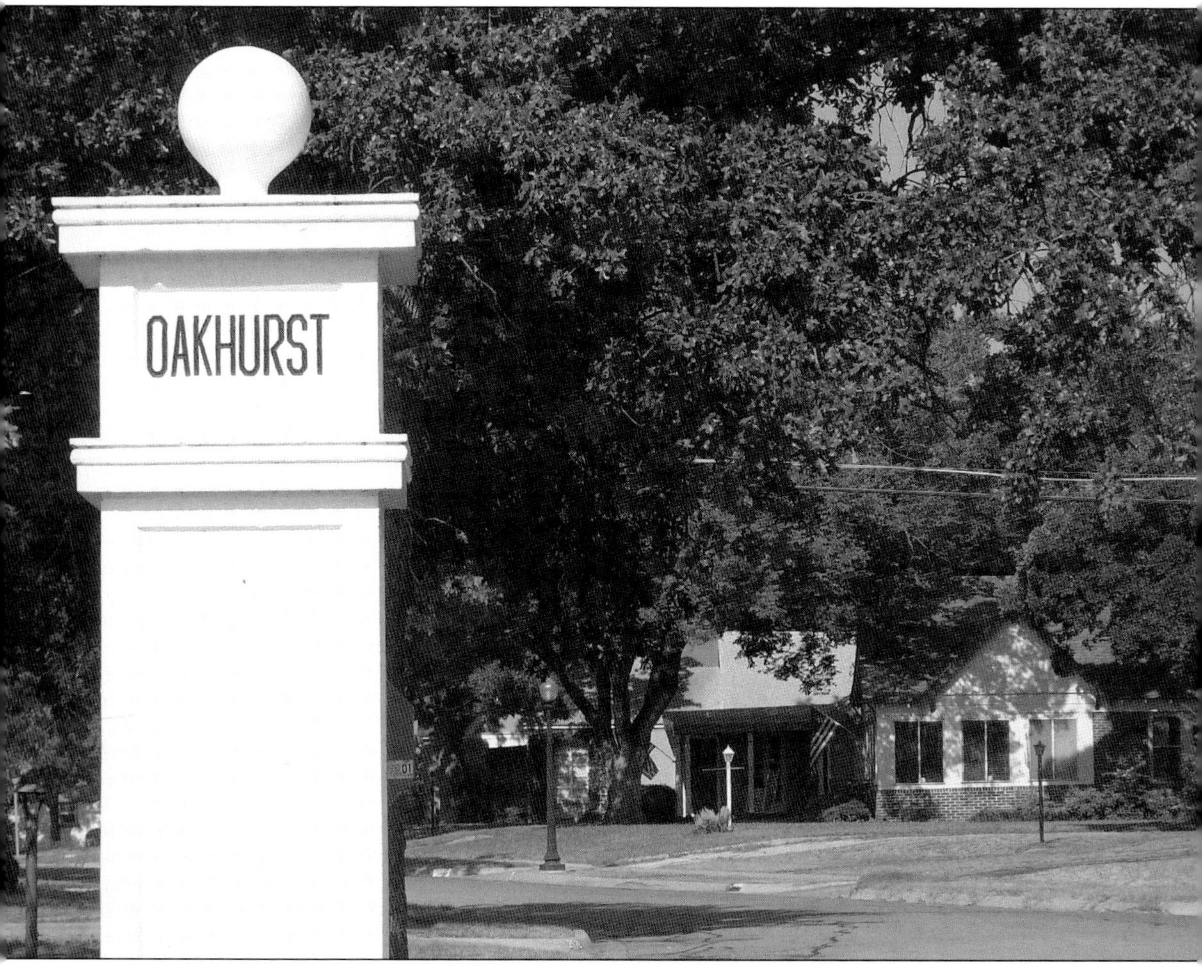

Oakhurst's columns have marked the entrance to the neighborhood at Daisy Lane and North Sylvania Avenue since its development in 1924. Columns also stand at the corner of North Sylvania Avenue and Watauga Road, and they once stood at the corner of North Sylvania and Yucca Avenues. They define Oakhurst as a distinct place within Riverside. (Courtesy of Doyle Willis Jr.)

On the Cover: This is a 1938 photograph of Marthe Frances Brown (left) and her Oakhurst playmate Janiece Wanamaker at 2312 Primrose Avenue. Oakhurst promoters asserted that "plentiful sunshine and fresh air are the rightful heritage of every boy and girl and those poor unfortunates who must live in crowded cities, playing in dirty streets, breathing dusty, germ-laden air will miss the keenest joys of childhood." Oakhurst, they said, was the perfect place for children. (Courtesy of Fran Brown Kerlin.)

IMAGES
of America

FORT WORTH'S OAKHURST NEIGHBORHOOD

Libby Willis

ARCADIA
PUBLISHING

ISBN 978-1-4671-3116-2

Published by Arcadia Publishing
Charleston, South Carolina

Printed in the United States of America

Library of Congress Control Number: 2013951498

For all general information, please contact Arcadia Publishing:
Telephone 843-853-2070
Fax 843-853-0044
E-mail sales@arcadiapublishing.com
For customer service and orders:
Toll-Free 1-888-313-2665

Visit us on the Internet at www.arcadiapublishing.com

Dedicated to the memory of John James and Duffy Lee, and to the enduring legacy of Ray Jefferson, Fran Brown Kerlin, Beverly and Dwight Mason, Beverly Sharp Germany, and Paul Griffin, who keep Oakhurst's history alive

Contents

ACKNOWLEDGMENTS

Dr. Rick Selcer, historian and former Oakhurst resident, deserves great credit for being the first to encourage me to compile this book. He heard my lecture on Oakhurst in September 2012 at the Billy W. Sills Center For Archives at the Fort Worth Independent School District and suggested the book.

So many shared their memories and images in personal visits or put out "calls for pictures" on Facebook, by e-mail, or by phone. Doyle Willis Jr. was my invaluable right arm, picking up photographs and taking and sharing his own. I am especially grateful to Ray Jefferson and Fran Brown Kerlin for sharing their own images and introducing me to others who shared photographs.

Thanks to every individual, family, and organization for lending photographs, especially to those who went "above and beyond." They deserve special mention. They are Susan Kline, Beverly Sharp Germany, Delia Brelsford Shiflet, Mary Womack Brelsford, Leslie James, Mildred Hogan, Beverly Mason, Wendy Vann Roach, Frances Lott Turella, Sue Shugart Drautz, Kathryn Dunson Wicker, Anna Beth Robinson, Dr. Ken Kirkham, Lazell Lambert Banowsky, and Mildred Lucas and Lucas Funeral Home. Others, like Nancy Ormston, Yve Martin, and Paul Griffin, gave me a tip or a contact that pointed the way to great history and photographs.

I particularly want to recognize the following organizations for their invaluable assistance. I note special helpers at each institution. The accompanying abbreviations appear with the photographs in this book: the Fort Worth Chamber of Commerce (FWCC), Marilyn Gilbert and Monta Noe; the Fort Worth Library's Genealogy, History, and Archives Unit (FWL), Renee Gomez; the TCU Library's Special Collections, Sarah Swain; the *Fort Worth Star-Telegram* Collection, in Special Collections, the University of Texas at Arlington (FWSTC/SCUTA), Cathy Spitzenberger; Tarrant County Archives, Dr. Dawn Youngblood; the Lyndon Baines Johnson Library and Museum, Chris Banks; Amon Carter Riverside High School; the Billy W. Sills Center for Archives at the Fort Worth Independent School District (BWSCA/FWISD), Lenna Hughes and Roy Housewright; Faith United Methodist Church archives (Faith UMC), Max Hill and Sallie Littlepage; the Oakhurst Historic District, listed in the National Register of Historic Places (OHD); Newsbank/Genealogy Bank (NGB); and Oakhurst Presbyterian Church, Thylis Chambless. Images from the author's collection are noted as AC. And thanks, of course, to Laura Bruns, my Arcadia editor.

INTRODUCTION

Oakhurst is a neighborhood in the Riverside area of Fort Worth, 2.8 miles north and east of downtown Fort Worth. Beginning in 1849, Texas pioneers settled Riverside, the area that is today bounded by the Trinity River and Interstate 35, Beach Street, Interstate 30, and Northeast 28th Street. Early settlers of Riverside included Charles B. Daggett, who owned and operated Daggett's ferry across the Trinity River and also owned the land that became Mount Olivet and Oakhurst.

Riverside was a rural community for its first 75 years. Many of its early residents were produce farmers, and a number were employees of several Riverside nurseries, including Baker Brothers Nursery. Riverside was a prosperous and growing rural community and suburb with schools, churches, businesses, and fine homes when the City of Fort Worth doubled its size by annexing it and many other suburbs in 1922. Annexation resulted in improved municipal services, including streetcars, buses, and firefighting and police services. These services allowed large-scale residential development to take place north of the original Riverside community.

In 1924, John P. King, owner of the King Candy Company in downtown Fort Worth, looked across the Trinity River and spotted acreage he thought would be perfect for the development of Oakhurst, "a sensibly restricted suburban residential district which the average family can afford—where life will be better." Typical Oakhurst deed restrictions included 35-foot front setbacks, the requirement that houses be built of brick, and the prohibition of commercial businesses in the neighborhood. King, along with his brother Henry and V.S. Wardlaw, created the Oakhurst Land Company, Inc., and began to sell lots for development.

The original development of the Oakhurst Addition, part of 175 acres owned by the Oakhurst Land Company, was one block deep and nine blocks wide, bounded by North Sylvania Avenue, Mapleleaf Street, Yucca Avenue, and Watauga Road. The second phase of development included the building of houses on the same streets, as well as on Primrose, Marigold, Honeysuckle, Carnation, Goldenrod, and Lotus Avenues, and Daisy Lane west from Mapleleaf Street to Balsam Street and Bluebonnet Drive (including Smilax Avenue, Marigold to Oakhurst Scenic Drive, and the east and west sides of Bluebonnet Drive to Wisteria Court).

In 1946, the West Oakhurst Addition, formerly known as Daggett's Woods, was platted. It extended west from Bluebonnet Drive at Wisteria Court to Oakhurst Scenic Drive. The streets in West Oakhurst are Bluebird, Morning Glory, and West Lotus Avenues and Cardinal Lane.

John P. and Henry King were evidently attracted to the nationally significant "Olmsted style" in suburban planning, with its curvilinear street patterns, parklike settings, and emphasis on nature. They developed the Oakhurst neighborhood around what would become a centrally located park. Their promotional brochure about the neighborhood emphasized that "everything grows in Oakhurst." One of the biggest selling points to potential buyers was that residents could grow their own orchards in their deep backyards and eat their own produce.

The neighborhood even included its own artesian water well, and, for a time, Oakhurst artesian water was available to residents from pipes separate from the City of Fort Worth water. Amenities included the Oakhurst columns at the ceremonial entrance to the neighborhood at Daisy Lane and North Sylvania Avenue, and also at Watauga Road and North Sylvania. Another feature was common green areas.

The Kings also promoted Oakhurst as Fort Worth's "most convenient and desirable residential neighborhood," only eight minutes from downtown. They emphasized the benefits of Oakhurst as a neighborhood where "high-class, restricted residential" lots were available for a modest sum, where families could raise their children in a healthy outdoor environment, and where happiness and independence were plentiful.

In the Depression years, the large, deep Oakhurst lots made "survival gardens" possible. Families were able to grow corn, pole beans, black-eyed peas, carrots, onions, potatoes, okra, tomatoes, figs, persimmons, and pecans. That ability helped tremendously with each family's income.

In those same years, minstrels would come and play a banjo and a trumpet or clarinet for 25¢ or 50¢ and walk the streets of Oakhurst and Sylvania. Beggars and hoboes knocked on Oakhurst doors. Depending on the hospitality they found, they would mark a pole near that house to note that its inhabitants would help a stranger, or that they would not.

Over the past 90 years, Oakhurst has developed into a neighborhood of attractive, mid-sized period revival houses. The most common house styles in the oldest parts of the neighborhood are Tudor homes and bungalows. In the newer part of the neighborhood, West Oakhurst, post–World War II homes and Ranch-style houses are the most common. The original Oakhurst Addition accounts for about two-thirds of all the houses, the great majority of which were built in the 1920s and 1930s. The West Oakhurst Addition comprises about 200 houses, a good many of which were built in the late 1940s and early 1950s.

The Oakhurst neighborhood is immediately adjacent to Oakhurst Scenic Drive, a Depression-era park drive that links the neighborhood to Belknap Street and downtown. The construction of Oakhurst Scenic Drive and the East Belknap Street Bridge were part of Fort Worth's great building program of the 1930s. In fact, Oakhurst Scenic Drive between Belknap Street and Watauga Road still features stone drainage culverts and pilings from that time.

Oakhurst is a charming early-20th-century neighborhood that retains many of its original characteristics. Because of its initial and subsequent development plans, produced by the well-known Kansas City landscape architecture firm Hare & Hare; its concentration of period architecture, from the 1920s through mid-century modern homes; and its connection to people of local and national fame; it is certainly noteworthy as one of Fort Worth's most interesting historic neighborhoods. Without question, Oakhurst is unique in Fort Worth.

One

John P. King

Fort Worth Leading Light and Oakhurst Developer

It is almost impossible to overstate the importance of early businessman, Oakhurst developer, and civic influence John Porter King to Fort Worth. Each of his real estate ventures still stand as testaments to his vision, commitment to design excellence, and perseverance. Oakhurst's history is linked to all of his accomplishments and takes on added importance in the development history of Fort Worth because of its association with King.

King was an earlier version of Amon Carter. When Carter came to Fort Worth in 1906, King was already a well-established businessman. King brokered real estate deals, built businesses, had a major impact on the development of Fort Worth's city government, left notable architecture and neighborhood developments, and was immensely respected by those who worked for and with him. He was born in Brenham during the Civil War and moved with his parents to Fort Worth in 1870. He graduated from TCU forerunner Add-Ran College and was elected Tarrant County clerk in 1888. After he married Lorena Blair in 1897, his first business was the Southern Ice & Cold Storage Company, founded in 1898. He began his flagship business, the King Candy Company, six years later. It would eventually distribute "King's Candies for America's Queens" in more than 20 states.

Besides his candy company, King held numerous board memberships and was prominent in the Fort Worth Chamber of Commerce, the Community Chest, and Fort Worth Power & Light, for which he was a director. He was president of four land development companies, including the Oakhurst Land Company and the Fort Worth Truck & Trailer Company, and he was vice president of the West Texas Production Company, an oil-drilling venture.

King was also known as the father of the council-manager form of government in Fort Worth. Though he was often urged to run for mayor, he steadfastly refused, preferring to work behind the scenes. He organized the Good Government League in the early 1920s, which worked to get a new council-manager charter adopted by the voters in 1925. He was a power behind the establishment of Camp Bowie and helped revamp the board of education and Tarrant County Water Control and Improvement District No. 1. In 1928, the Exchange Club honored him with the Golden Deeds Award as the city's most outstanding citizen for his huge impact on Fort Worth civic and governmental affairs for more than 50 years.

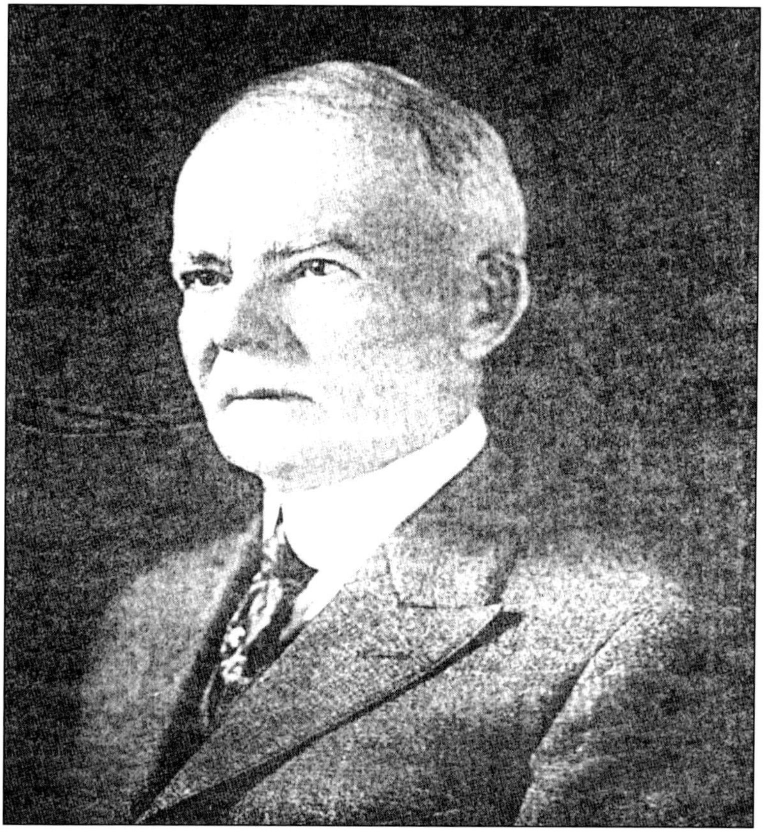

John P. King is seen here about 1922, during the time the City of Fort Worth annexed Riverside and numerous other areas into the city. King began the development of Oakhurst in 1924. He had already had a very successful business career before he started Oakhurst's development, when he was about 62. (OHD.)

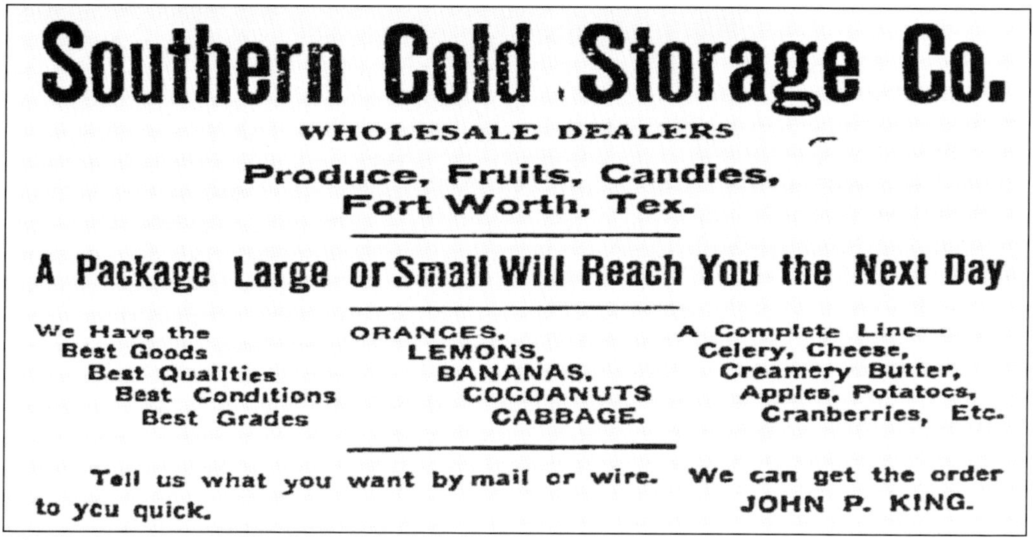

John P. King's Southern Cold Storage Company predated the King Candy Company, although he said the idea for the candy company started with the need for his produce salesmen to carry a product more exotic than fruits and vegetables. That item was candy. Eventually, King sold his wholesale produce company to the concern that went on to become industry giant Ben E. Keith. "Maybe I sold the wrong business," King said, "for just look what Ben E. Keith has done with the produce business." (NGB.)

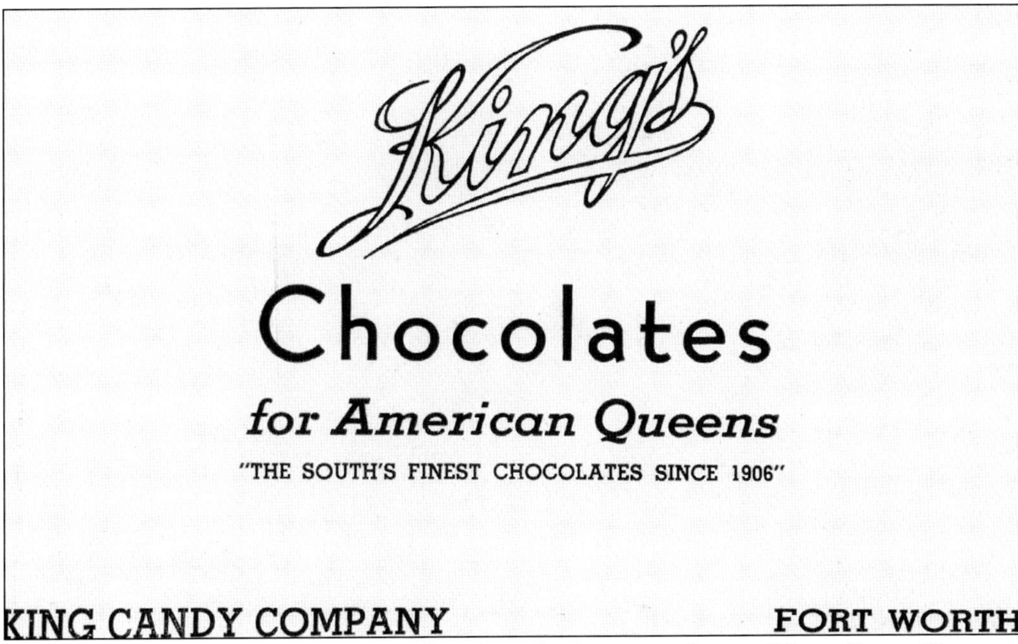

John P. King used this slogan, "King's Chocolates for American Queens," for well over 50 years to promote the candy produced at his East Ninth Street factory. He got the idea for the slogan one day from a passing reporter. "Hello there, Mr. King's Candy for American Queens," the reporter said. Soon, King began placing the phrase on every box of his chocolates. (FWCC.)

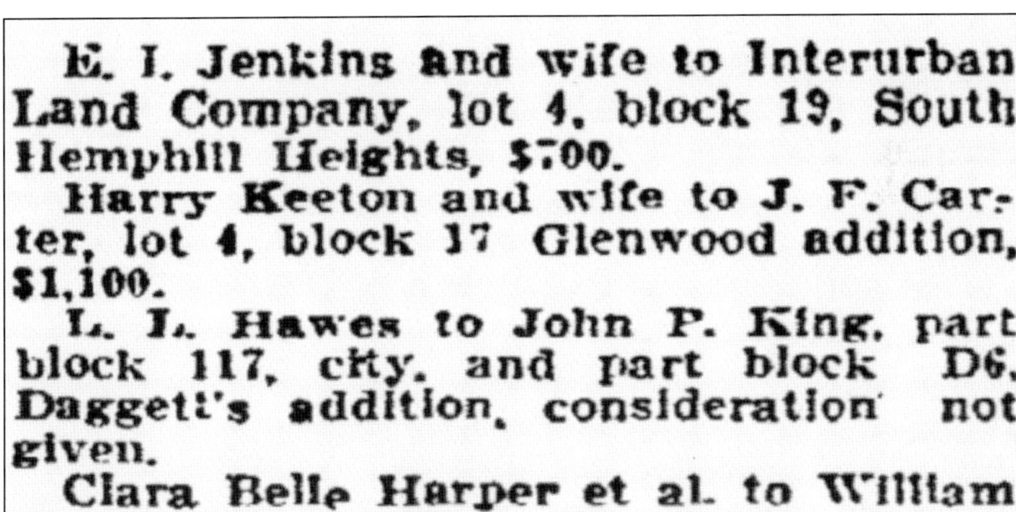

E. I. Jenkins and wife to Interurban Land Company, lot 4, block 19, South Hemphill Heights, $700.

Harry Keeton and wife to J. F. Carter, lot 4, block 17 Glenwood addition, $1,100.

L. L. Hawes to John P. King, part block 117, city, and part block D6, Daggett's addition, consideration not given.

Clara Belle Harper et al. to William Capps, lot 21, block 22, South Hemphill Heights, $300.

This excerpt from the *Fort Worth Star-Telegram*'s March 26, 1910, "Day's Transfers in Real Estate" column shows that King was purchasing land for investment as early as that date. One of King's skills, used in business and real estate development, was to always think and plan ahead, and real estate development was always a strong interest of his. (NGB.)

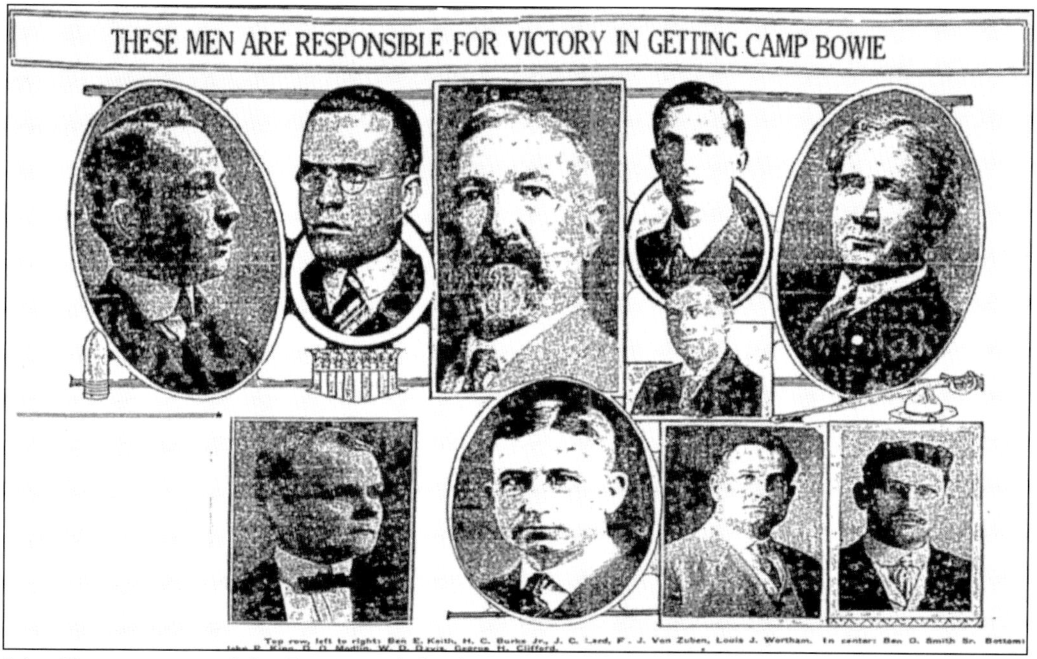

THESE MEN ARE RESPONSIBLE FOR VICTORY IN GETTING CAMP BOWIE

Top row, left to right: Ben E. Keith, H. C. Burke Jr., J. C. Lord, F. J. Von Zuben, Louis J. Wortham. In center: Ben O. Smith Sr. Bottom: John P. King, D. O. Modlin, W. D. Davis, George H. Clifford.

John King was one of the Fort Worth leaders who together amassed over 2,000 rent-free acres to attract the federal government's establishment of Camp Bowie during World War I. In 1919, King, William Bryce, D.O. Modlin, and others sold 330 acres in Arlington Heights known as "the Hill Crest Addition" to Tulsa developers Frank and Fred Hammond for $200,000. This project set King and his family on the course for their permanent success with real estate projects, including Oakhurst and Monticello. In this collage, King is on the bottom row, far left. (NGB.)

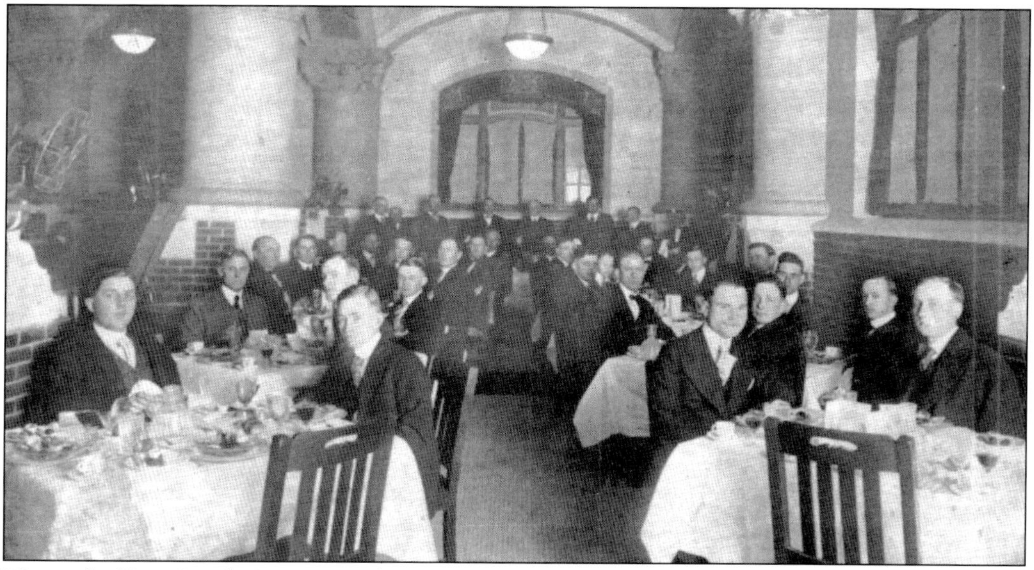

This is the King Candy Company sales force at a 10th-anniversary celebration at the Metropolitan Hotel in downtown Fort Worth in 1916. In 1922, John P. King opened King's Candy Store and Tea Rooms at 810 Main Street, which was referred to in the *Fort Worth Star-Telegram* as "the Store Beautiful." The newspaper also quoted "an attractive gowned" visitor as saying, "I'm sure Mr. King won't spoil it with a jazz band." (FWCC.)

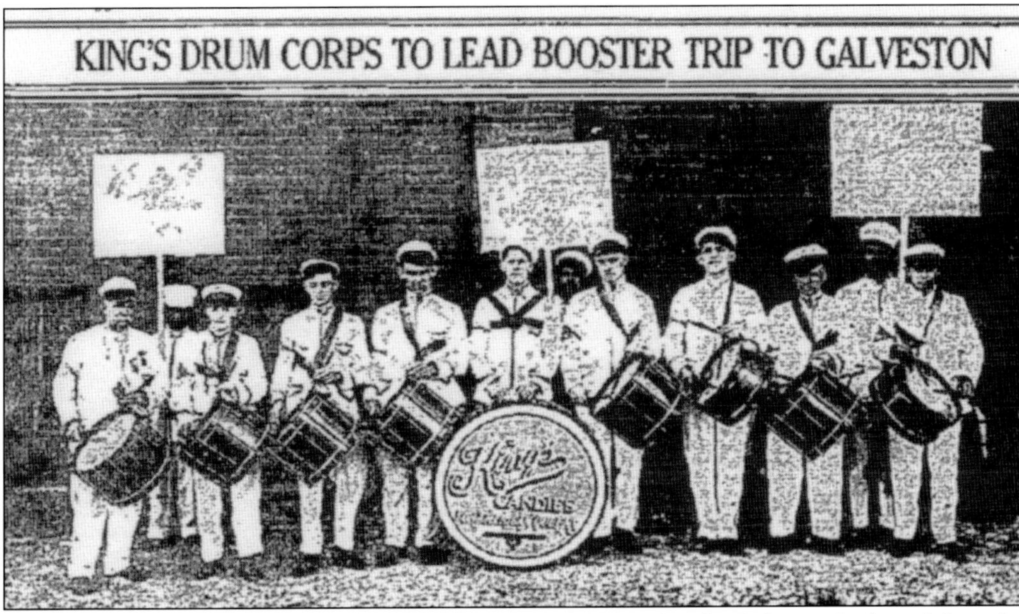

On July 4, 1916, members of John P. King's Drum Corps finished their whirlwind four-day tour of Texas in Galveston, parading through downtown promoting King's Candies in front of thousands. King estimated in 1909 that Fort Worthians were consuming seven tons of candy a week. "We have always made quality our first consideration," King said, "and this is the reason for our success." (NGB.)

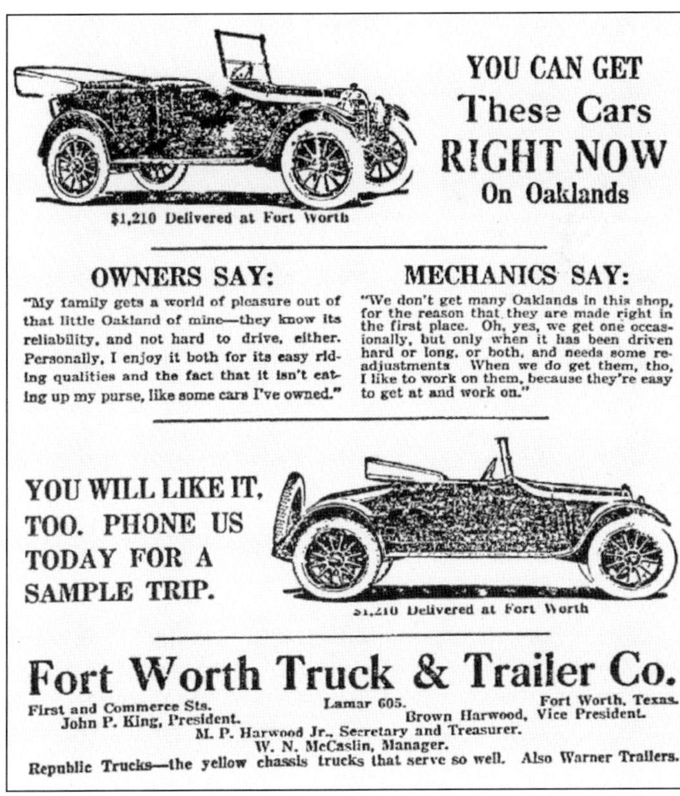

This 1918 advertisement for the Fort Worth Truck & Trailer Company shows the wide variety of businesses King owned. He was president of a number of car and truck businesses on top of his ice, cold storage, and candy company ventures. King also threw in his lot with at least one company that drilled for West Texas oil. (NGB.)

ANNOUNCING CHANGE IN NAME

A charter has been granted by the Secretary of State changing the name of the undersigned to "KING ICE COMPANY," therefore, beginning with this date all business heretofore transacted under the name of the undersigned will hereafter be in the name of the "KING ICE COMPANY."

The new company by the addition of a 75-ton Electric Unit is increasing its present ice capacity from 85 tons to 160 tons daily, and when finished will have the largest ice plant in this city.

There is no change in ownership of the KING ICE COMPANY. The owners and officers are John P. King, President; Olin Davis, Vice President; Porter King, Secretary; Henry King, Treasurer.

Extending our deep appreciation to our patrons and to the public in general for the many favors shown us, we are,

Very respectfully,

SOUTHERN ICE COMPANY

King was always a family man, as illustrated by this 1921 advertisement announcing the change in name from the Southern Ice Company to the King Ice Company. John P. King served as president, his son Porter was secretary, and his brother Henry, an agent for the Oakhurst Land Company, was treasurer. Olin Davis was vice president. Davis was still giving birthday parties for King well into his 80s. (NGB.)

OAK KNOLL ADDITION (Riverside) lying between Grapevine rd and Parrish rd
Oakes Leonard (Gertrude) polisher Panther Mfg Co rms 1313 Main
" Leonidas barber 1265 Evans av
" Littleton H waiter rms 1208 E Leuda
" Wesley rms 1010 E 4th
OAKHURST LAND CO, John P King Pres, Henry King V-Pres and Agent, Frank P Culver Jr Sec, Wm D Morris Asst Sec, Owners and Agents Oakhurst Addition N E Fort Worth, General Office 906-7 First National Bank Bldg, Tel Lamar 2777, Addition Office Lamar 6480
OAKLAND MOTOR CARS, Gladish Motor Co Distributors, 300 Throckmorton, Tel Laar 7660
" Studio The (J E Long) photogs 208½ W 6th
OAKLAWN ADDITION, 6½ mi se of Court House e of Oaklawn Stop on Cleburne Interurban, ½ mi s of Masonic Home

The 1926 Fort Worth City Directory listed the Oakhurst Land Company phone number in the First National Bank Building, as well as the number of the sales office, at 1805 North Sylvania Avenue. Sales of lots picked up considerably after the Fort Worth City Council passed an ordinance allowing the North Texas Traction Company to operate buses in conjunction with the streetcar system. A line to Oakhurst, one of the first, was installed as an experiment. (FWL.)

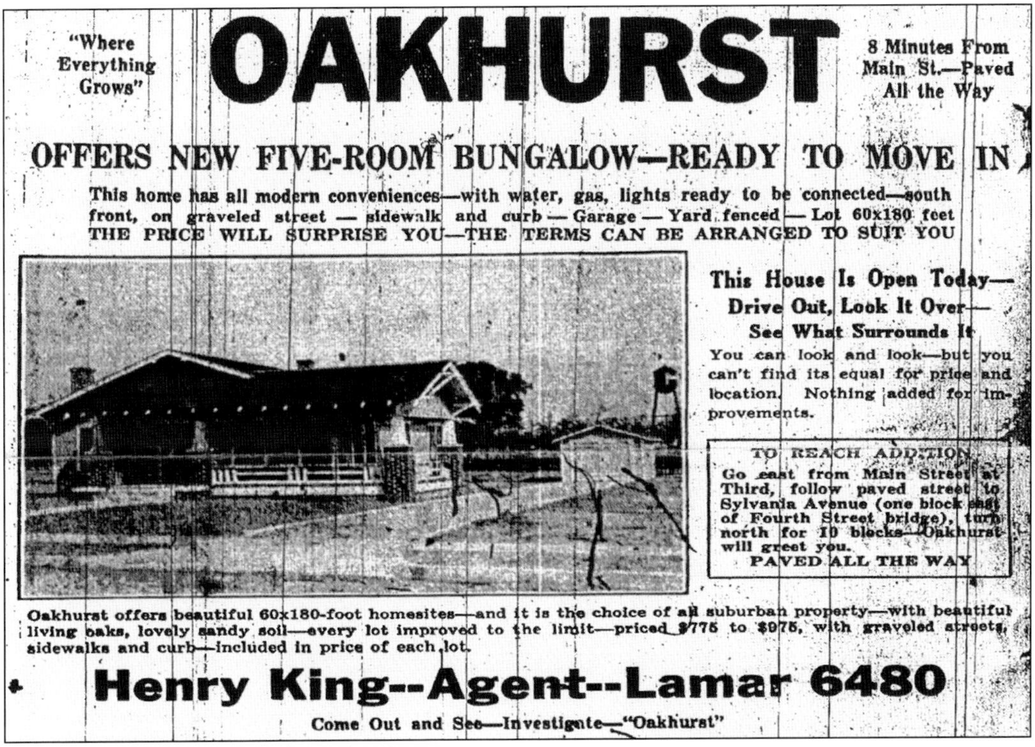

The 1925 advertisement above for the new Oakhurst Addition shows that it was possible to buy not just a lot but also a new house from the Oakhurst Land Company. The house in the advertisement is on North Sylvania Avenue, along the easternmost border of the neighborhood. Note the detached garage, a hallmark of Oakhurst Addition houses, and the water tower in the background. (OHD.)

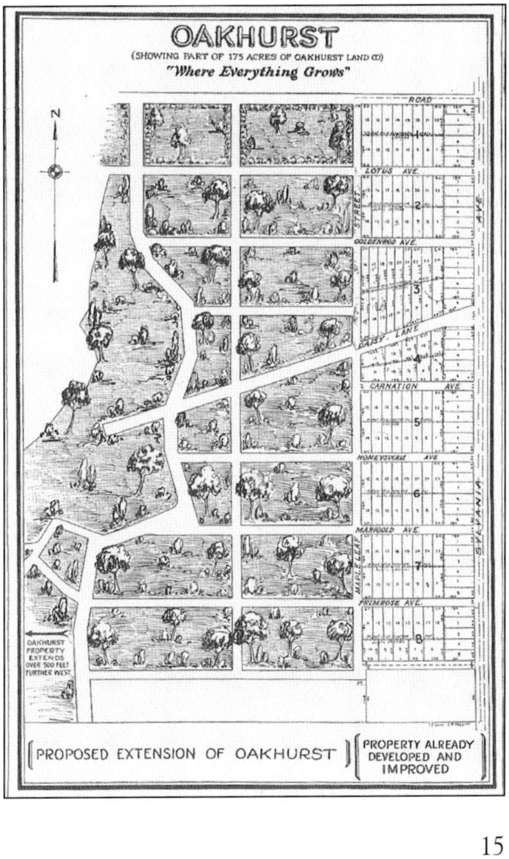

This drawing from John P. King's original 1924 Oakhurst marketing brochure shows how the neighborhood developed. The first platted area, one block deep, was situated between Sylvania Avenue and Mapleleaf Street and ran from Watauga Road to Yucca Avenue. Carnation Avenue did not originally extend west to Daisy Lane, in order to leave more room for the eventual Oakhurst Park. (OHD.)

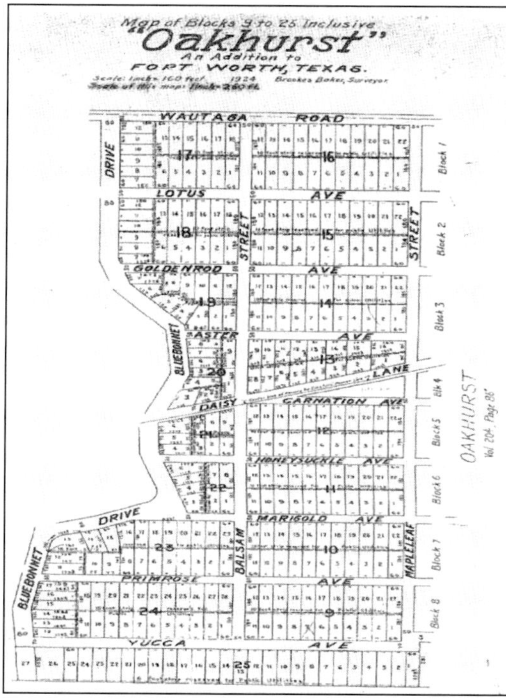

This is the 1925 plat map of the Oakhurst Addition, blocks 9–25. By the time of this platting, the development in Oakhurst had expanded beyond its original block-long depth to include the area from Mapleleaf Street to Bluebonnet Drive. The long, deep lots attracted buyers who wanted to live in the increasingly urban Fort Worth but still grow and tend gardens as if they were in the country. (OHD.)

The map below, platted in 1926, shows the addition of Oakhurst blocks 26 and 27 west of Bluebonnet Drive. Note the triangular piece of land left undeveloped between Daisy Lane and Carnation Avenue for 20 years. At various times, the land housed an office for the Oakhurst Land Company and a Red Cross station during World War II. (AC.)

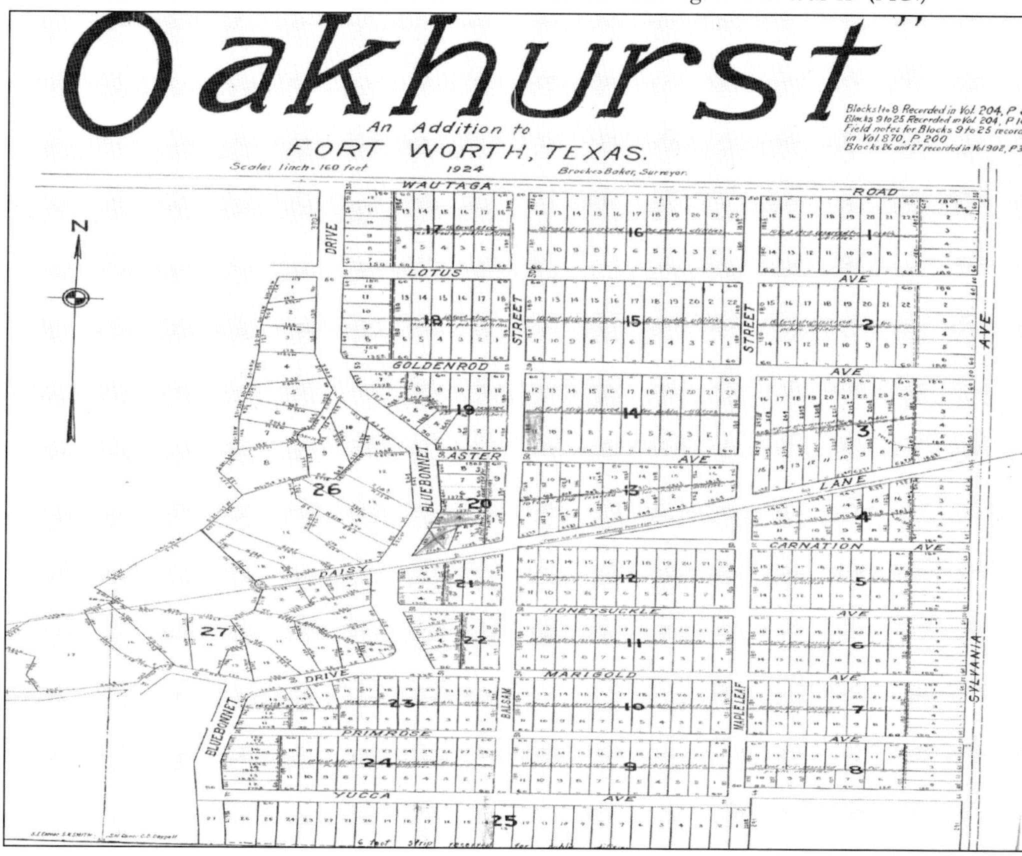

This 1925 advertisement for the Oakhurst development highlighted all its physical amenities and its reasonable lot fees. Henry King, John P. King's brother, represented the Oakhurst Land Company and other West Side real estate concerns until his untimely death in a car accident in 1937. (OHD.)

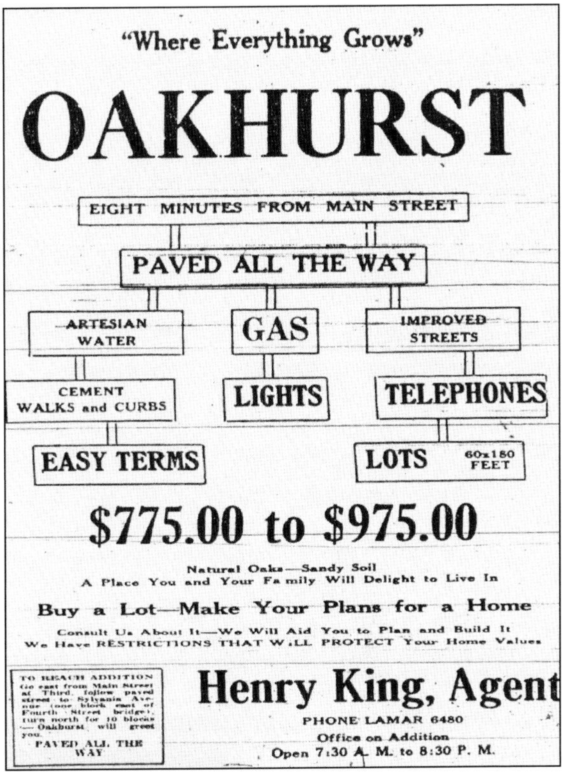

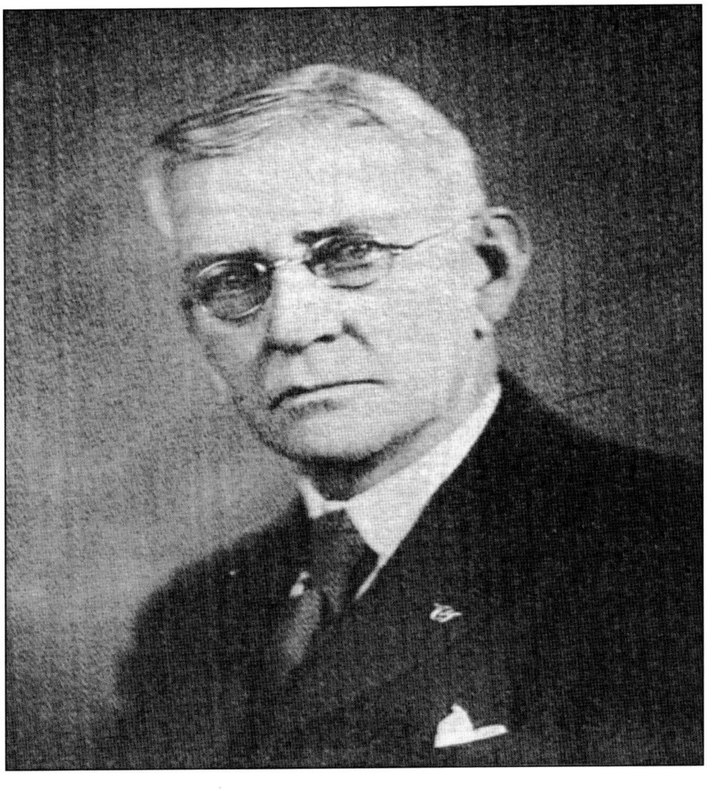

Verner Stuart "V.S." Wardlaw was an early officer of the Oakhurst Land Company. Once general manager of the Union Stockyards Company and president of the Exchange State Bank, Wardlaw was among the first citizens elected in the 1920s to the board of Tarrant Water Control & Improvement District No. 1 to manage the Trinity River in Fort Worth. (OHD.)

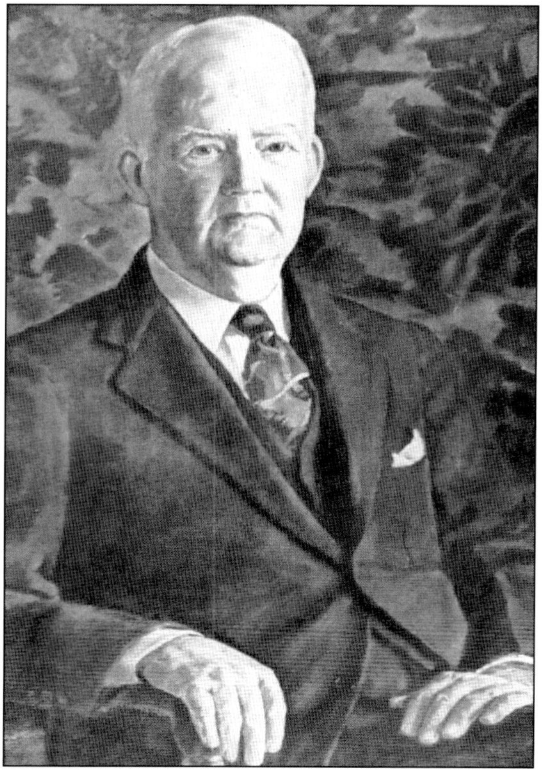

Here is John Porter King as painted by his son, noted Texas regionalist Clinton B. King, in the 1940s. This portrait appeared in a 1948 Fort Worth Chamber of Commerce tribute to King after his death. (FWCC.)

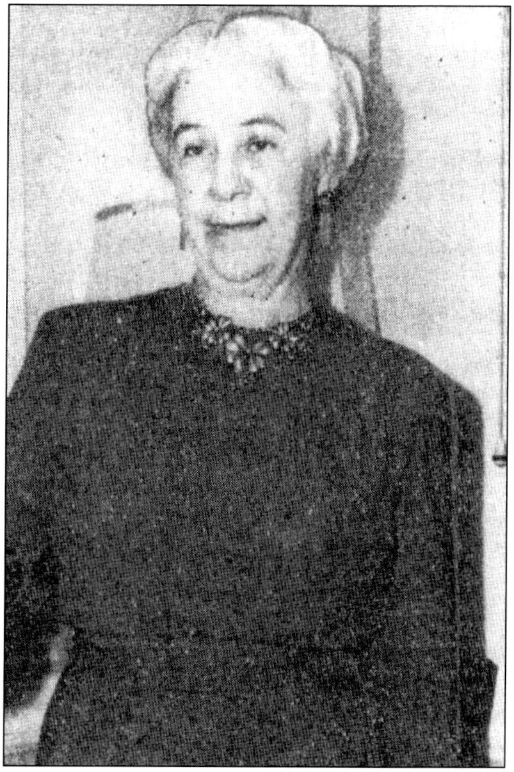

Lorena Blair King married John P. King in 1897. She gave parties where 10-pound boxes of King's bonbons were the prizes. She also worked on notable civic projects, such as raising funds for Texas Woman's College by managing sales at G.W. Haltom's Jewelers and Haltom's Optical Parlor. In 1927, Lorena and John King purchased a lot on the west side of River Crest Country Club and commissioned architect John F. Staub to design a Federal-style, two-story house at 4926 Crestline Road. (AC.)

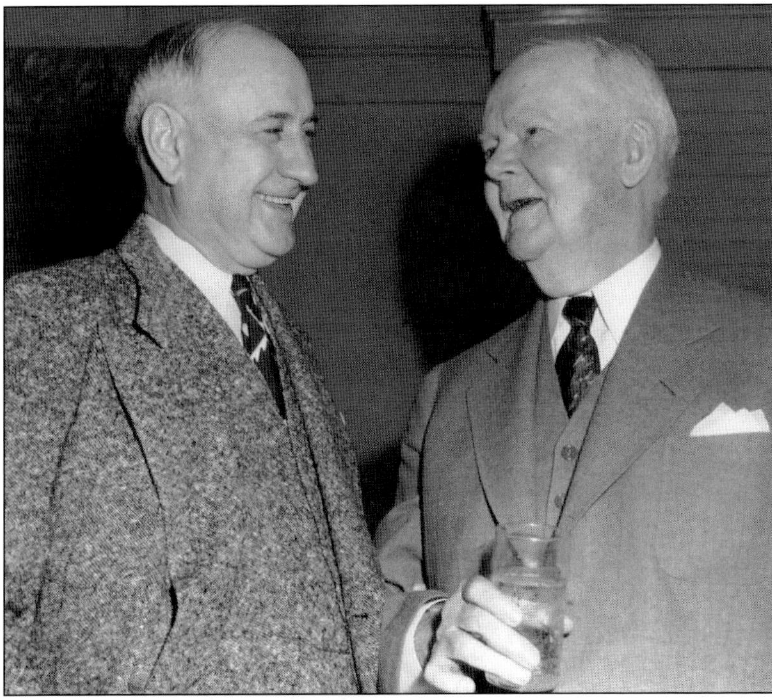

Amon Carter (left) and John P. King are shown at King's surprise 80th birthday dinner, given by his son Porter King on December 5, 1941, at River Crest Country Club. The event took place two days before the Japanese attack on Pearl Harbor. Many of Fort Worth's most prominent men were present at the party. At one time, Carter owned property in Oakhurst. (FWSTC/SCUTA.)

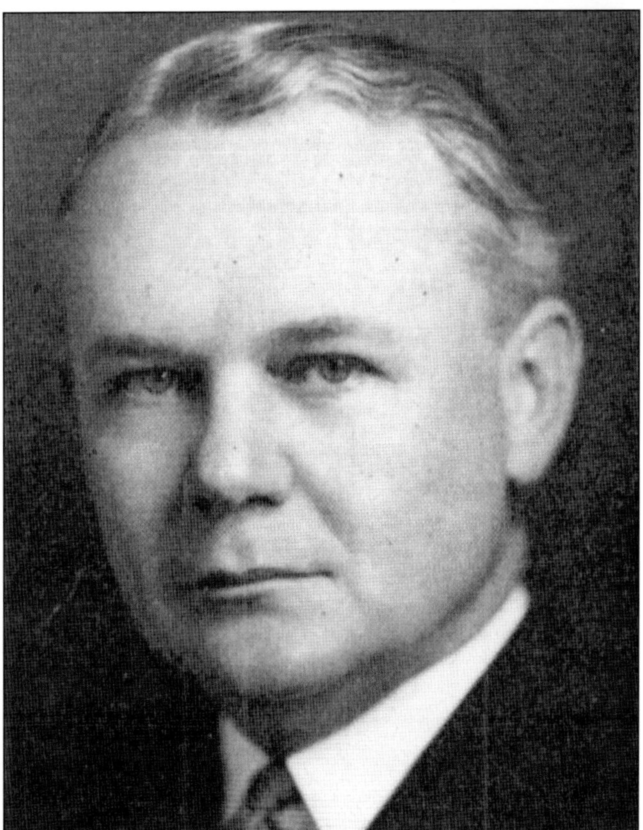

Porter King, the eldest of Lorena and John P. King's three sons, followed in his father's footsteps in the various King-run businesses. He became president of the King Candy Company. He was also a civic leader as a member of the board of directors of the Fort Worth Chamber of Commerce in the 1940s. He was chairman of the chamber's Fire Prevention Committee. (FWCC.)

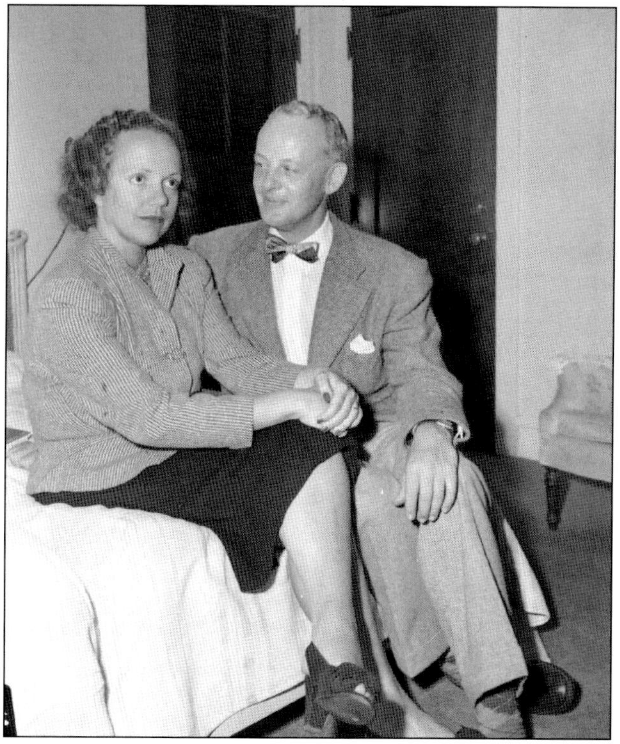

Narcissa Swift King and artist Clinton King visited his parents and other Fort Worth relatives in 1946 at the Fort Worth Club, where the elder Kings were living. Narcissa was his second wife. She was a great friend of artist Georgia O'Keefe. Clinton's first wife, Lady Duff Twysden of England, was a companion of Ernest Hemingway in Paris and Spain in the 1920s. Hemingway modeled the character Brett Ashley, in his 1926 novel *The Sun Also Rises*, on Twysden. (FWSTC/SCUTA.)

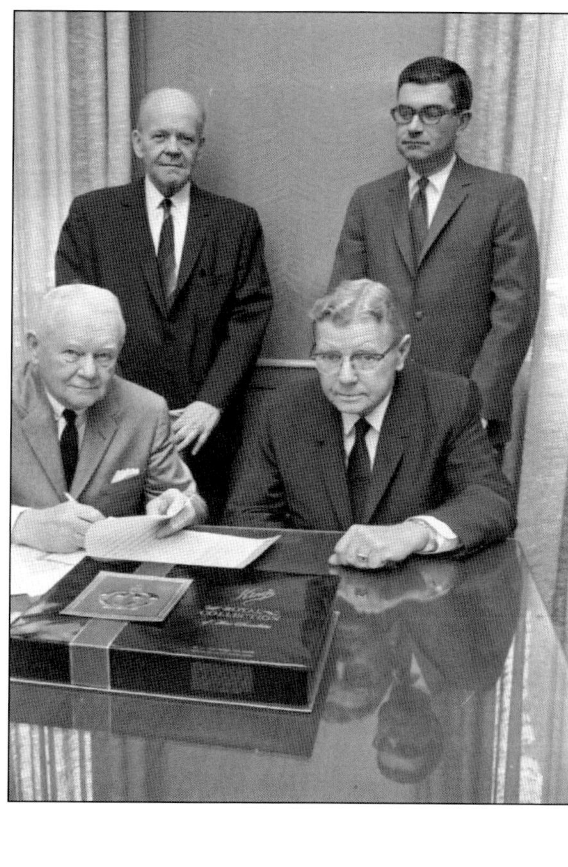

This 1968 photograph shows Porter King (seated, left) signing the documents selling King Candy Company to Galbraith McFadden Weaver of Southland Royalty Company. After 62 years, the King Candy Company was no more. Also shown is Porter's brother Robert L. King (standing, left). In the 1950s, Robert took on a greater role with Oakhurst Land Company as it continued to sell lots in West Oakhurst. (FWSTC/SCUTA.)

Two

The 1920s

Boom Times in Fort Worth and Oakhurst Becomes a Reality

In 1923, just a year before John P. King began the development of Oakhurst, the city was casting a look backward at its history. It had been almost 75 years since the establishment of the military outpost above the Trinity River in 1849 and exactly 50 years since Fort Worth had been incorporated as a city in 1873. What community leaders and residents saw was a great history, as Fort Worth had become the rail, commercial, cattle, grain, and cotton hub of the region and state. Added to those attributes was the great West Texas oil boom and its impact on the city. Between 1916 and 1923, Fort Worth doubled in population.

By 1925, Fort Worth was the literal center of the five-state region of Arkansas, Louisiana, Oklahoma, Texas, and New Mexico. The 1920 census revealed that of the 10.5 million people in those five states, one million lived within 75 miles of Fort Worth; two million lived within 125 miles of the city.

The Swift and Armour packing plants on the North Side, only 20 years old at the time, were emblematic of other large industries locating in Fort Worth. The companies found their labor costs lower at their Fort Worth plants than in any other city where they operated. The Fort Worth Chamber of Commerce reported that the Texas commissioner of labor said Fort Worth experienced less "trouble" with labor than any other Texas city. For the workers, energy, housing, clothing, and food costs were low. The city was also touted as having one of the lowest death rates in the United States.

All of these factors played into the successful development of the Oakhurst neighborhood, strategically located near downtown with railroad and industrial centers to the north and the stockyards nearby. Oakhurst appealed to workers, who found the lots and houses affordable and were attracted by the recent benefits of Fort Worth city services, added by annexation in 1922. The parklike setting of the neighborhood and the ability to grow almost any fruit or vegetable added to the overall pull of the development.

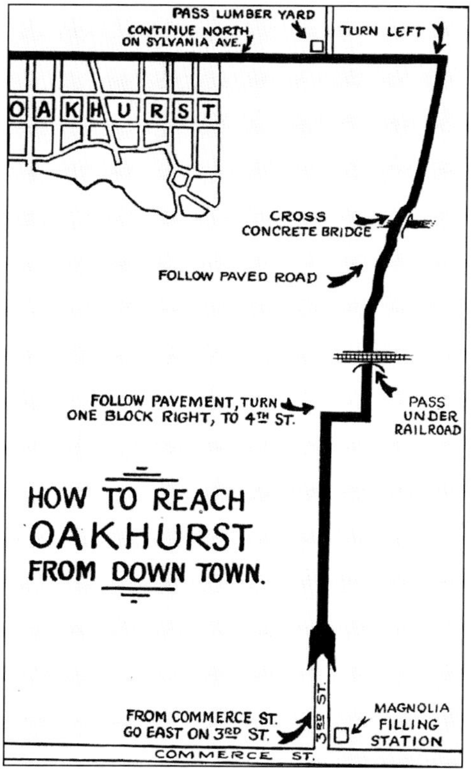

The 1924 Oakhurst Land Company marketing brochure stressed not only the proximity of the development to downtown but also the effect of country life in the city. "It is so much cooler!" because of its bluff location, said the brochure. Oakhurst was "graded, graveled, and bordered with cement curbings . . . without additional cost" to the home buyer. (AC.)

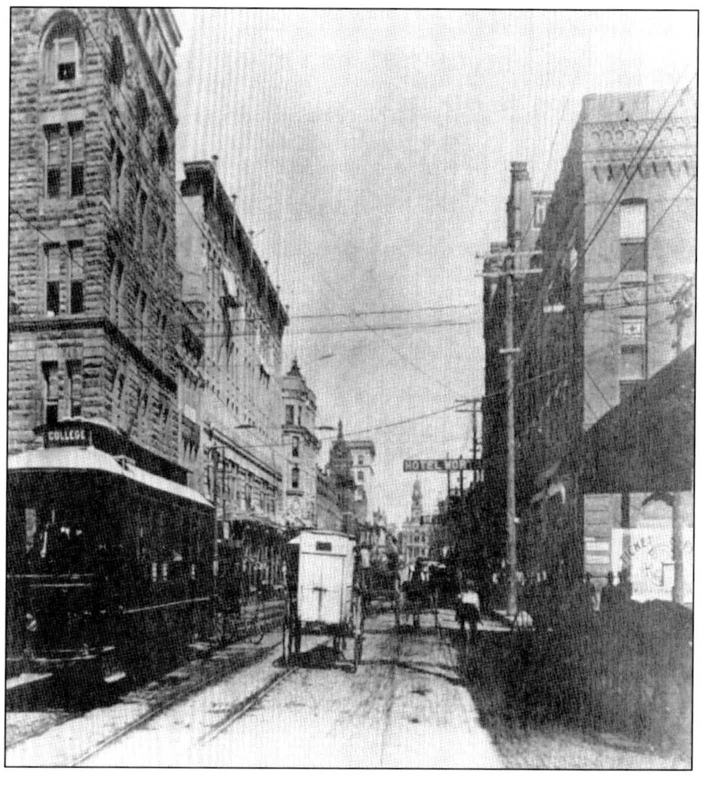

This is Fort Worth's Main Street in 1920, two years before Riverside was annexed to the city and four years before the Oakhurst development opened. The oil boom of the late 1910s stretched the resources of the city for housing and services for the thousands who poured into Fort Worth. New residents were looking for jobs in a multitude of fields and for places to live, like Oakhurst. (Beverly Sharp Germany.)

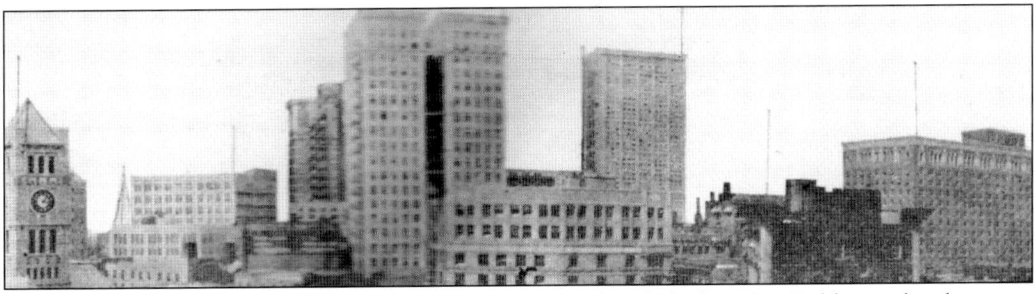

This is a view of downtown Fort Worth in late 1923, shortly before the Oakhurst development was opened 2.8 miles away. Already, the city's skyline looks more modern than in the 1920 view on the previous page. (FWCC.)

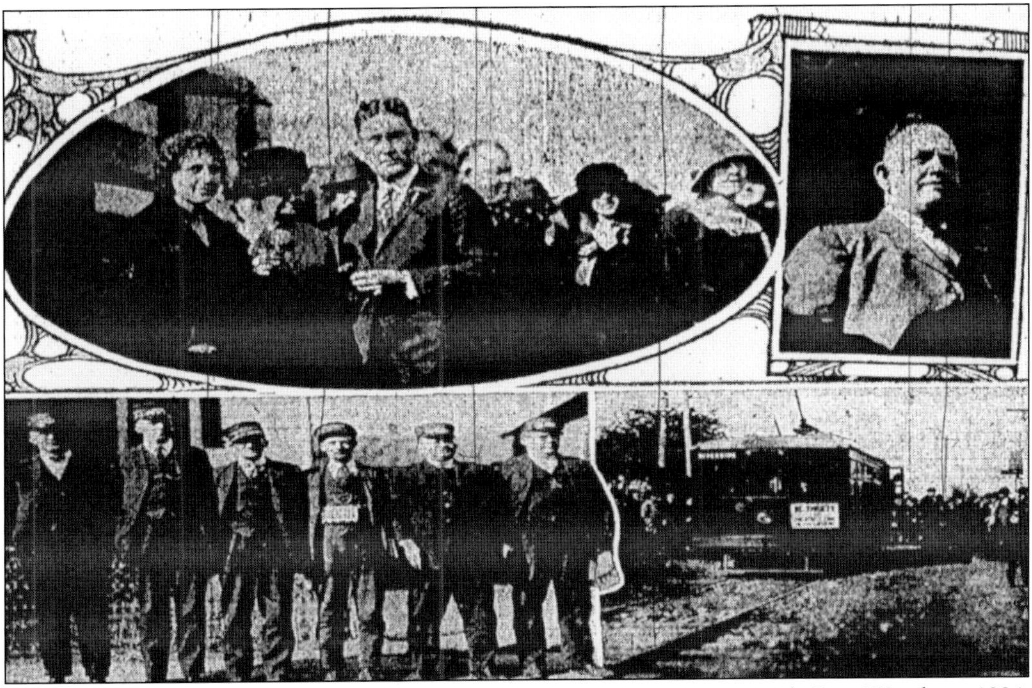

Riverside's new streetcar line created a way for residents to connect with Fort Worth in 1924. This composite image shows the celebration of the initial run of the Northern Texas Traction Company line from East Third Street downtown to Riverside. (NGB.)

KING WILL NOT RUN

Declares He Will Not Become Candidate for Mayor

John P. King, who has been mentioned prominently this week in connection with the coming mayoralty race will not be a candidate. The candidacy of Mr. King was sought by a number of men looking for a business candidate.

When seen today in regard to the matter Mr. King declared he had never considered running for mayor and that he could not consent to do so under any circumstances.

John P. King preferred to work behind the scenes as an influential businessman to ensure that projects with major civic benefits, like schools and bridges, were approved. After his early 10-year stint as Tarrant County clerk, he never ran for public office again, as evidenced by this 1905 news item in the *Fort Worth Star-Telegram*. (NGB.)

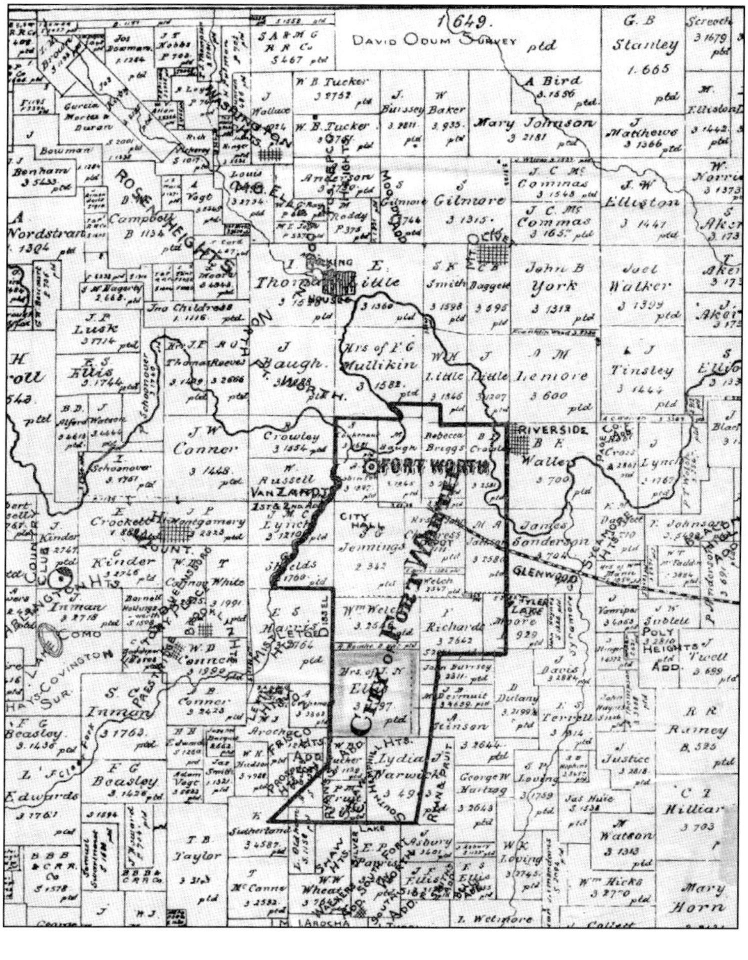

This Guaranty Abstract & Title Company map shows Fort Worth's city limits in 1909. The C.B. Daggett and S.K. Smith surveys are near the top of the map, and the community of Riverside is just east of the city limits. Just at the top of what would become Oakhurst, two-year-old Mount Olivet is already noted on the map. (OHD.)

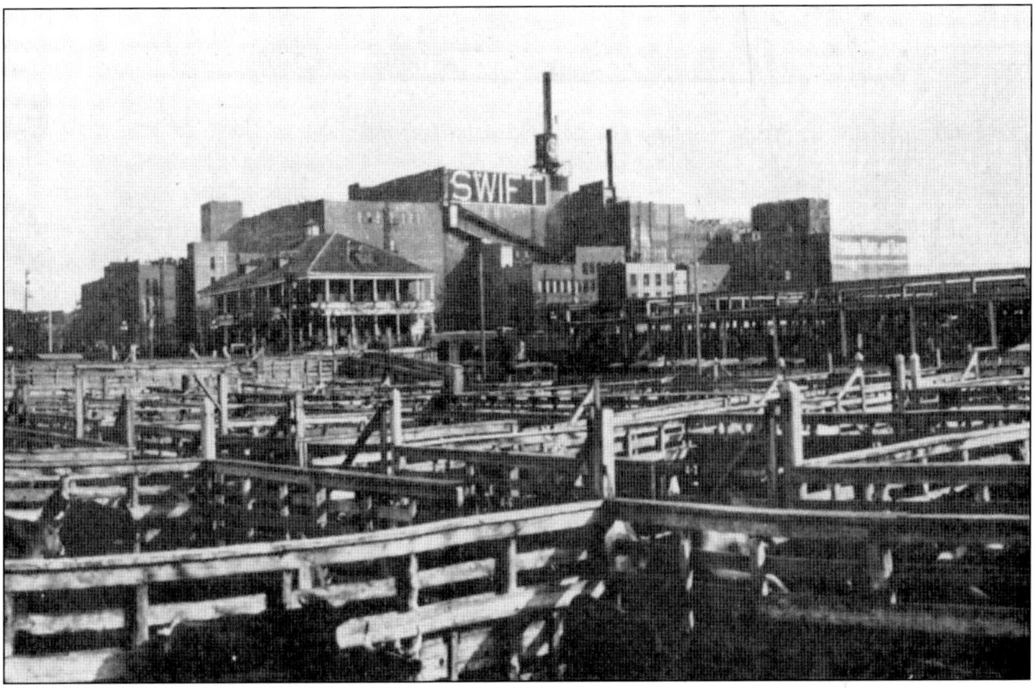

This is an early photograph of Swift & Company's meatpacking plant, established in the Fort Worth Stockyards in 1902. Some Swift employees chose Oakhurst over North Side neighborhoods because they could buy affordable, more substantial brick homes there. (FWCC.)

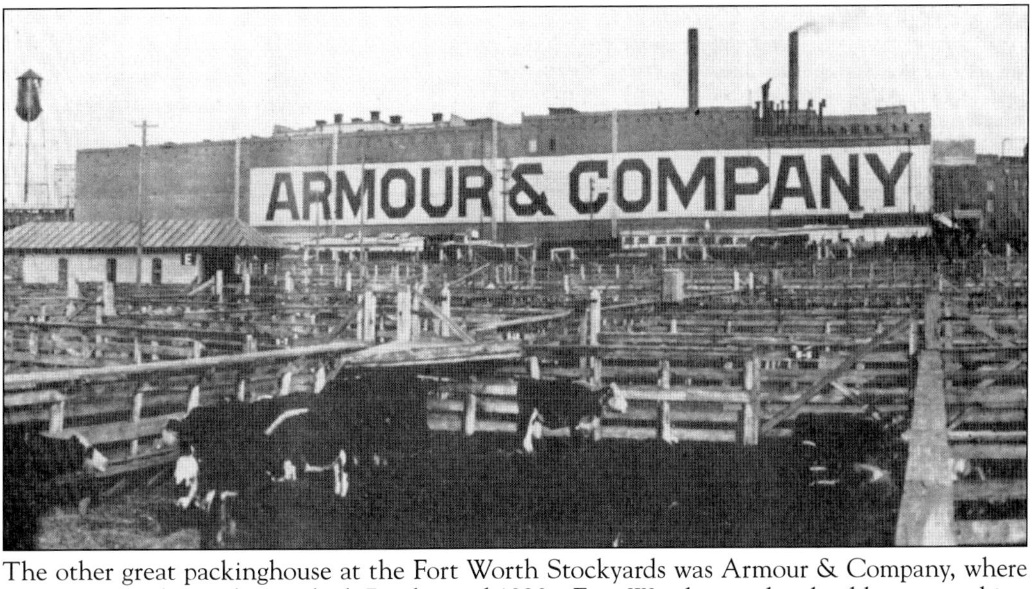

The other great packinghouse at the Fort Worth Stockyards was Armour & Company, where Oakhurst residents also worked. By the mid-1920s, Fort Worth was the third-largest packing center in the United States. The connection between the North Side and residents of Oakhurst was strong. Not only did residents work there, they also often sent their children to North Side High School before Riverside High School was built in 1935–1936. (FWCC.)

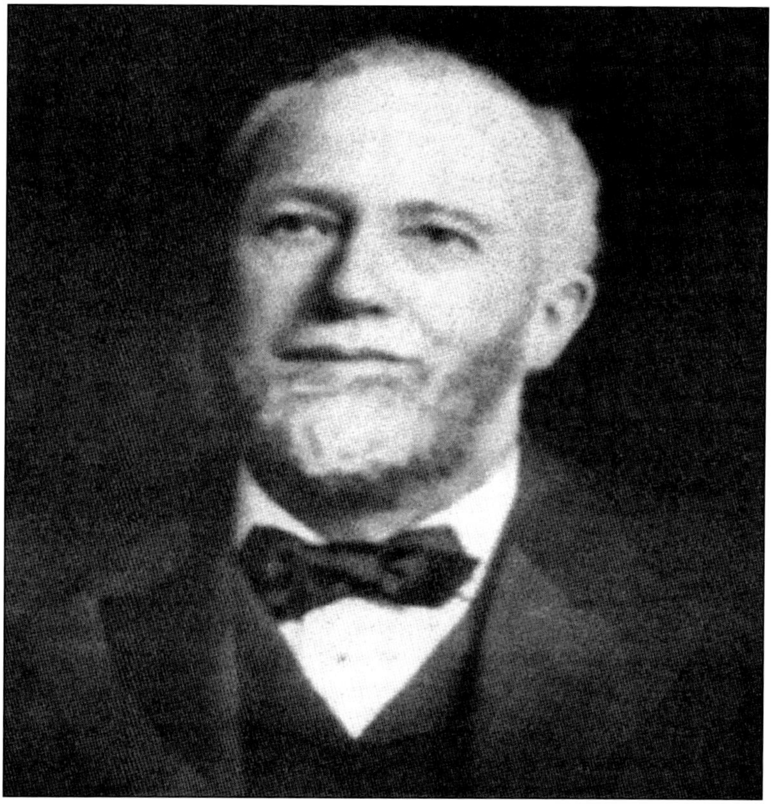

Gustavus F. Swift was the founder of Swift & Company in Chicago and the inventor of the refrigerated railway car, a groundbreaking innovation for the storage and transport of fresh meat to large urban markets in the Northeast. Oakhurst developer John P. King's son Clinton married Narcissa Swift, Gustavus's great-granddaughter, in Chicago in 1941. (AC.)

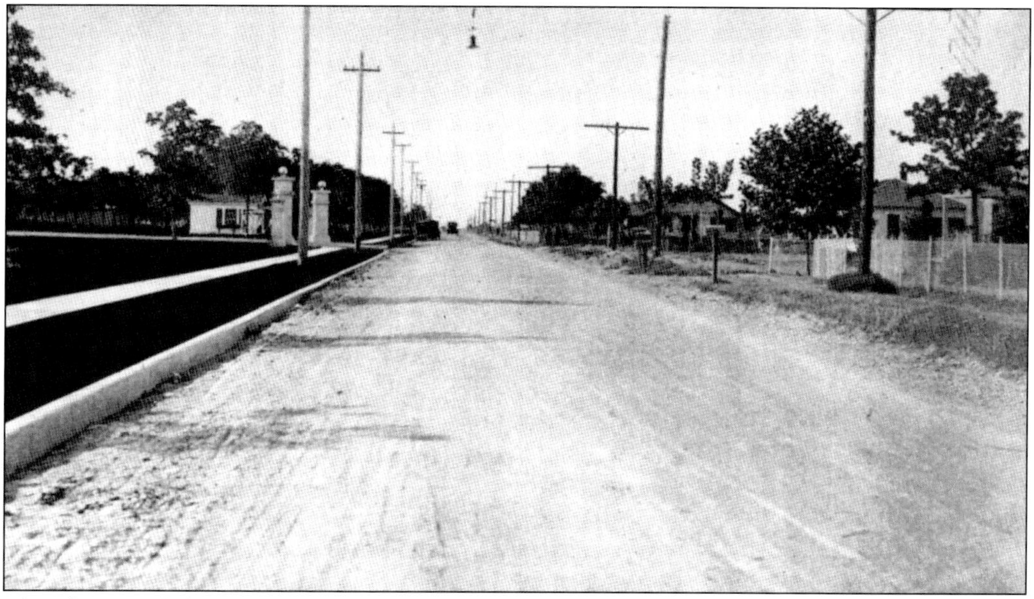

This photograph from a 1924 Oakhurst Land Company marketing brochure shows North Sylvania Avenue heading north, with the new Oakhurst development on the left. The structure beyond the columns may be the early Oakhurst Land Company sales office, at 1805 North Sylvania Avenue. By 1928, the company office was at 1703 Mapleleaf Street, as was the Oakhurst Sand & Gravel Company. The Sylvan Heights West Addition is to the east. (AC.)

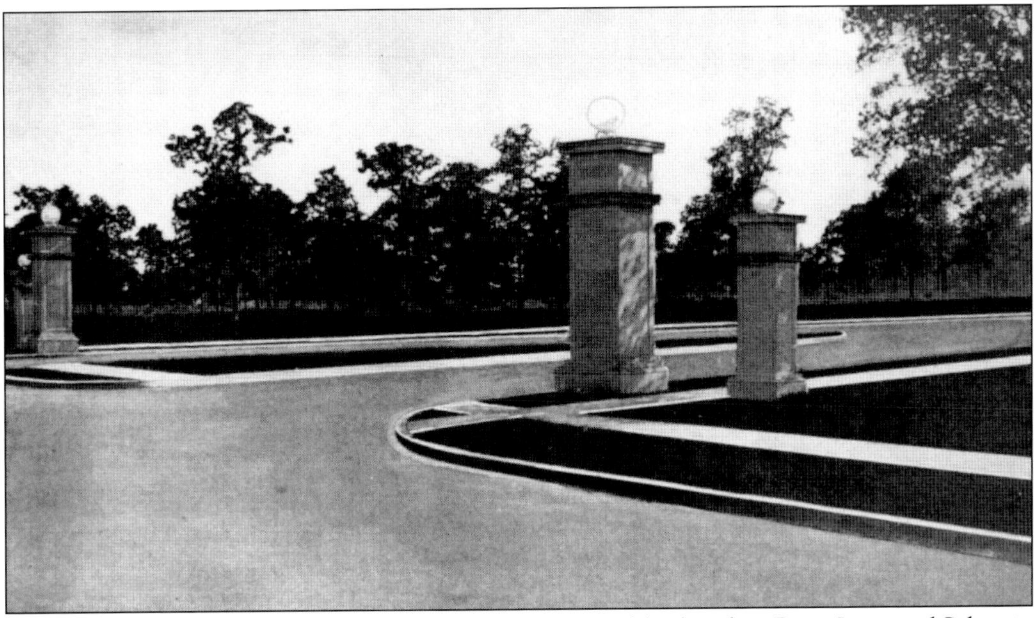

Oakhurst's columns at the ceremonial entrance to the neighborhood on Daisy Lane and Sylvania Avenue created a dramatic scene. Visitors knew they had reached Oakhurst when they saw the columns. The presence of the columns may be the reason some have thought incorrectly through the years that Oakhurst was not part of Riverside, although many merchants and institutions far from the neighborhood's boundaries often used the name. (AC.)

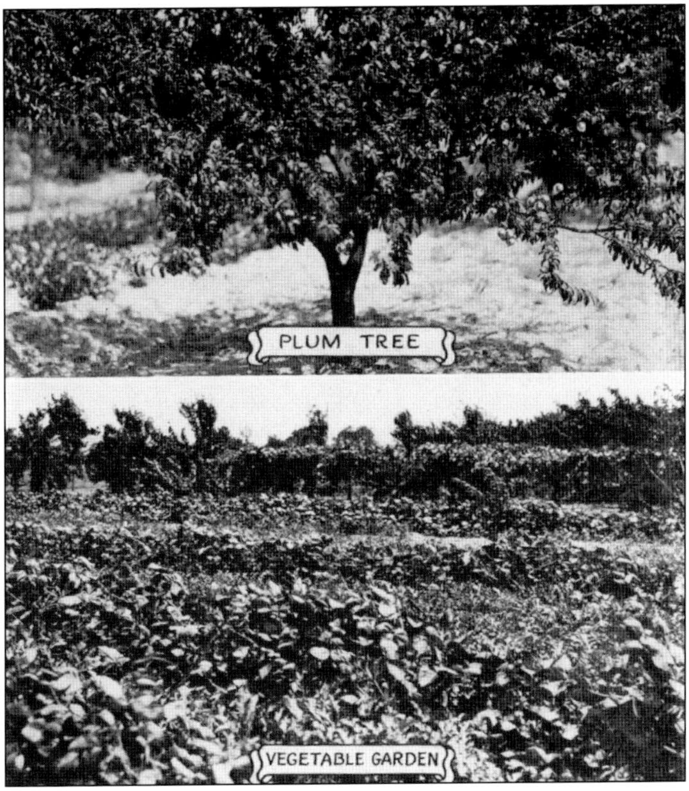

Tarrant County was a horticultural paradise, and Riverside, including Oakhurst, was the sweet spot. "Everything Grows in Oakhurst" was more than a marketing slogan. It was literally true. These two 1924 images show the variety of fruits and vegetables that proliferated in the area's sandy loam soil. The streets were named for flowers (Aster, Carnation, Daisy, Goldenrod, and Primrose), reportedly by one of the founders of Riverside's Baker Brothers Nursery. (AC.)

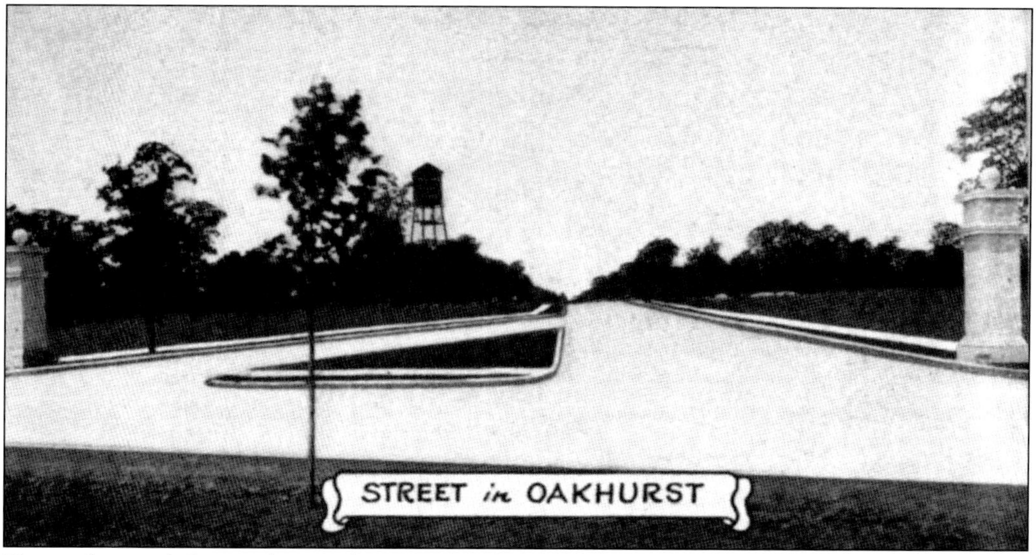

Vacant lots and the newly paved Daisy Lane beckoned would-be Oakhurst home owners to go deeper into the neighborhood in 1924 and explore the beauty and promise of life there. Note the concrete sidewalks, touted in the marketing brochure of the Oakhurst Land Company. (AC.)

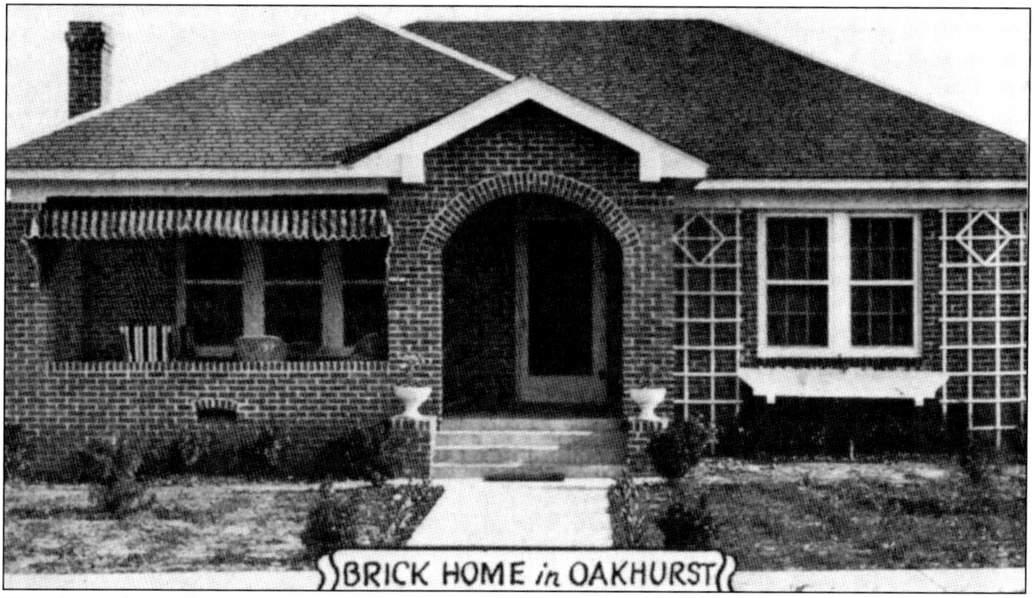

This brick bungalow, seen in Oakhurst's 1924 marketing brochure, was an example of a home that a buyer in Oakhurst could afford. The Oakhurst Land Company built some of the houses that appeared on their lots. They stressed that Oakhurst lots "cost no more than you can afford to pay." Prices ranged from $625 to $925. No two brick houses in Oakhurst are alike, a noteworthy feature of the neighborhood. (AC.)

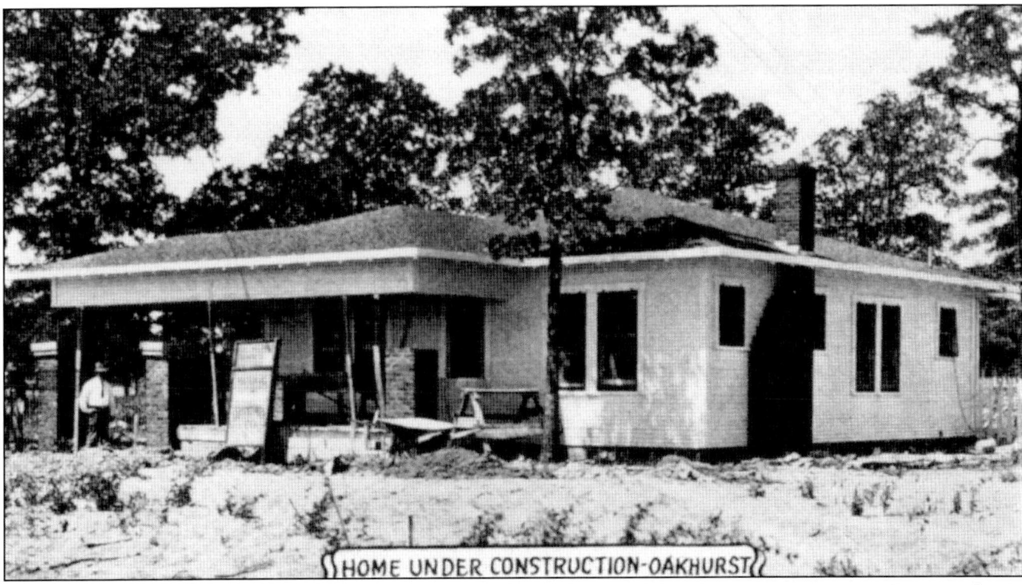

This frame house with brick columns was under construction when Oakhurst was first marketed in 1924. By 1927, the Sanborn Fire Insurance maps of Oakhurst showed that 150 houses had been built in the development. (AC.)

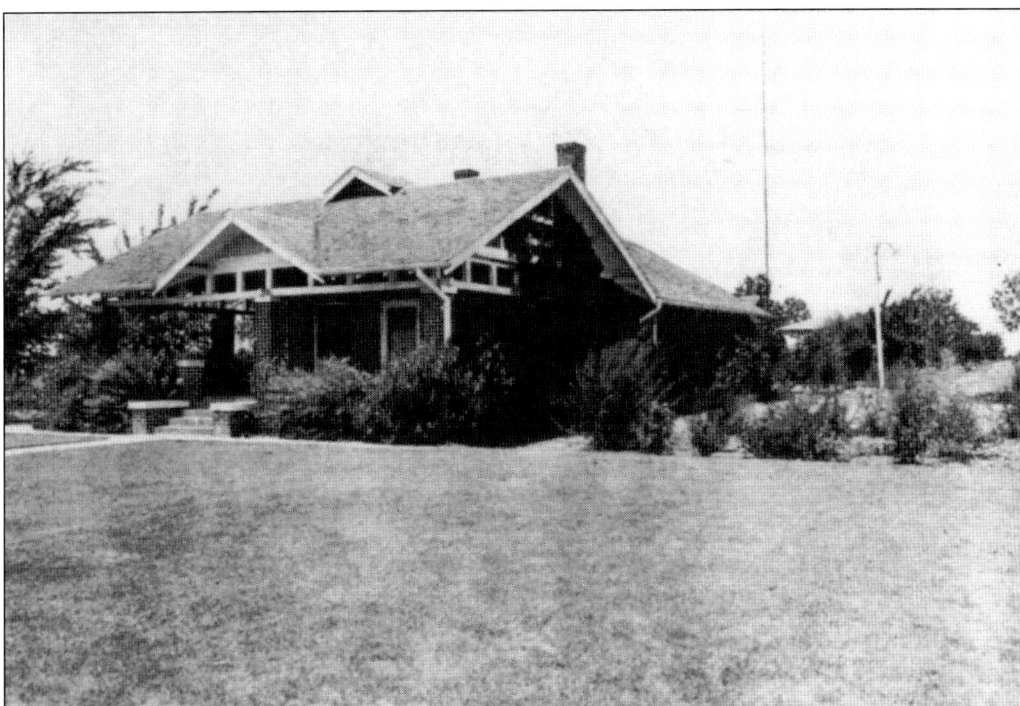

The large lots of Oakhurst homes provided planting space as well as room for children to play. This 1924 photograph illustrates a marketing brochure's statement that Oakhurst was "the ideal place for happy, healthy children." (AC.)

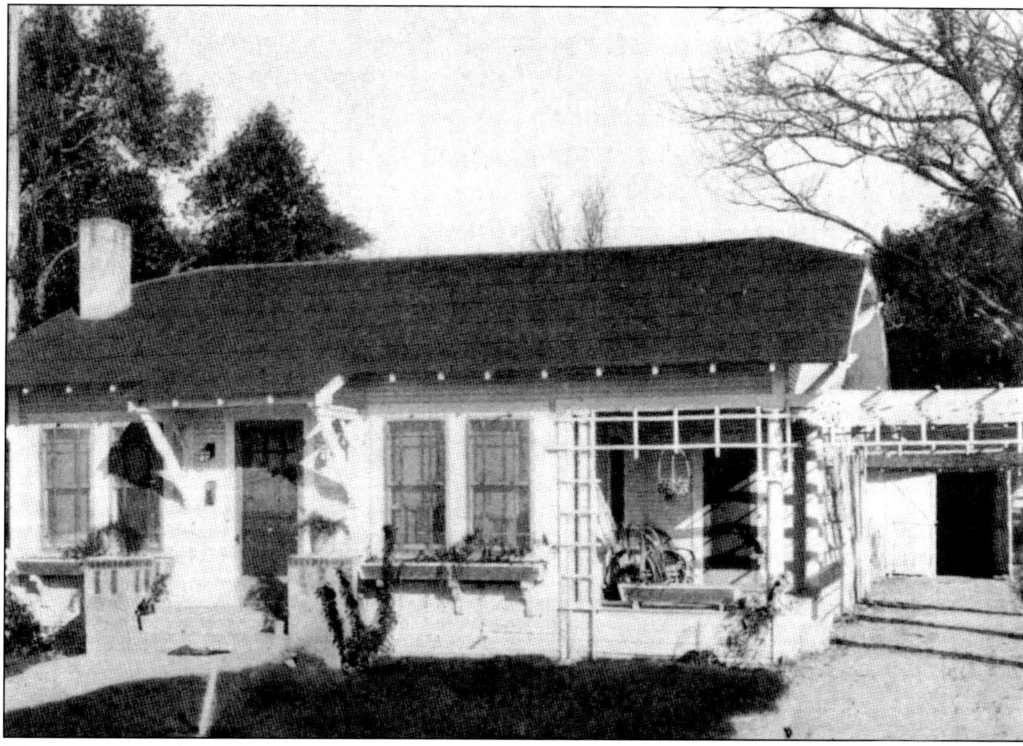

This quaint Oakhurst bungalow, shown in 1924, has a hanging flower basket on the side porch—a common feature of Oakhurst houses—and window boxes with flowers. The narrow driveway is a reminder of the size of 1920s cars. The detached garage was, and still is, a usual feature of houses in the neighborhood. (AC.)

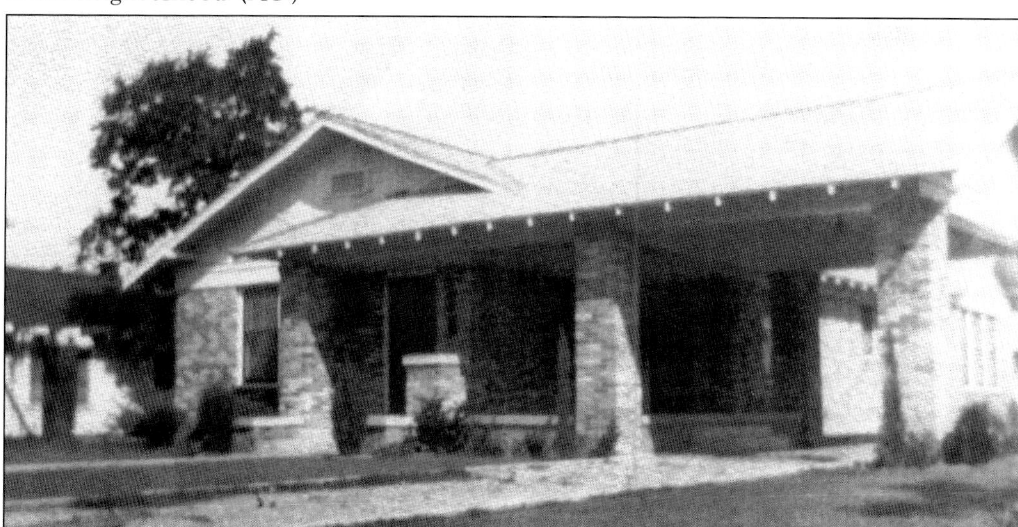

The Sharp house, at 2313 Aster Avenue, is seen here in 1928, when newlyweds Ruby and W.E. Sharp built it. It was typical of the brick bungalows built in Oakhurst in the 1920s. With no air-conditioning in those days, open windows were a necessity. "We did have oscillating fans," remembers daughter Beverly Sharp Germany, "but we kept our windows open all of the time." (Beverly Sharp Germany.)

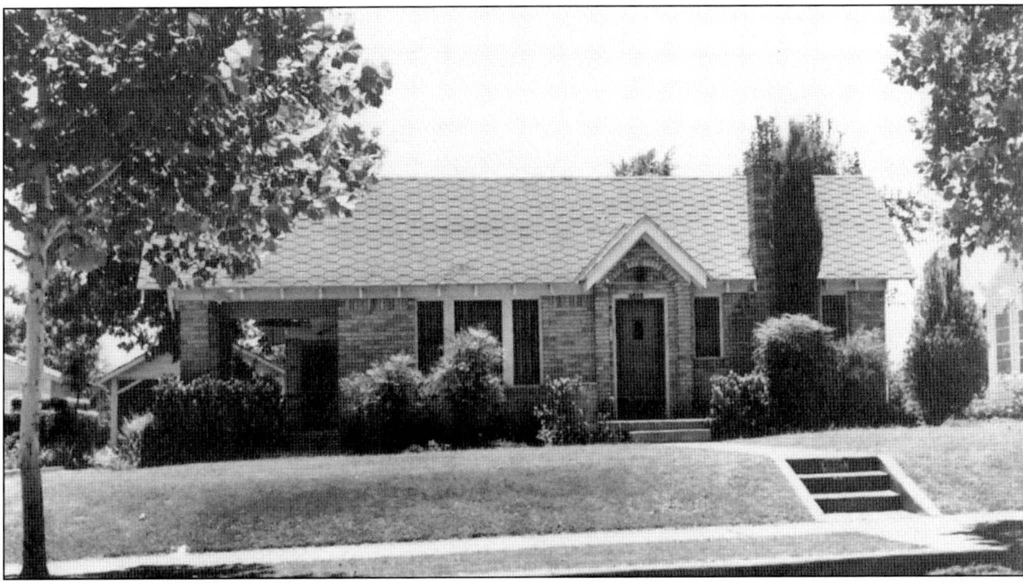

The brick Tudor house at 2508 Primrose Avenue was professionally photographed for a publication called "Our Home in Fort Worth." It also appeared as a model of Oakhurst homes on a postcard. Bertha and W.A. Womack's family lived here for almost 50 years. (Delia Brelsford Shiflet.)

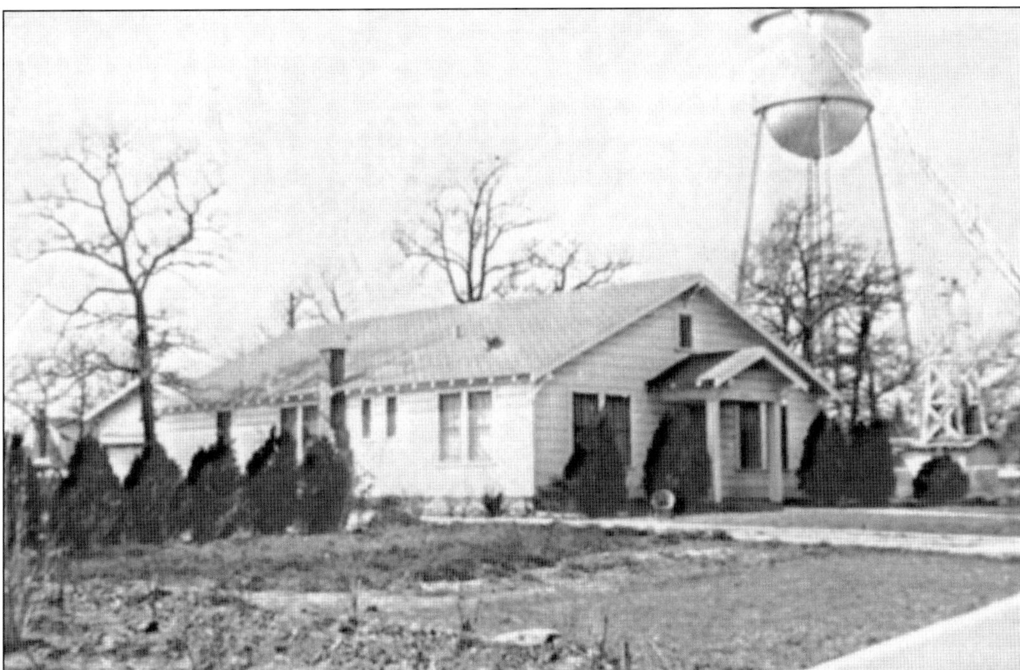

This is an early photograph of 2516 Daisy Lane, with the Oakhurst water tower in the background. An artesian water well, also in the background, served Oakhurst in the early years. The tower and well were on lot 12 of block 4, the only area reserved for commercial activity, which was otherwise prohibited by Oakhurst deed restrictions. Bertha Jo and Houston C. Story bought the house for $2,500 in 1939. (Carolyn Story Bailey.)

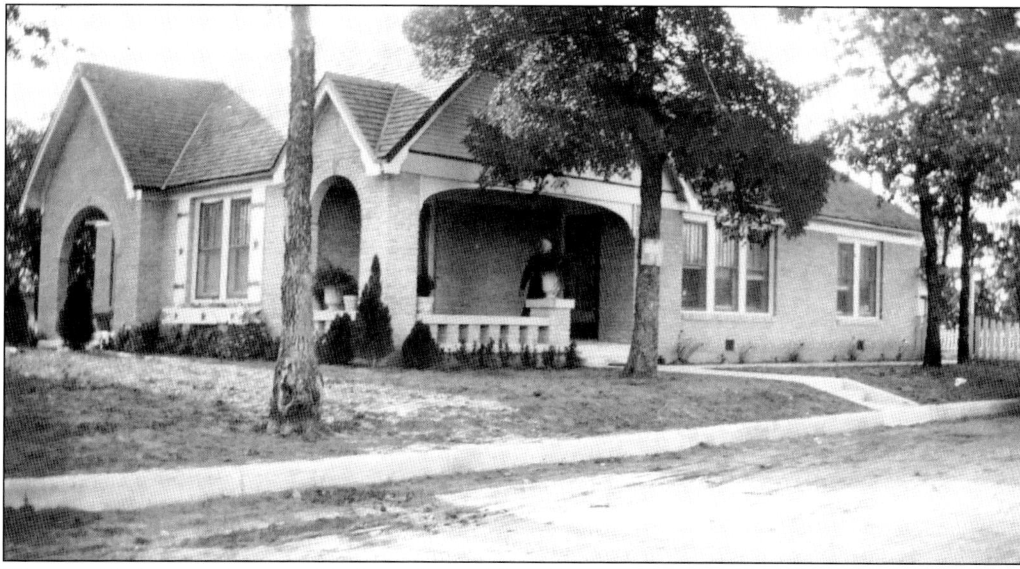

The new Tudor-style home of Dr. Jesse C. and Dora Bennett, at 2341 Goldenrod Avenue, is seen here about 1929. Dr. Bennett operated his medical and obstetrics office at 602 North Sylvania Avenue. Sadly, Dora was a widow by 1931. Note the dirt street in the foreground, before Oakhurst's streets were paved. (Cathy Kyle.)

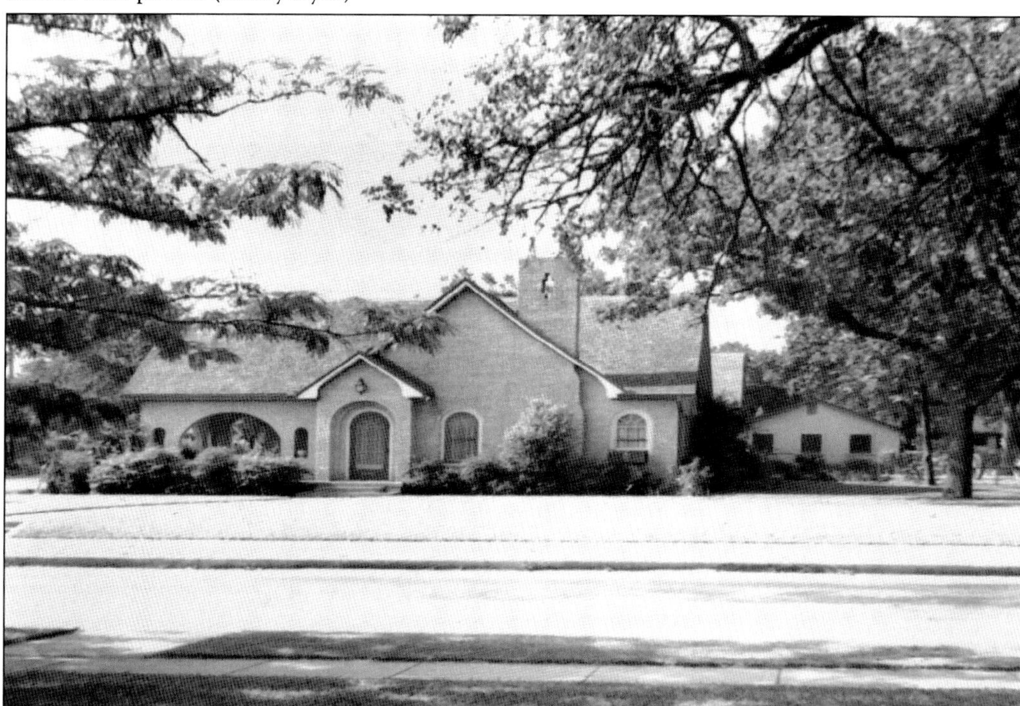

This 1930s-era brick Tudor-style house at 2346 Lotus Avenue, pictured here in July 1955, is a good example of the style of architecture many early residents built their homes in. Later, home buyers were drawn to this style in the Oakhurst Addition. Lee and Tom Archer were listed at this address in 1931. He owned Tom B. Archer & Company, a sand and gravel business. (Leslie James.)

Three

1930s Oakhurst

Depression and New Building

When the 1930s began in Oakhurst, the nation and Fort Worth had sunk into the crippling Great Depression. Oakhurst was six years old, a neighborhood in its infancy, home to mostly middle-class residents whose men worked and whose women stayed home with the young children. It was hard to make ends meet, but the foresight of the Fort Worth Chamber of Commerce's Five Year Plan, written before the Depression, along with the financial support of federal building programs, helped Oakhurst families survive.

The independent Fort Worth Board of Park Commissioners and the city were busy building everything from the Fort Worth Botanic Garden to the 1934 East Belknap Street Bridge, which was important for Oakhurst residents who worked downtown. Commuters could now drive the 2.8 miles home across the new span. In 1936, with help from the federal Public Works Administration and the Works Progress Administration (WPA), Riverside High School was built six blocks from Oakhurst. Kansas City landscape architects Hare & Hare provided the plans for the school grounds and its esplanade.

Closer to home, S. Herbert Hare designed Oakhurst Scenic Drive, a park drive, for the board of park commissioners. John P. King ensured its development by donating 17 acres of his land toward the eventual 41-acre parkway and park drive. The WPA built the road in 1936–1937, a pastoral drive connecting downtown to Oakhurst and nearby neighborhoods. In 1939, again seeing a possibility, King commissioned Herbert Hare to design a landscape plan for what he conceived as the new addition of West Oakhurst. This development would not begin to be platted until 1946.

King also leased his land on the west side of the new Oakhurst Scenic Drive for the development of the nine-hole Oakhurst Golf and Country Club. Internationally famous professional golfers Byron Nelson and Ben Hogan caddied at the course in the mid-1930s, just a stone's throw from what was left of Daggett's Woods and "the river road," the new Oakhurst Scenic Drive.

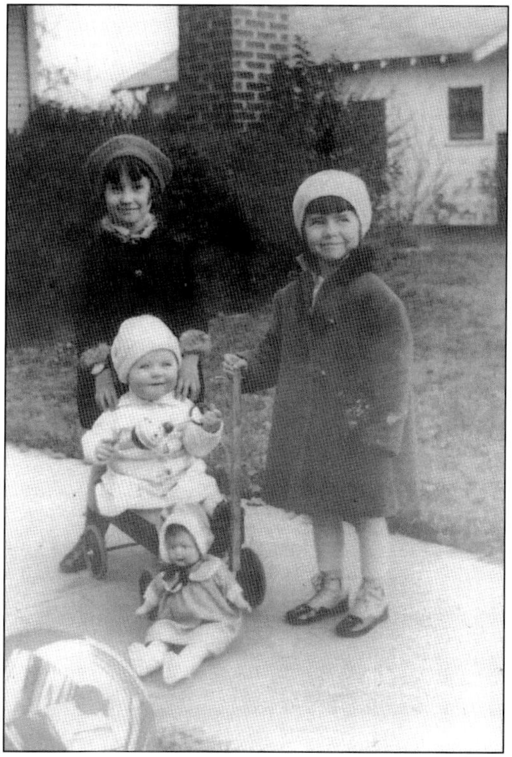

Betty Jane (left), Anna Belle (right), and baby Ray Jefferson stand outside their home at 2501 Goldenrod Avenue in 1931. Ray Jefferson remembered: "It was the Depression and we didn't have any money. Nobody had any money, but Mother always dressed us well. I don't know how she did it. My Grandmother Jefferson was a seamstress and worked downtown for a tailor. She may have made some of these things for us." (Ray Jefferson.)

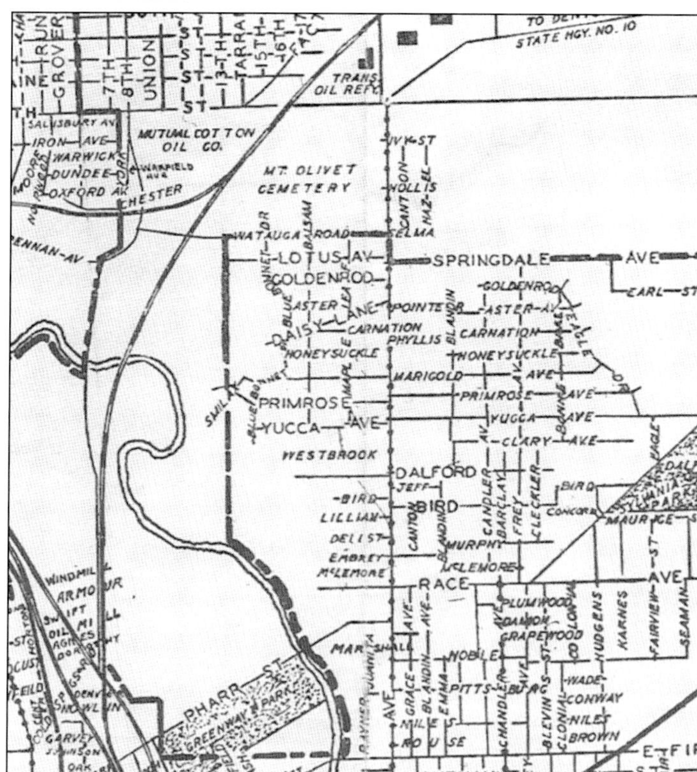

This is a 1931 map of Oakhurst from the Western Map Company. Note that the Oakhurst Addition is located just within the city limits. Some Oakhurst residents worked at nearby oil companies and refineries. (OHD.)

Manager Harry Whitaker gets ready for the Free Milk & Ice Fund Golf Tournament, held in 1932 at the Oakhurst Golf and Country Club, just west of Oakhurst. The King-owned property was a nine-hole course "with grass greens, watered fairways, plenty of hazards, a keen little clubhouse and all the attractions of a golf course." King sold the property in 1944. Later, the construction of Interstate 35 took half of the former course property in the late 1950s and early 1960s. (FWL.)

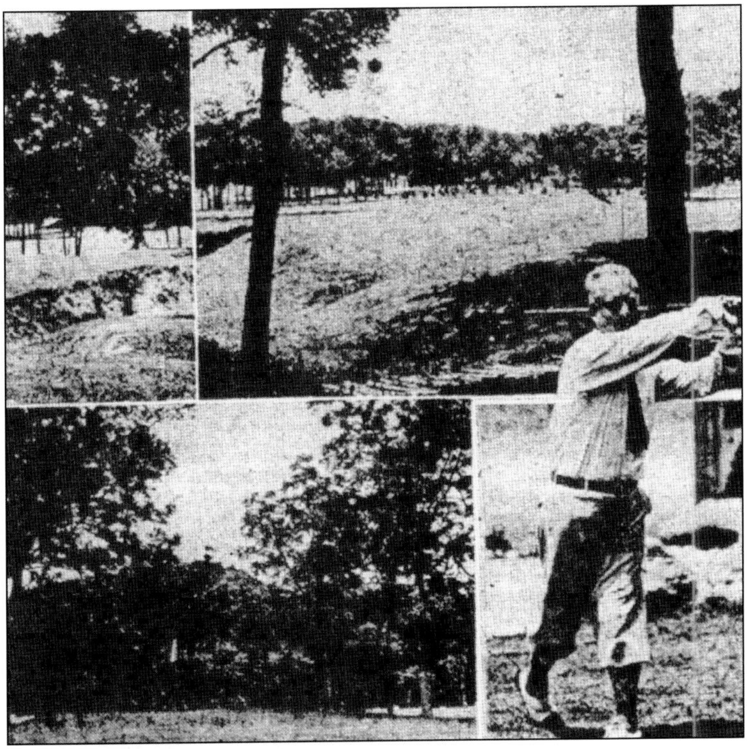

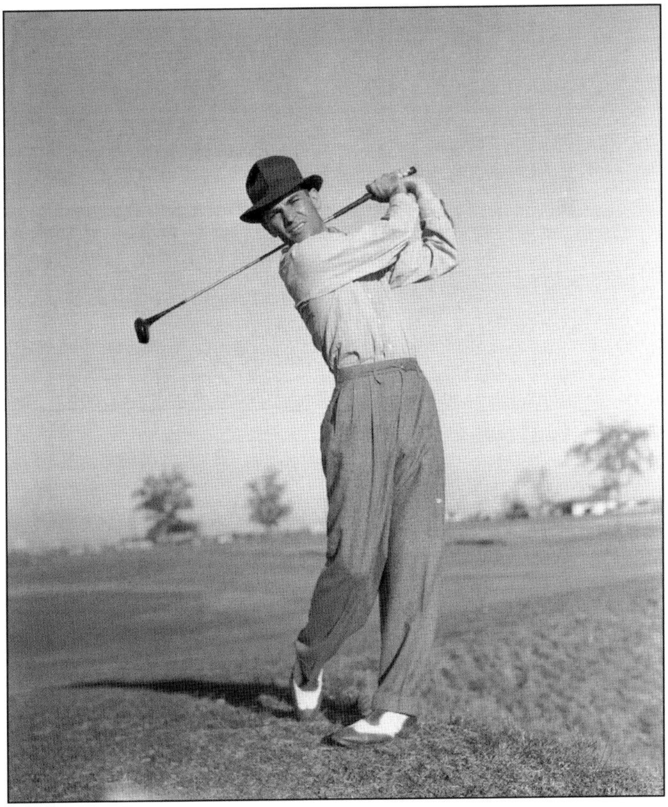

Internationally famous professional golfer Ben Hogan is seen here in 1938. In 1937, he was the playing pro for the nine-hole Oakhurst Golf Course. His mentor, Ted Longworth, who had been the pro for Glen Garden, leased the 54.4-acre Oakhurst course with Harry Lee Whitaker. Once, two Dallas golfers playing at the course were robbed by two men who had hidden in the thick Oakhurst woods. Hogan wanted to chase them using the rifle he had in his car. Friends dissuaded him. (FWSTC/SCUTA.)

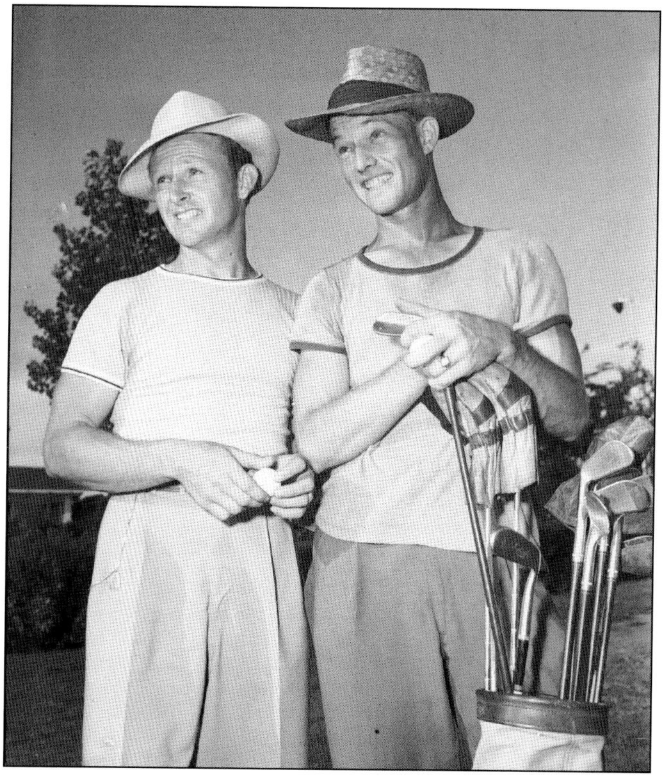

Golfer Bobby Morris (left) lived in Oakhurst for a time. He and Ben Hogan shared the course record of 67 beginning in 1935. He is shown here in 1941 with another great golfer, Iverson Martin. Both were known for their play at the Oakhurst Golf Course. (FWSTC/SCUTA.)

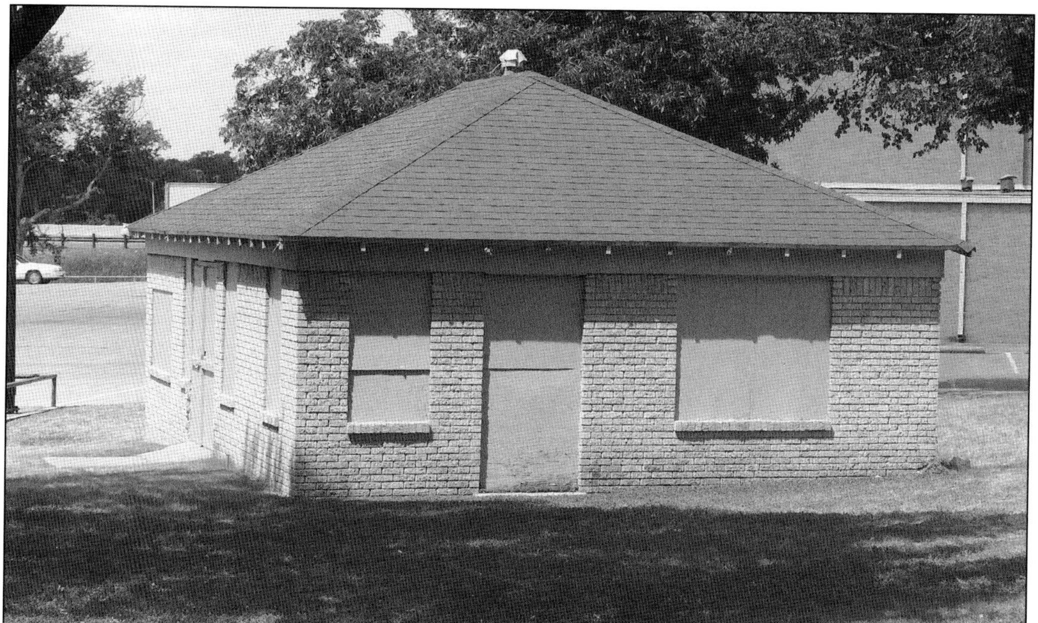

This is the only remaining building from the 1930s-era Oakhurst Golf and Country Club. Professional golfing greats Ben Hogan and Byron Nelson, as well as Bobby Morris, Jimmy Walkup, and Iverson Martin, no doubt knew this building well. It is now the property of Calvary Cathedral International. (Doyle Willis Jr.)

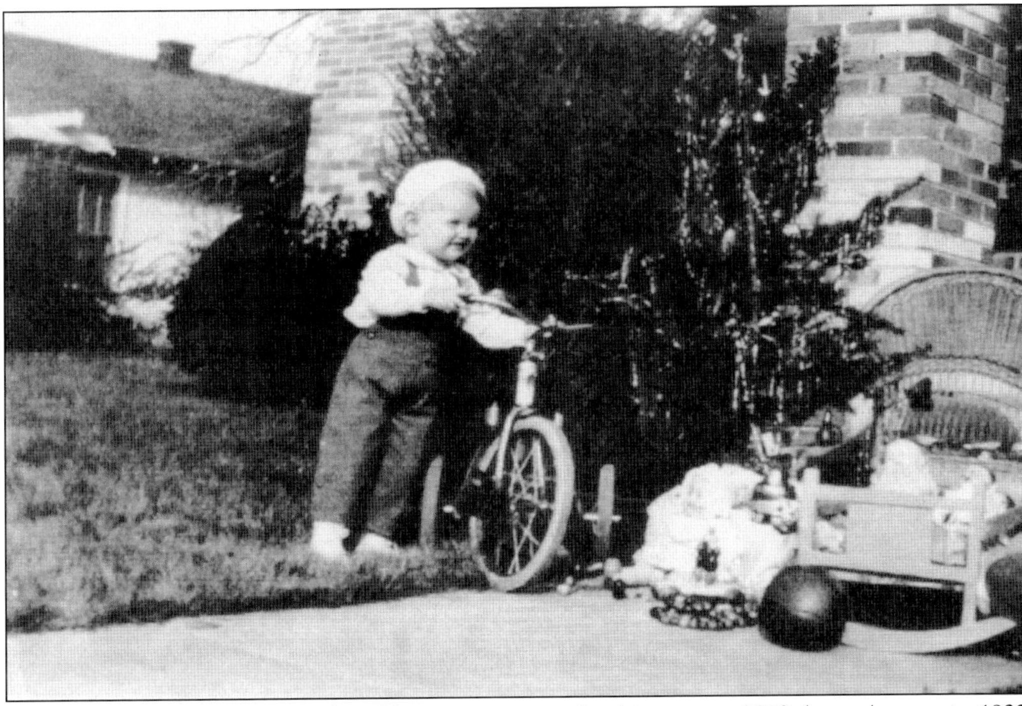

Young Beverly Sharp inspects her Christmas toys in the driveway at 2313 Aster Avenue in 1933. Before Prohibition was repealed in December 1933, there were rumors of bootleggers in Oakhurst. According to Sharp, "My parents always thought those neighbors [just west of us] were selling bootleg out of their garage because cars would drive up . . . right under our kitchen window and into their garage . . . stay just a minute . . . and be gone." (Beverly Sharp Germany.)

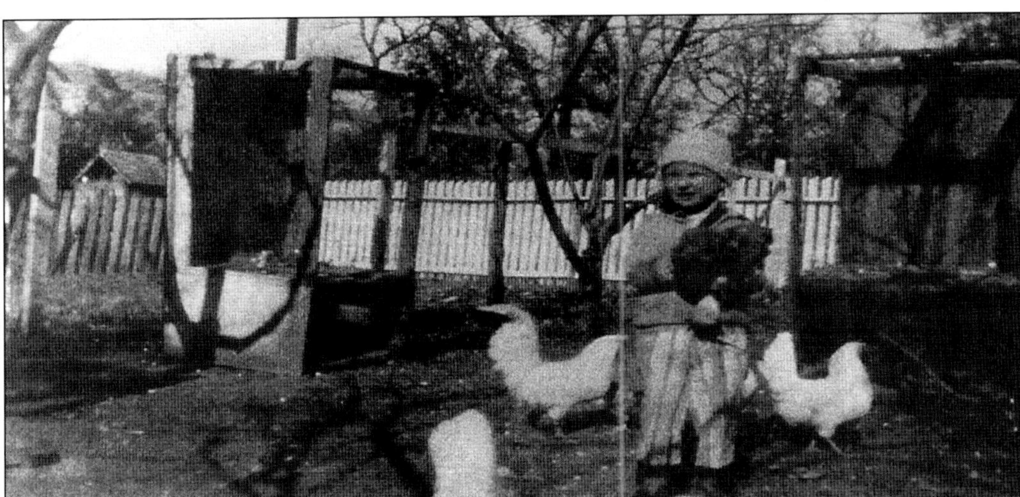

In this early-1930s photograph, Beverly Sharp is with the family's chickens in their backyard on Aster. She recalled, "My mother sold eggs to the neighbors at 12¢ a dozen. She saved quite a little sum of money. In 1934, my brother was born at the new Harris Hospital downtown. When Dad took Mother to the hospital, they wouldn't admit her until my dad paid them $100. Dad had to come home and get Mother's egg money to fill out the charge." (Beverly Sharp Germany.)

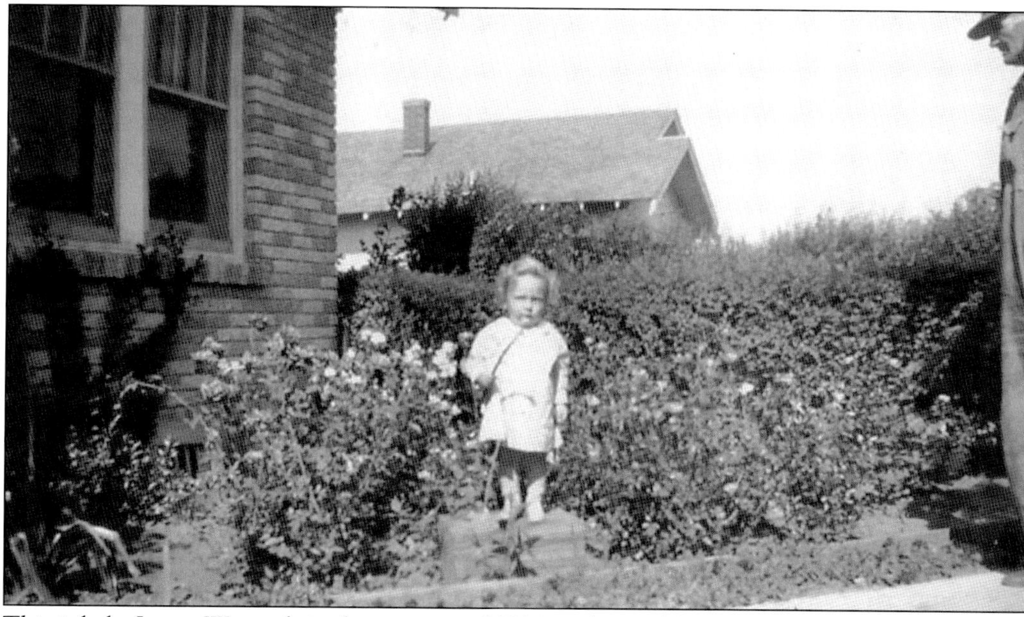

This is baby James Womack in the summer of 1934 in the prolific rose garden on the east side of the house at 2508 Primrose Avenue. His father, W.A. Womack, is visible in the far right of the photograph. Womack worked as a fireman for the Chicago, Rock Island & Gulf Railway Company. Many early Oakhurst residents worked for railroad companies. (Delia Brelsford Shiflet.)

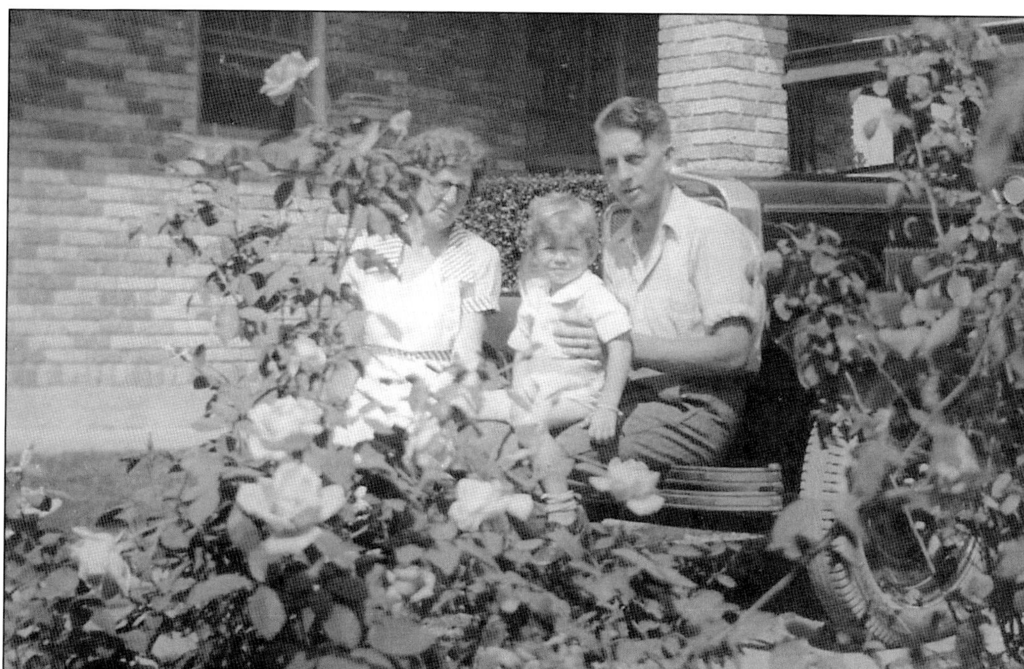

The Womack family took full advantage of the sandy loam soil in Oakhurst to grow a lush rose garden on the east side of their house at 2508 Primrose Avenue. Shown here in 1934 are Bertha Womack, her son John Carver, and a neighbor boy, Bob Hall (on Carver's lap), in the midst of the rose bushes. (Delia Brelsford Shiflet.)

Beginning in 1928, Tarrant County commissioner S.A. "Sandy" Wall and his wife, Mamie, lived at 2340 Carnation Avenue. Elected in 1924, he served until 1930. In 1933, he was appointed to the court to succeed the late J.A. Davis. Wall was a member of the court that called for the $4.8 million county highway road-building program. Part of that program was the construction of the Belknap Street overpass, which eventually made possible a short trip from downtown to Riverside and Oakhurst. Wall died in 1934. (Tarrant County Archives.)

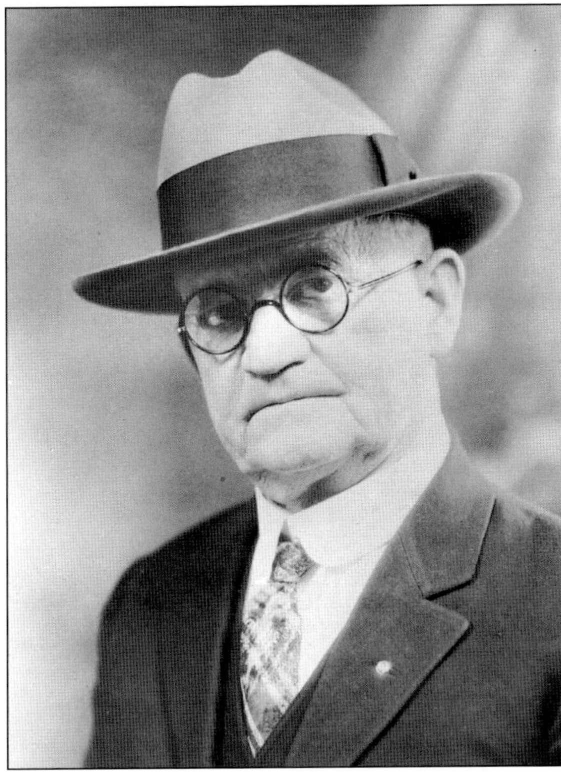

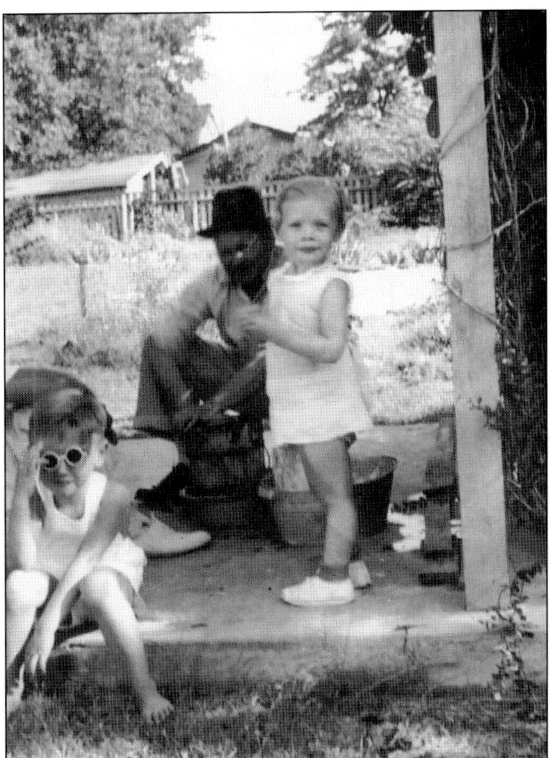

Fran Brown plays in the backyard at 2310 Primrose Avenue in July 1938. She recalls, "I was 2 and a half when we met our next door neighbors. I stuck my hand through the back fence and the 18-month-old baby—Billy Jack Ferguson—bit it. Mrs. Ferguson said, 'Bite him back. It's the only way he will learn not to bite people.' So I did." (Fran Brown Kerlin.)

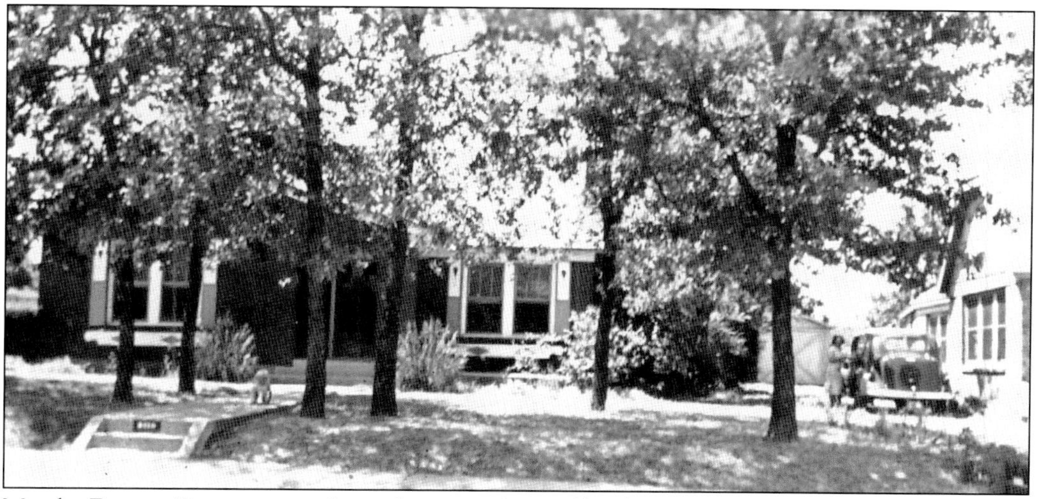

Marthe Frances Brown is seen here playing in front of her home at 2310 Primrose Avenue in the late 1930s. Her mother, Martha, worked at Armour & Company, and her father, Paul, worked at Swift & Company for 30 years in the accounting department. They paid $3,750 for the house, which was close to the Swift plant. Garwin Hutcheson, a salesman for the King Candy Company, and his wife lived here in the late 1920s. (Fran Brown Kerlin.)

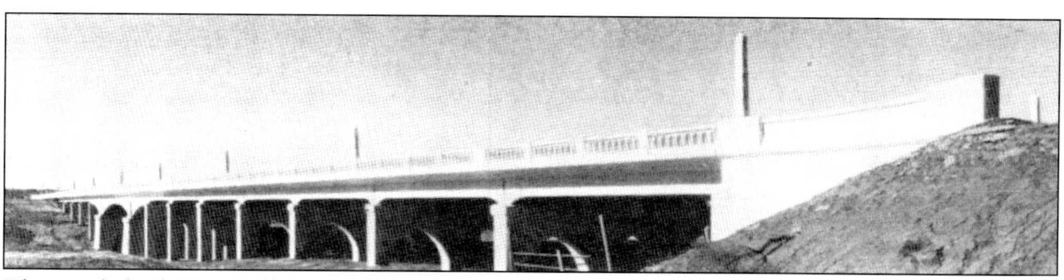

The newly built East Belknap Street Bridge (1934) between downtown and Riverside was a great boon to the Oakhurst development. For the first time, residents and visitors had a direct 2.8-mile connection between the two. This was an enhancement for the original Oakhurst neighborhood and for the West Oakhurst development, which followed in the late 1940s. (FWCC.)

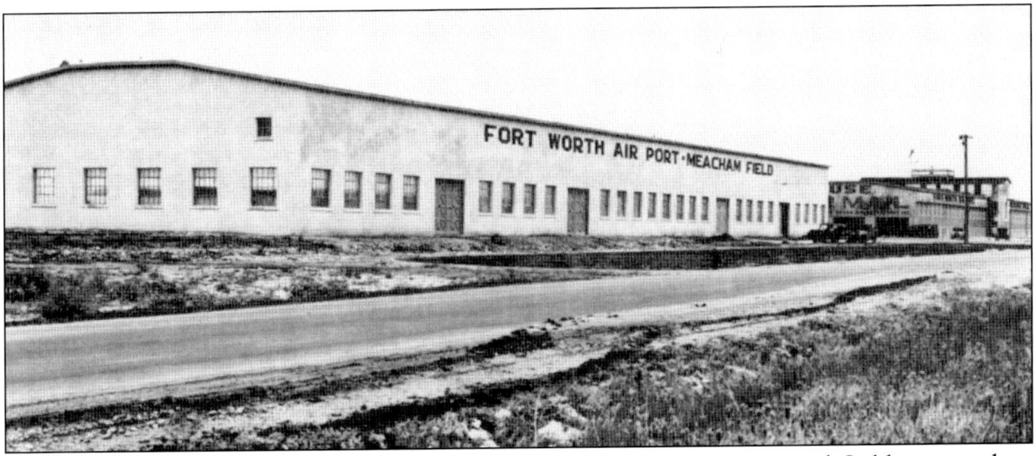

This 1930s-era hangar at Meacham Field was designed by city engineer and Oakhurst resident C. Milo Thelin. The airport, with its close proximity to Oakhurst, has long been a workplace for countless pilots, aviation workers, and aviation-related government workers who have lived in Oakhurst. (FWL.)

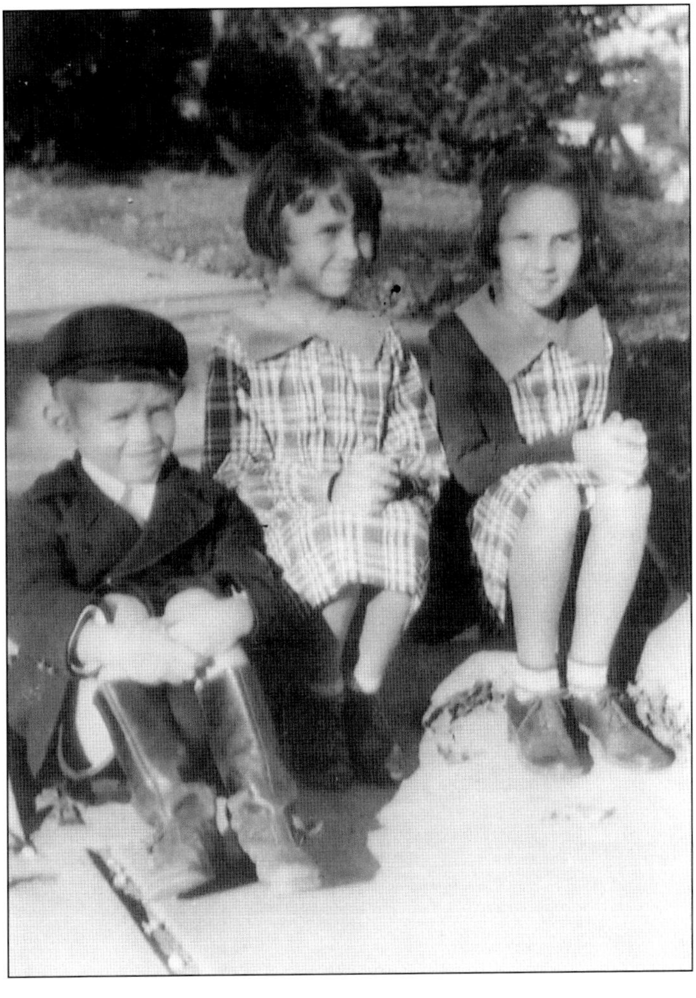

The Jefferson children, Ray (left), Anna Belle (center), and Betty Jane, are seen here in 1935 at 2501 Goldenrod Avenue. When he was six, Ray's father "cut off two little clubs" and taught him to swing at the Oakhurst Golf Course. "I could swing the clubs," he said. "It was a natural thing." And so started Ray's career in golf. He also played basketball and football. (Ray Jefferson.)

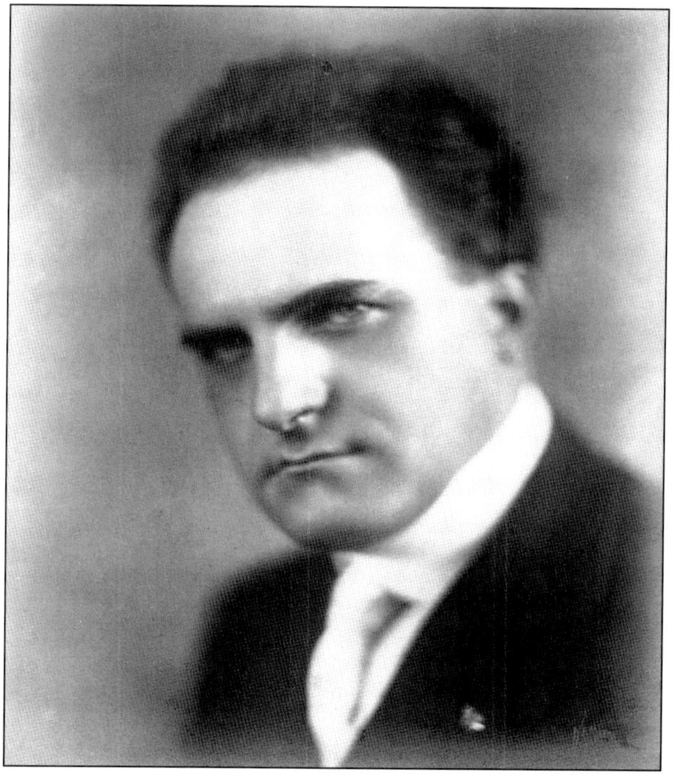

Samuel S. Losh taught music at TCU and was an important early musician in Fort Worth. He taught soldiers to sing at Camp Bowie during World War I, believing that the singing soldier could lift more weight and march farther because he was distracted by the music. Losh led many great community sings and was the choir or music director for several well-known congregations. He and his wife, Ada May, moved to 1408 Bluebonnet Drive in Oakhurst in 1937. (Mildred Hogan.)

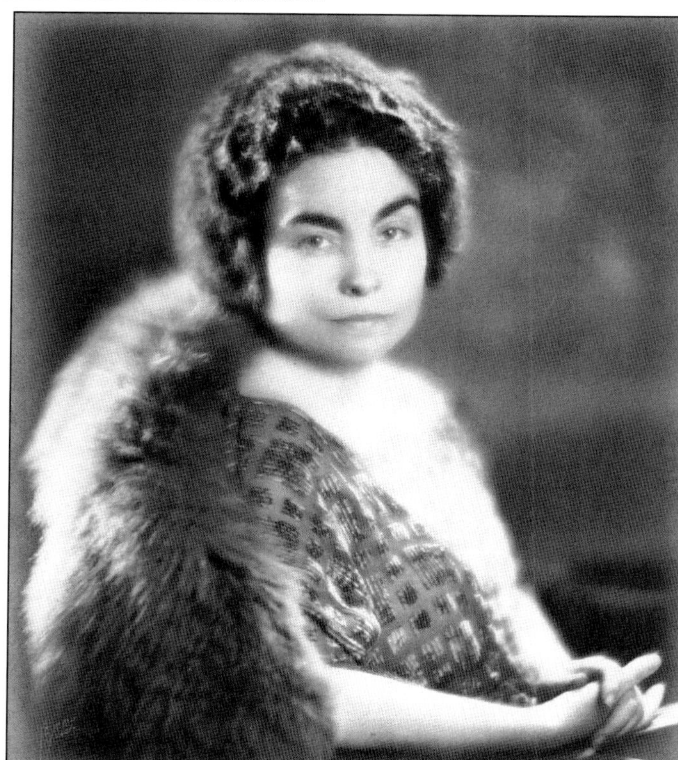

Ada May Hogan Losh was a music teacher before she met Sam Losh. Together, they operated the Losh Institute of Music and Expression and had a music studio in their Oakhurst home, where she taught piano to many neighborhood children. Their former home on Bluebonnet Drive includes a stained-glass window with the word "Losh." (Mildred Hogan.)

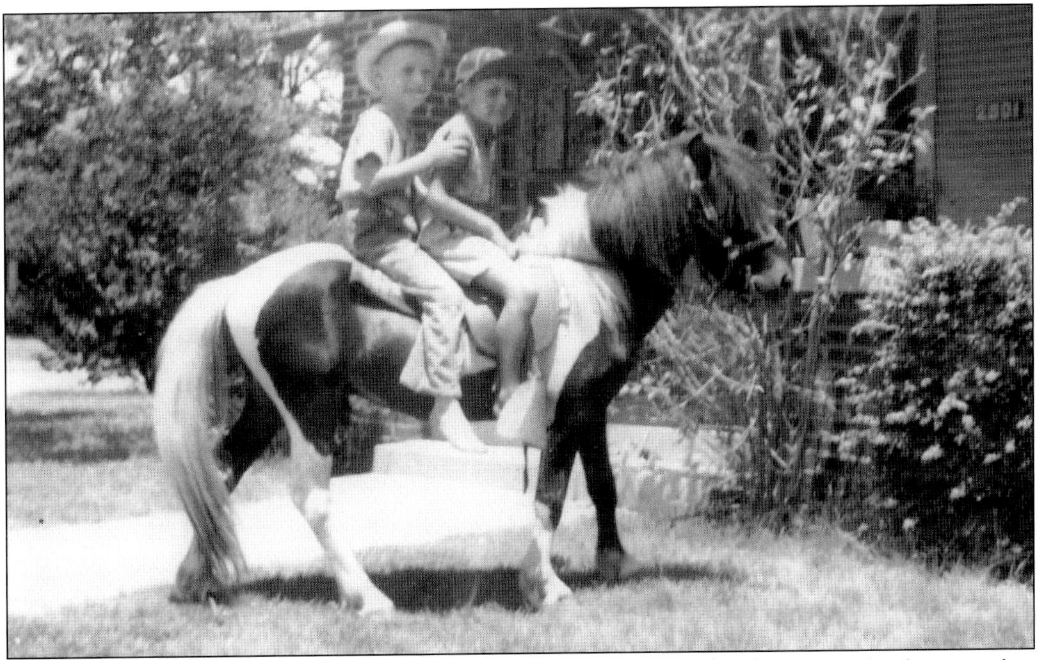

Ray Jefferson (left) and Johnny Freeman pose on Freeman's Shetland pony in the front yard at 2501 Goldenrod Avenue in 1937. Freeman kept the pony in his backyard. In Oakhurst's early days, it was not unusual for residents to keep cows or chickens in their ample backyards. Most of the houses sat on 60-foot-by-180-foot plots, providing lots of room for gardens or animals. (Ray Jefferson.)

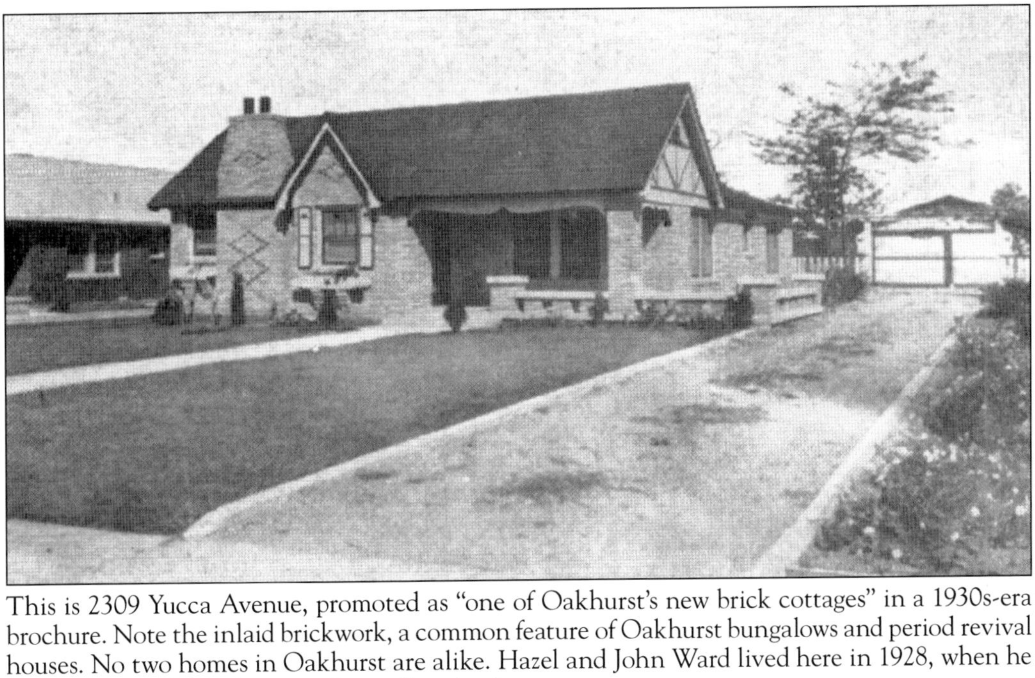

This is 2309 Yucca Avenue, promoted as "one of Oakhurst's new brick cottages" in a 1930s-era brochure. Note the inlaid brickwork, a common feature of Oakhurst bungalows and period revival houses. No two homes in Oakhurst are alike. Hazel and John Ward lived here in 1928, when he was an automobile salesman. (Larry Fanning.)

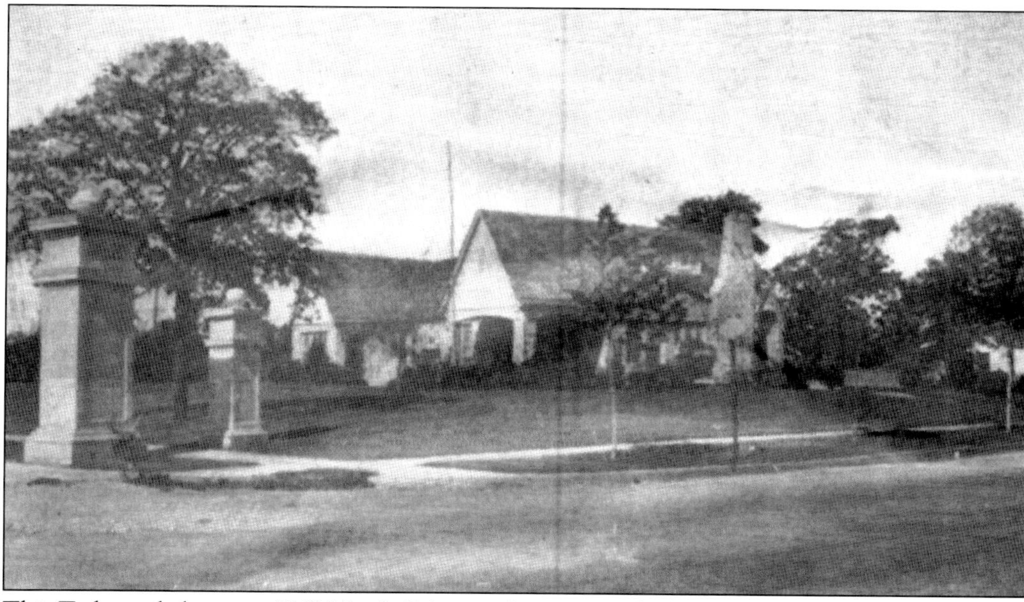

This Tudor-style home at 1803 North Sylvania Avenue was built in 1932 at the intersection with Daisy Lane and the Oakhurst entrance columns. The federal government made loans available for home improvement, "modernization," or purchase as a way to assist home owners during the Great Depression. A brochure featuring this home called it "an outstanding homeplace." Bertha and Fred H. Barney lived here in 1933, when he was vice president of the American Manufacturing Company of Texas, located north of Oakhurst on Sylvania Avenue. (Larry Fanning.)

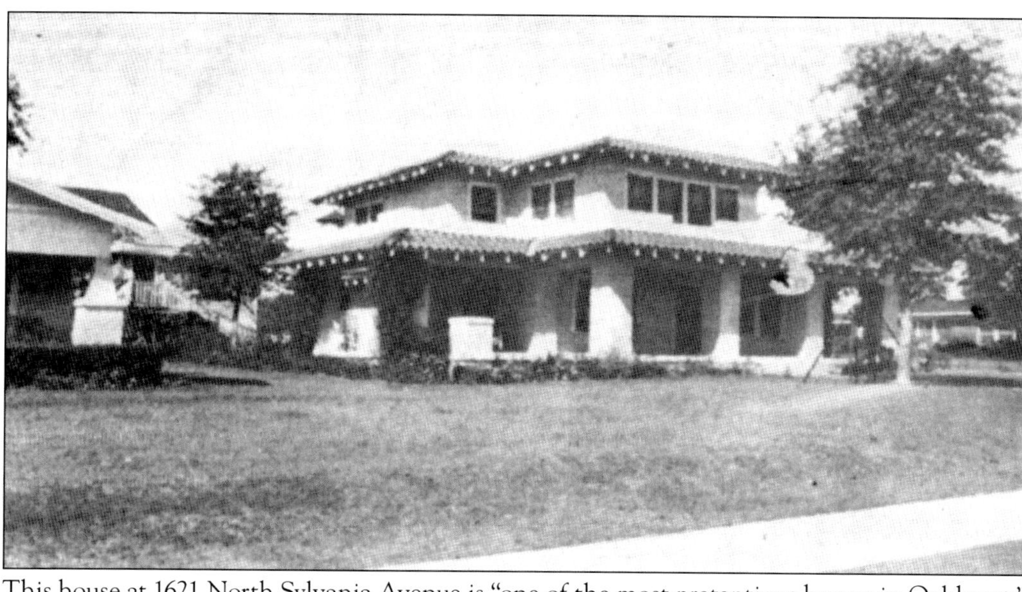

This house at 1621 North Sylvania Avenue is "one of the most pretentious homes in Oakhurst," according to the 1930s brochure in which this photograph appeared. The Mission-style house, at the corner of North Sylvania and Carnation Avenues, was constructed in 1927. Minnie and Clarence G. Worsham lived here in 1928, when he was a clerk for a railway mail service. (Larry Fanning.)

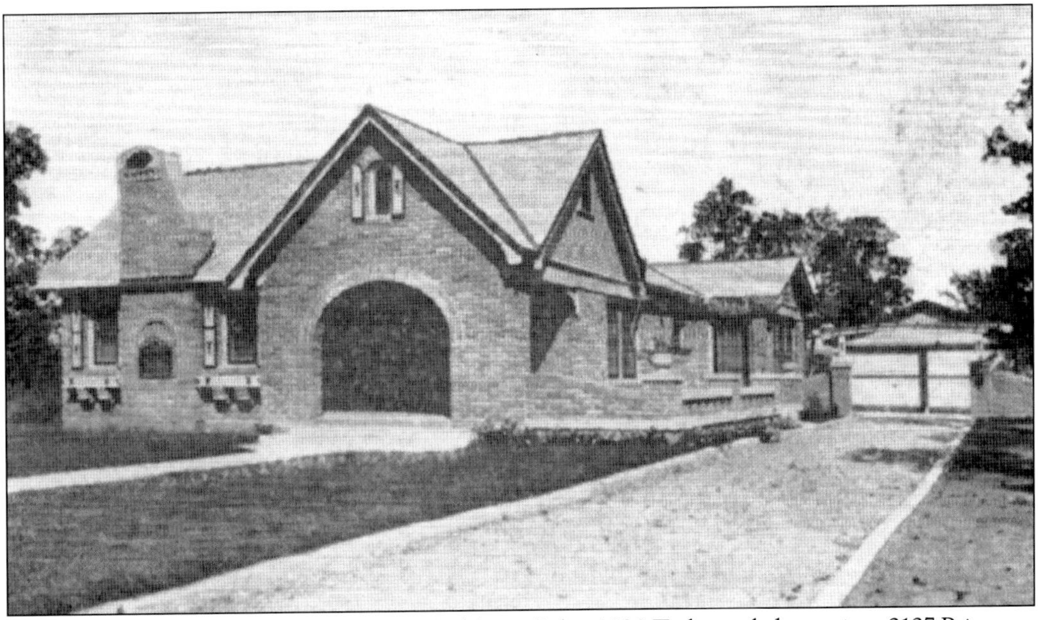

"One of the many new brick cottages in Oakhurst," this 1930 Tudor-style house is at 2127 Primrose Avenue. The curved arches are common to many Oakhurst homes. Promoters made a lot of the fact that many Oakhurst houses were constructed of brick, as that produced a substantial house. Agnes and Al Weaver lived here in 1931, when he was vice president of the National Live Stock Commission Company. (Larry Fanning.)

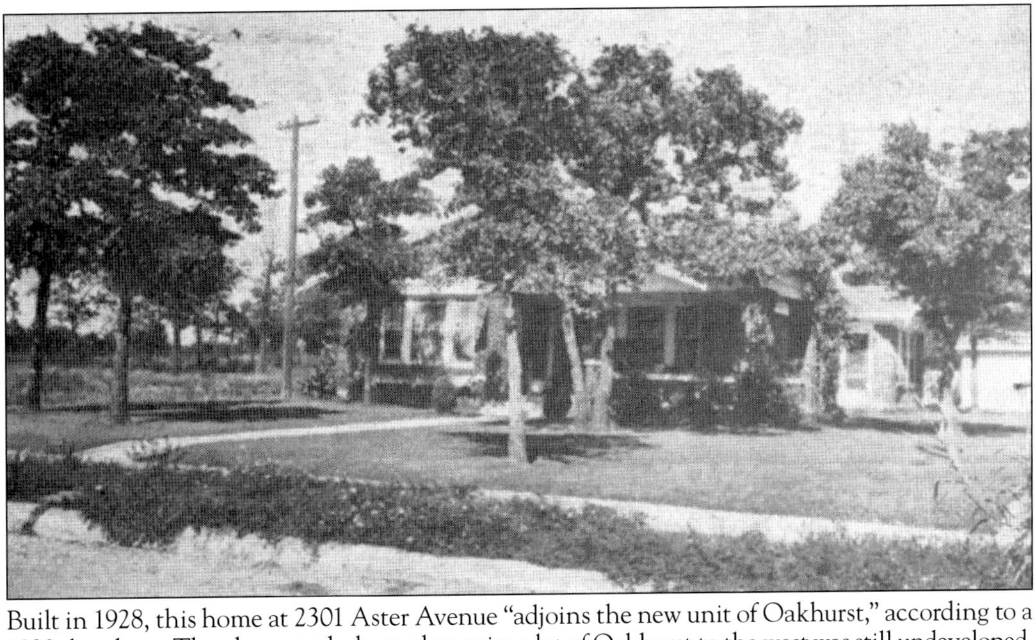

Built in 1928, this home at 2301 Aster Avenue "adjoins the new unit of Oakhurst," according to a 1930s brochure. The photograph shows that quite a lot of Oakhurst to the west was still undeveloped. The original owner was Alf Gregg, who was a "helper" at the Magnolia Petroleum Company. By 1931, Gardner W. Key of Key Brothers Real Estate owned the house. (Larry Fanning.)

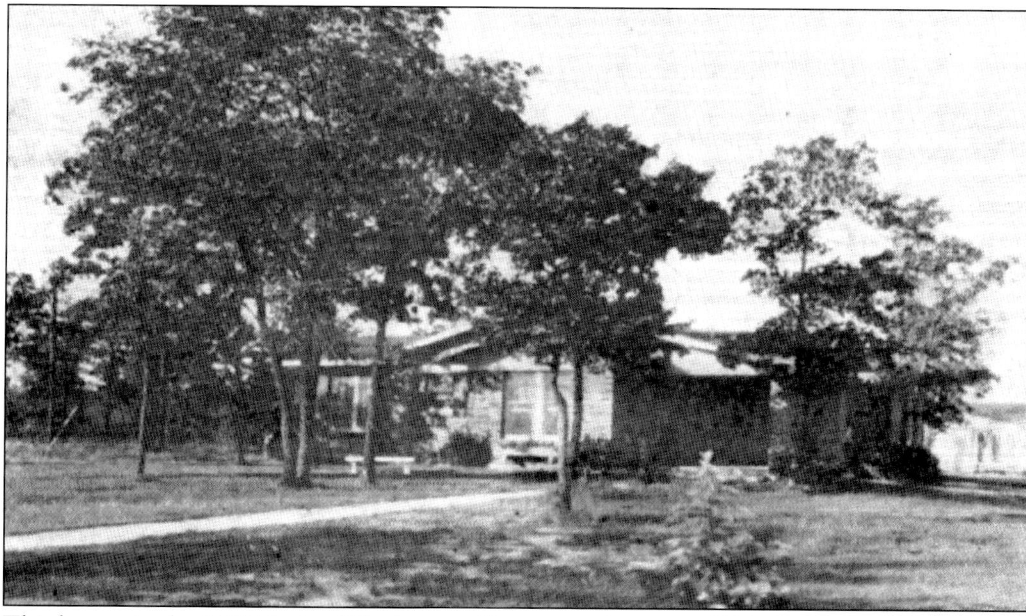

This house, in the 2100 block of Bluebonnet Drive, seen here in a 1930s Oakhurst brochure, was noted for its "profusion of native oak trees." The home appears to be almost entirely surrounded by trees and may actually be the building in Mount Olivet Cemetery just off Watauga Road now used for Advance Planning. When the home was built, Daggett's Woods still lay to the west. (Larry Fanning.)

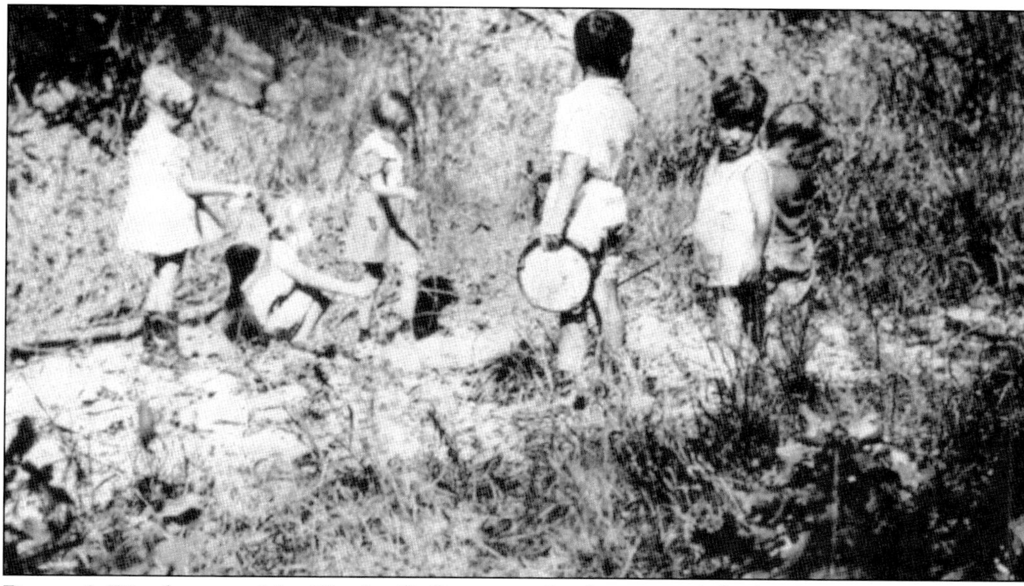

Daggett's Woods, named for Charles B. Daggett, who first owned the land, was a favorite place for Oakhurst children to play until it became West Oakhurst in the late 1940s. Beverly Germany remembers, "The Moses family [on Aster] had a black woman working for them named Roberta. She'd gather up a few of us and walk down to the wooded area on the west side of Bluebonnet Drive. There was a dry creek bed full of white rocks. She would build a fire in that creek bed and we would roast wieners or marshmallows. Even our mothers didn't do this with us." This is a 1938 photograph of that idyllic place with some of Beverly's playmates. (Beverly Sharp Germany.)

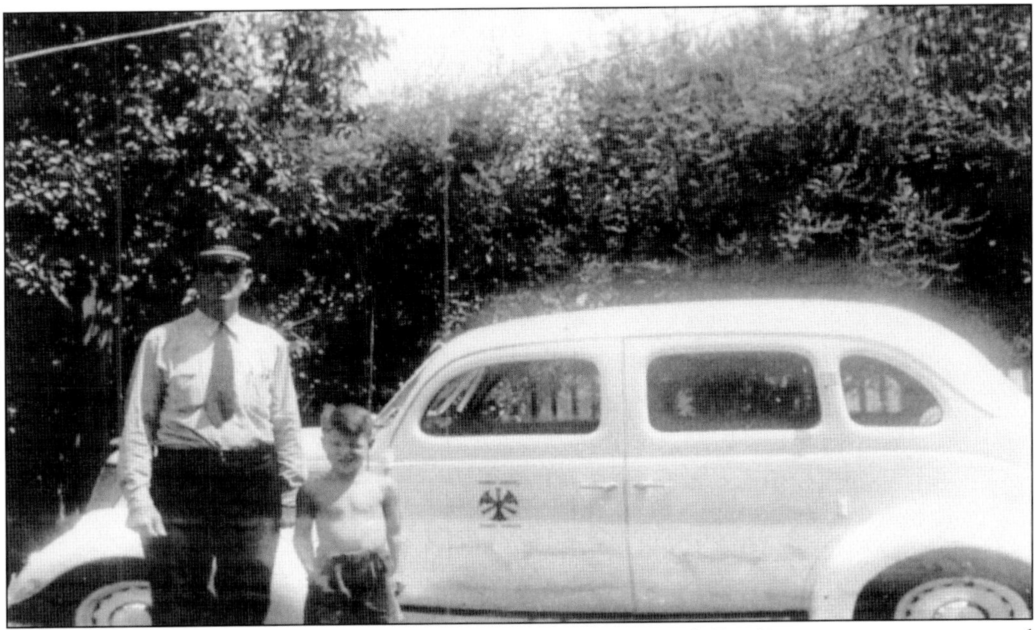

Southside District battalion chief William Sharp of the Fort Worth Fire Department was promoted to deputy fire chief when he lived in Oakhurst in 1939. He is seen here with his son Billy. The car was a perk of the position, as was a phone in his house, at a time when not everyone had one. "Many times he was called out in the middle of the night to a second alarm fire," remembers his daughter Beverly Sharp Germany. Many public servants have called Oakhurst home since its beginning. (Beverly Sharp Germany.)

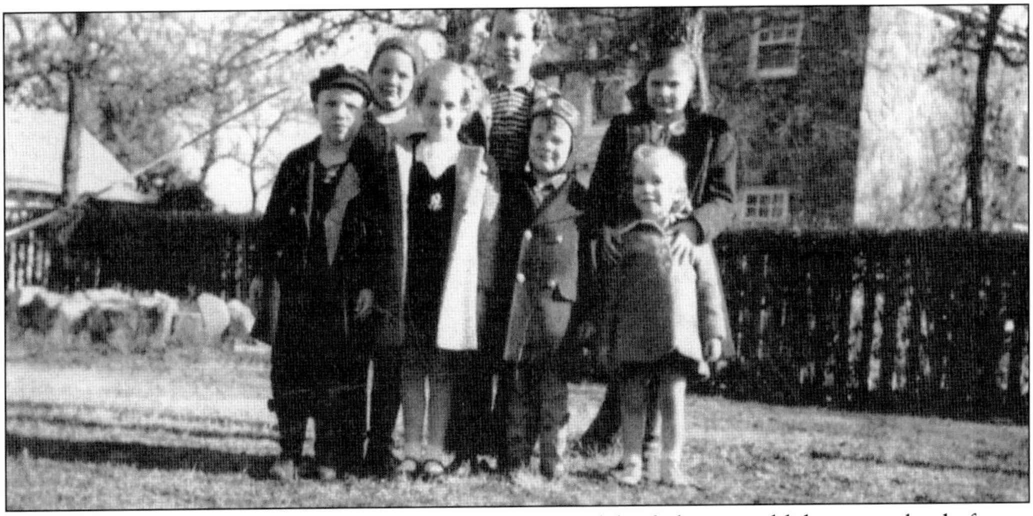

"Saturdays were special," said Beverly Germany. "One of the fathers would drive a carload of us to the Texan movie theater down on Sylvania. For 9¢, we spent the afternoon watching a Western, Roy Rogers or Gene Autry, a couple of cartoons, a short comedy such as *The Three Stooges* and there was always a serial." There were 15 kids among the 19 houses in the 2300 block of Aster Avenue in 1939. Here, the gang is just back from the movies. (Beverly Sharp Germany.)

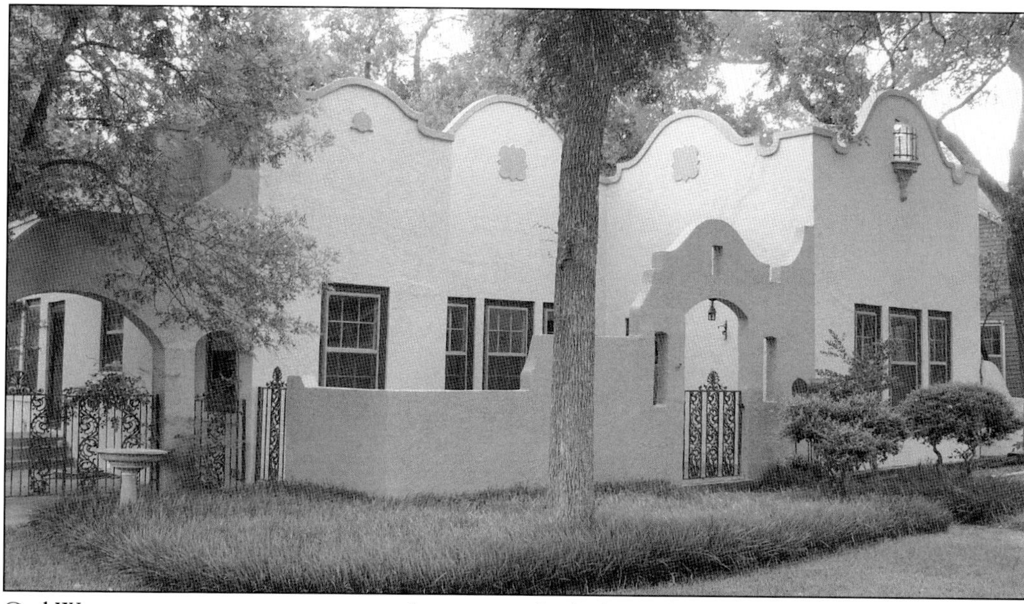

Carl Warner, a masonry contractor and carpenter, built this 1930 Mission Revival house with his wife, Velma. He was a craftsman who helped construct the Buccaneer Hotel in Galveston and the Baker Hotel in Mineral Wells. The house is unique in the neighborhood in its extensive use of stucco and interior plaster work. Known as the "Alamo House," it is a much-loved landmark in the original Oakhurst Addition. In the 1980s, it was identified as architecturally significant in the Tarrant County Historic Resources Survey. (Doyle Willis Jr.)

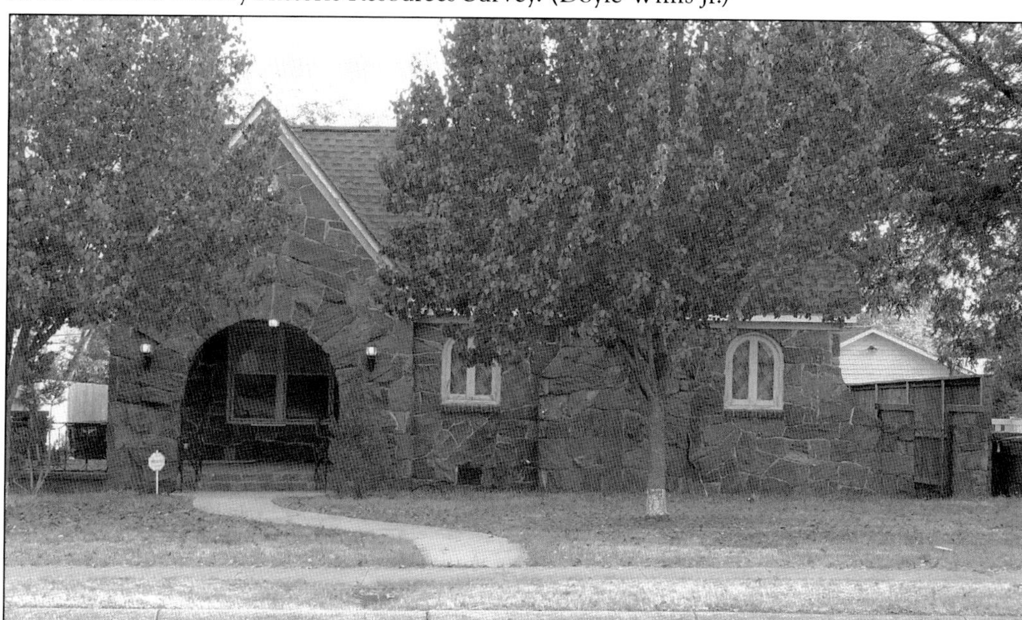

The 1933 Register-McLean House, at 2320 Yucca Avenue, combines traditional Tudor Revival style (stained-glass front windows) and arches with a sandstone exterior. Mildred and Frank Register built it for $3,000 when he was a clerk for the Gulf Refining Company. Several Oakhurst houses have sandstone exteriors. Some of the material is from Palo Pinto County, west of Fort Worth. (Doyle Willis Jr.)

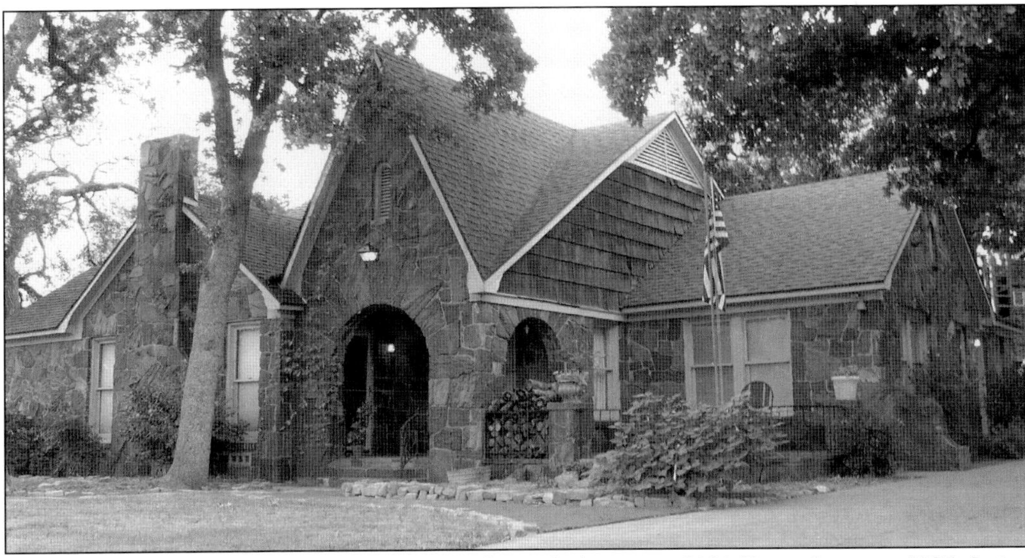

Mabel and Howard Williams built this Tudor-style house at 2201 Daisy Lane in 1936. It is a contributing structure in the Oakhurst National Register Historic District. After Mrs. Williams complained that the city would not pave Balsam Street in the 1930s, county commissioner Frank Estill said he would provide "hot topping" if the residents would pay for it. Mr. Williams, Mr. Key, and banker Charles B. "Tubby" Duke then collected $5 from each property owner on the street to pay for the paving. (Doyle Willis Jr.)

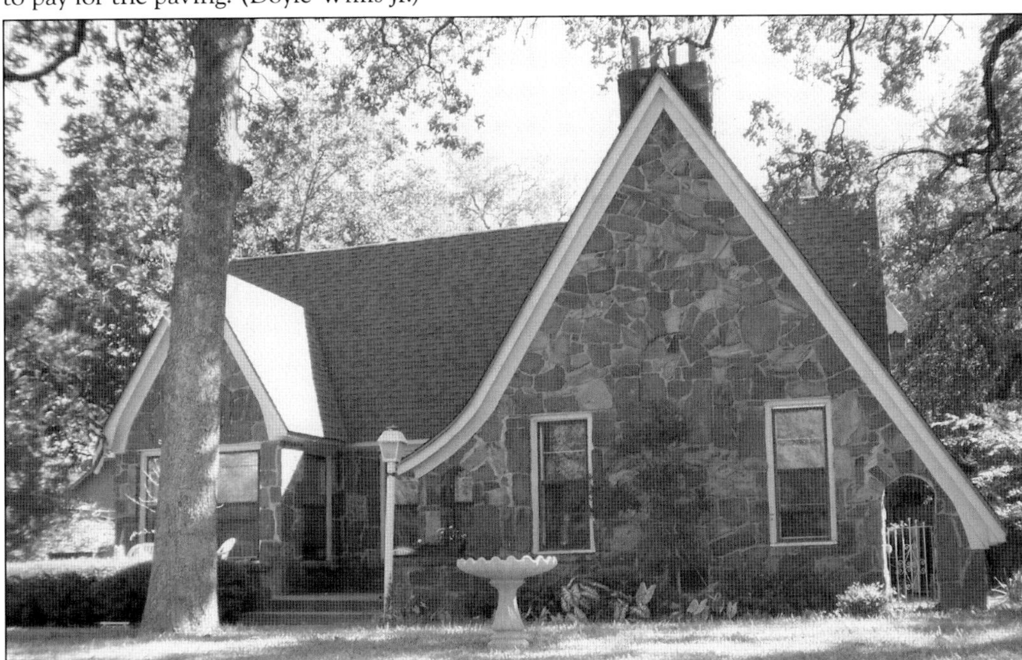

This "fairy tale style" house from 1937 makes passersby think they might see Hansel and Gretel, or perhaps Goldilocks, emerging from it. The Thornton House, at 2200 Marigold Avenue, is a stone-veneered Tudor Revival home. A contributing structure in the Oakhurst National Register Historic District, it was built by Otis Thornton, the manager of the Finley-Kitchens Commission Company. (Julie Lawless.)

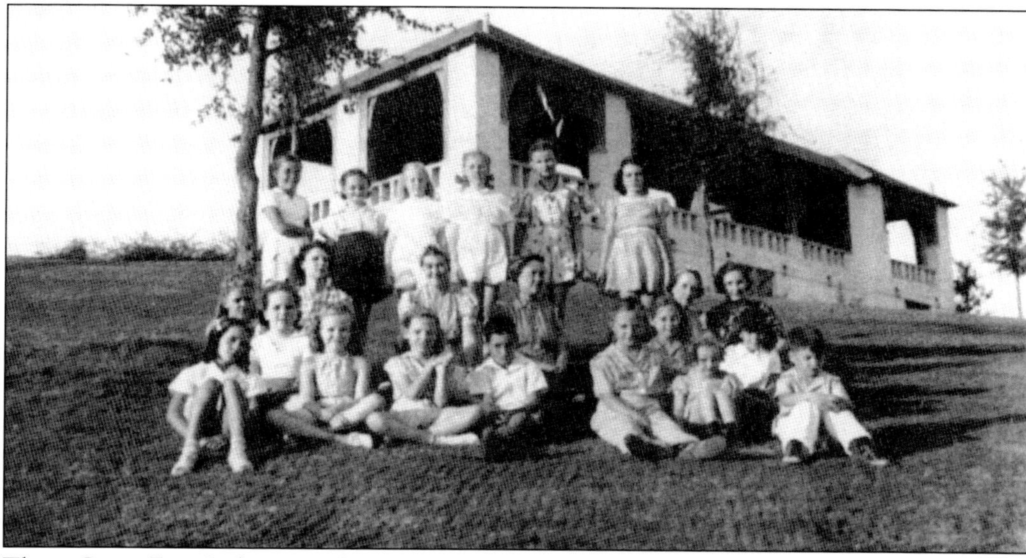

These Camp Fire Girls, many from Oakhurst, are on an outing in Trail Drivers Park in 1939. Oakhurst Scenic Drive, complete for two years at the time of this photograph, was originally intended to link to the park as part of the system of parks and connecting park roads completely encircling Fort Worth in S. Herbert Hare's 1930 Park Master Plan for Fort Worth. (Beverly Sharp Germany.)

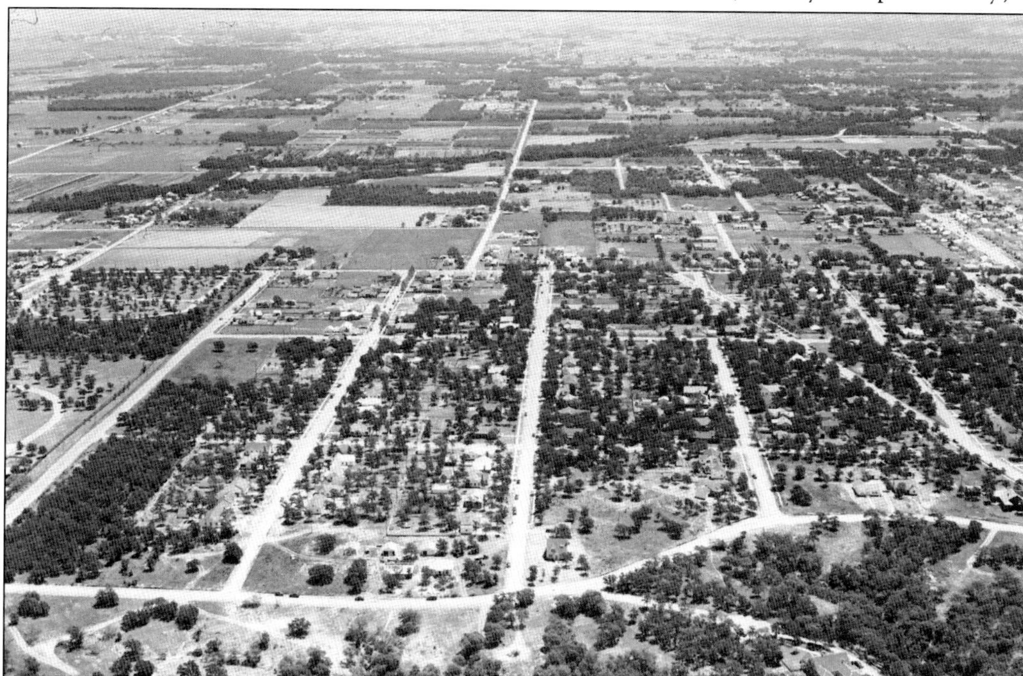

This aerial photograph of Oakhurst was taken in 1939. The neighborhood is still largely woods, with a few homes. Mount Olivet Cemetery, developed in 1907, is visible on the northern (left) edge of the neighborhood. Bluebonnet Drive (foreground) is the major north-south street bordering the Oakhurst Addition. This view is looking east. (FWSTC/SCUTA.)

Four

THE 1940S

WORLD WAR II YEARS AND BEYOND IN OAKHURST

Like people in every American neighborhood, Oakhurst residents were focused on World War II from the dropping of Japanese bombs on Pearl Harbor on December 7, 1941, to the dropping of American bombs on Hiroshima and Nagasaki, Japan, on August 6 and 9, 1945. One resident remembered Sunday lunch on December 7, 1941. When her father heard the announcer break into John Charles Thomas's radio broadcast with the news bulletin about the bombing, "he stood up, picked up his plate of food, walked to our console radio and stood there to eat."

Oakhurst residents from that era remember where they were when President Roosevelt died, as later generations would remember where they were when President Kennedy was assassinated almost 20 years later. One said, "When President Roosevelt died, we all went out to the flag pole at Oakhurst Elementary and someone prayed a prayer."

Most families had at least one relative serving in the armed forces during the war. The city's aeronautics industry ramped up to meet the need for equipment, and Fort Worth obliged with some of the largest warplane assembly lines in the country. Oakhurst sent male and female workers to those factories. War shortages and rationing turned up in the usual places, but Amon Carter Riverside High School students in 1944 and 1945 made a most unusual sacrifice, which saddens some to this day: unlike most other Fort Worth high schools, ACRHS students gave up their traditional senior annual for a smaller booklet version as a contribution to the war effort.

After the war, as the men returned home to old jobs or found new ones, families were again looking at Oakhurst as a place to settle down. The West Oakhurst Addition suddenly sprang to life. By 1949, Ranch homes were popping up all over the newly opened area, which had been a private woods for Oakhurst children for the first 25 years of the neighborhood's existence. Not only did architectural styles change, the neighborhood actually added about another 30 percent of its eventual total population beginning in the late 1940s.

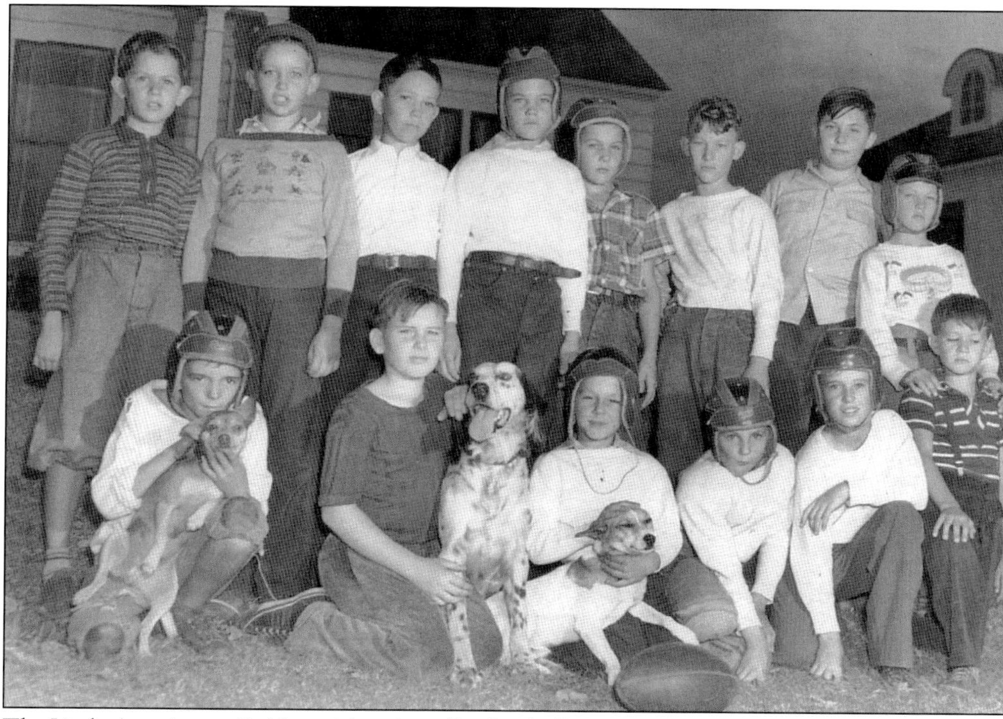

The Little Americans, Oakhurst's boys' sandlot football team, is shown in 1941, just before America's entry into World War II. The team practiced at Mount Olivet and at Oakhurst Elementary's field. They played Arlington Heights and Polytechnic Heights teams and others for several years. Seen here are, from left to right, (first row) Pete McDonald, Lonnie Price, Dinky Blankenship, Bruce Dillon, Ray Jefferson, and Bob Hardie; (second row) David Anderton, Harry Redell, James Johnston, Donald Blankenship, Johnny Freeman, Charles Sides, Ronald Walker, and Brooks Feland. The team mascots are, from left to right, Snuffy, Buck, and Tony. (Ray Jefferson.)

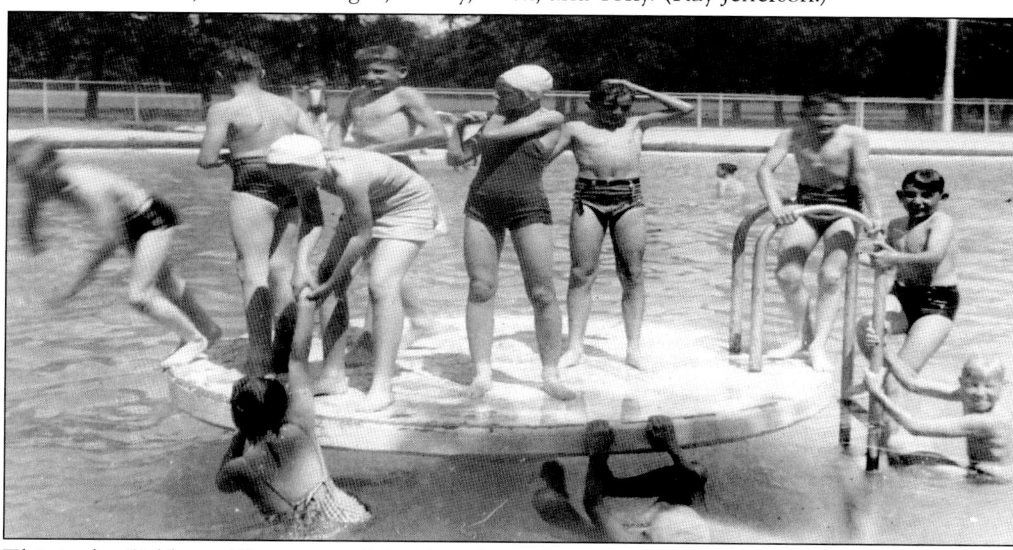

This is the Oakhurst Elementary School sixth-grade graduation swim party, in 1941 at Sylvania Park Pool. From its establishment in the 1920s, Sylvania Park was the central focus of recreation in Riverside. (Beverly Sharp Germany.)

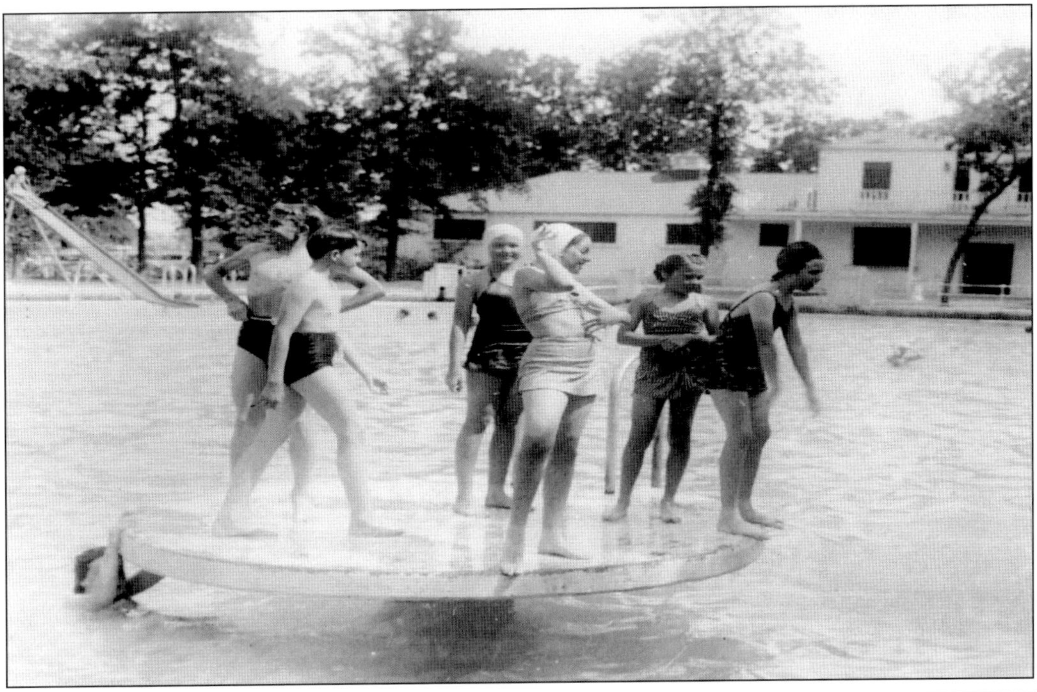

Above is another photograph of the 1941 Oakhurst Elementary School sixth-grade party at Sylvania Park Pool. The old Sylvania Park bathhouse is in the background. (Beverly Sharp Germany.)

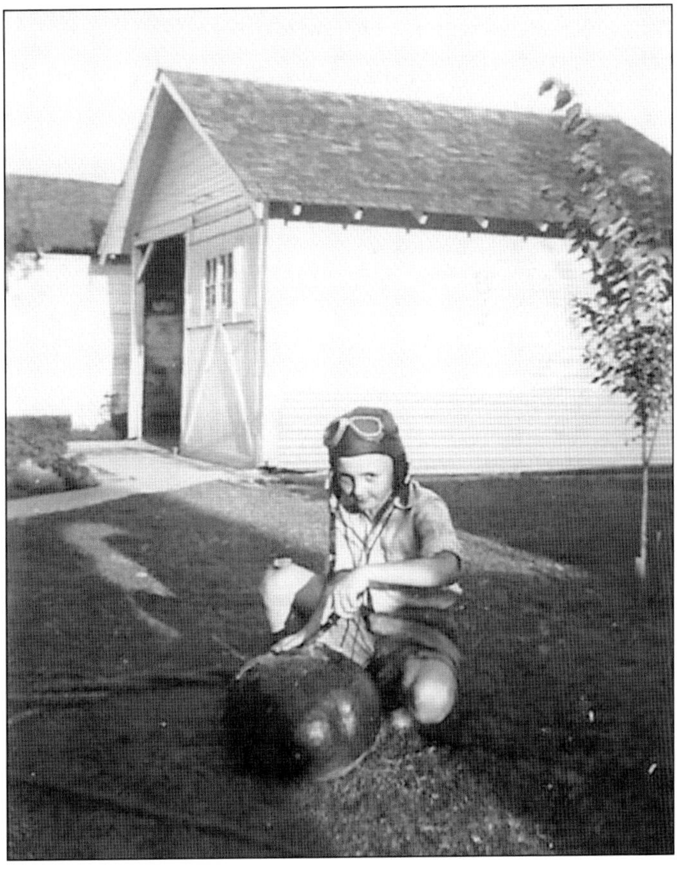

James Womack is in popular aviator goggles in the early 1940s at his parents' home at 2508 Primrose Avenue. David Martin of Daisy Lane remembered seeing a Navy Corsair plane flying from Meacham Field over Oakhurst during the war and disappearing before it crashed just east of North Sylvania Avenue, between Primrose and Marigold Avenues, killing the pilot but no residents. His school friend Buford Brian turned crash wreckage over to the FBI. (Delia Brelsford Shiflet.)

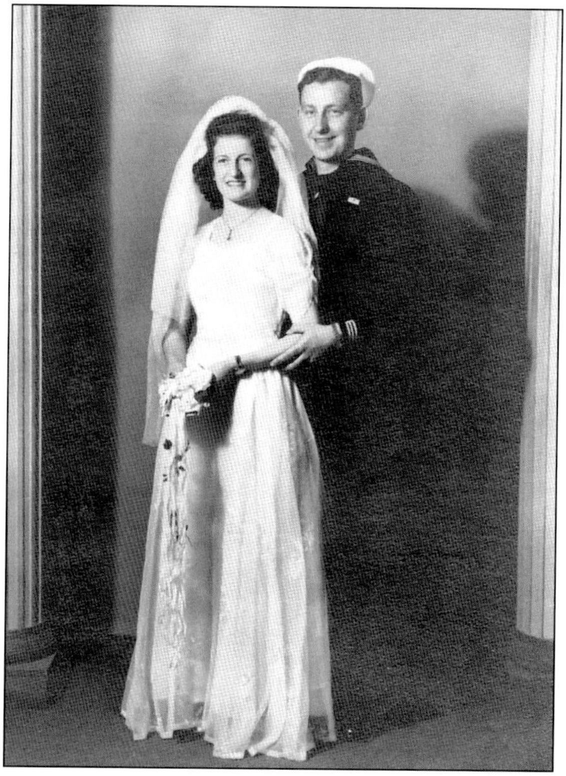

Mary Womack and Joe Brelsford married in October 1942 in San Francisco. Mary, a Primrose Avenue resident, met Joe at Riverside Christian Church when she was 15. Joe, 16, told a friend that day that he would "marry that girl." But Pearl Harbor dashed marriage plans, and Brelsford signed up to serve on the USS *Pennsylvania*. Mary followed him to San Francisco, where they married. She went to work for the federal government, monitoring Japanese propaganda broadcasts. (Delia Brelsford Shiflet.)

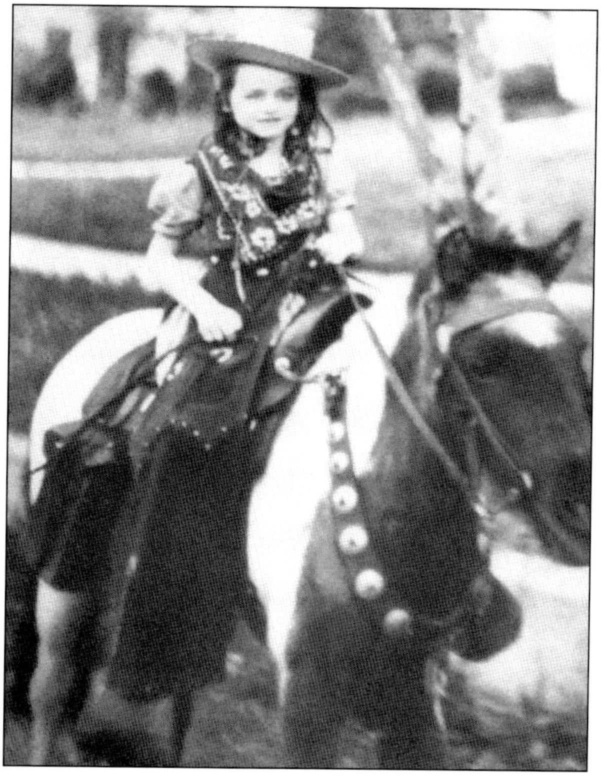

Carolyn Story rides a pony near her home at 2516 Daisy Lane about 1943. She remembers, "A man would come around the neighborhood and offer a short ride and a picture for a price—kind of like ice cream vendors now." She and David Martin attended Mrs. Regan's Nursery School on Springdale Road. Martin recalls, "During recess the boys pretended to be soldiers fighting and girls pretended to be Army nurses or WACS. There was a World War I gas mask hanging in the barn that provided a great prop." (Carolyn Story Bailey.)

Mary Margaret Thompson poses in front of her 1941 home at 2221 Primrose Avenue in the early 1940s. Note the screened-in front porch on the right, a common feature of Oakhurst homes. In later years, as the Thompson family grew, the porch was converted into a bedroom. (CeCe Thompson.)

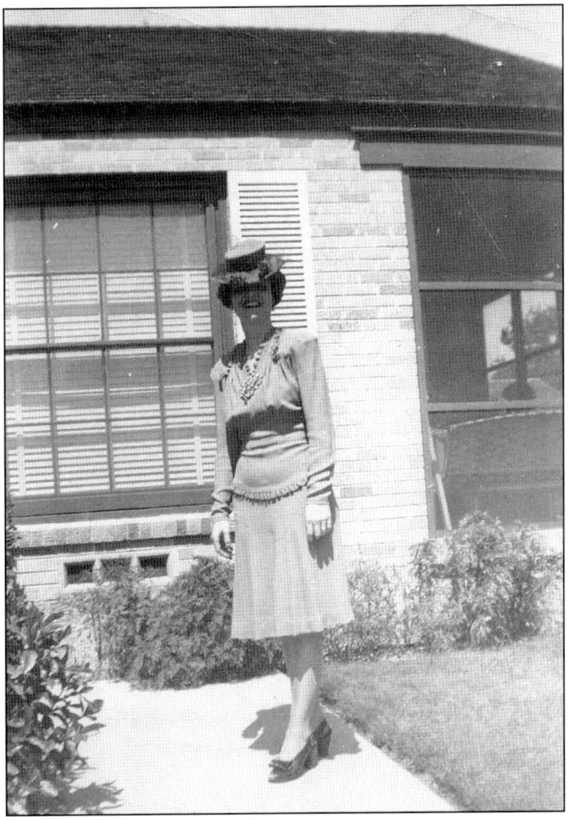

Below, children of Oakhurst Methodist Church pose in a Tom Thumb wedding in 1943. Many Oakhurst residents were church members. "We met in the cafeteria at Oakhurst Elementary until money could be raised to build the church," remembered Sue Shugart Drautz. That building, constructed in 1942, was at 1516 North Sylvania Avenue, at its intersection with Honeysuckle Avenue, across from Oakhurst. (Sue Shugart Drautz.)

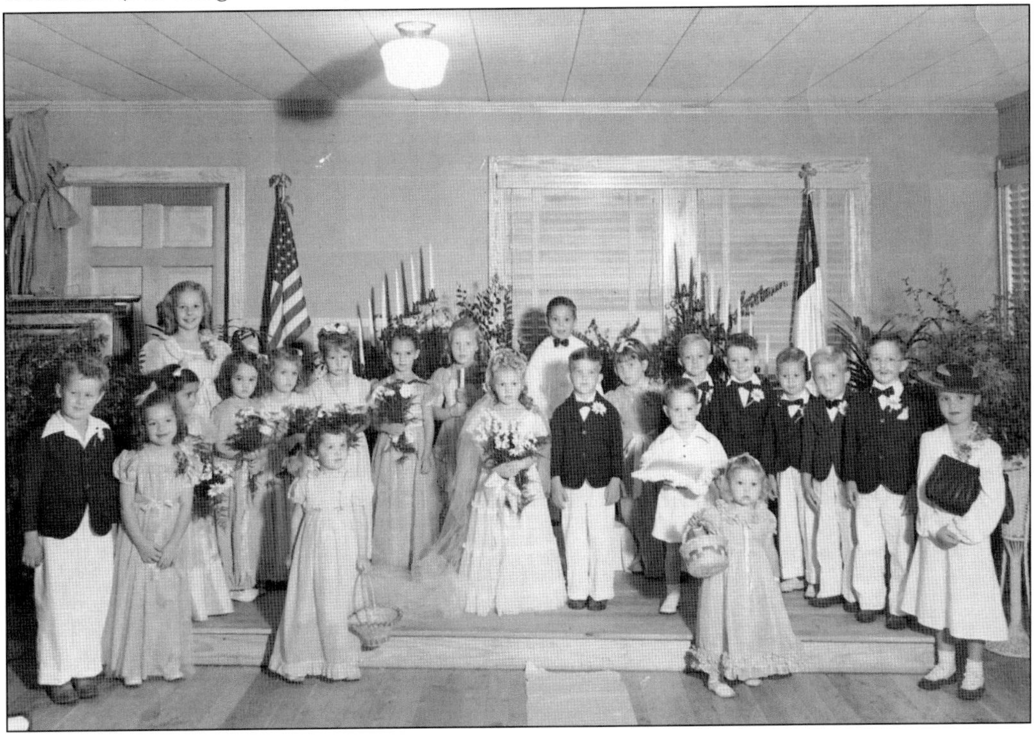

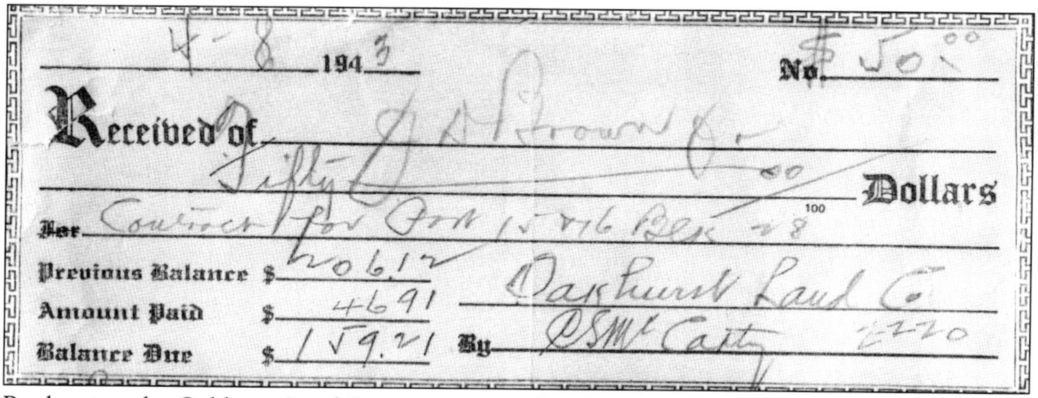

4-8 1943 No. $50.00

Received of J.D. Brown Jr.

Fifty 00/100 Dollars

For Contract for Lot 15 776 Blk 8

Previous Balance $206.12

Amount Paid $46.91

Balance Due $159.21

Oakhurst Land Co.

By RSMcCarty 2220

By the time the Oakhurst Land Company wrote this receipt to J.D. Brown in 1943 for payment on a lot at 2220 Marigold Avenue, the company had been in business for almost 20 years. Lots were still available in Oakhurst during World War II. (Graham Brizendine.)

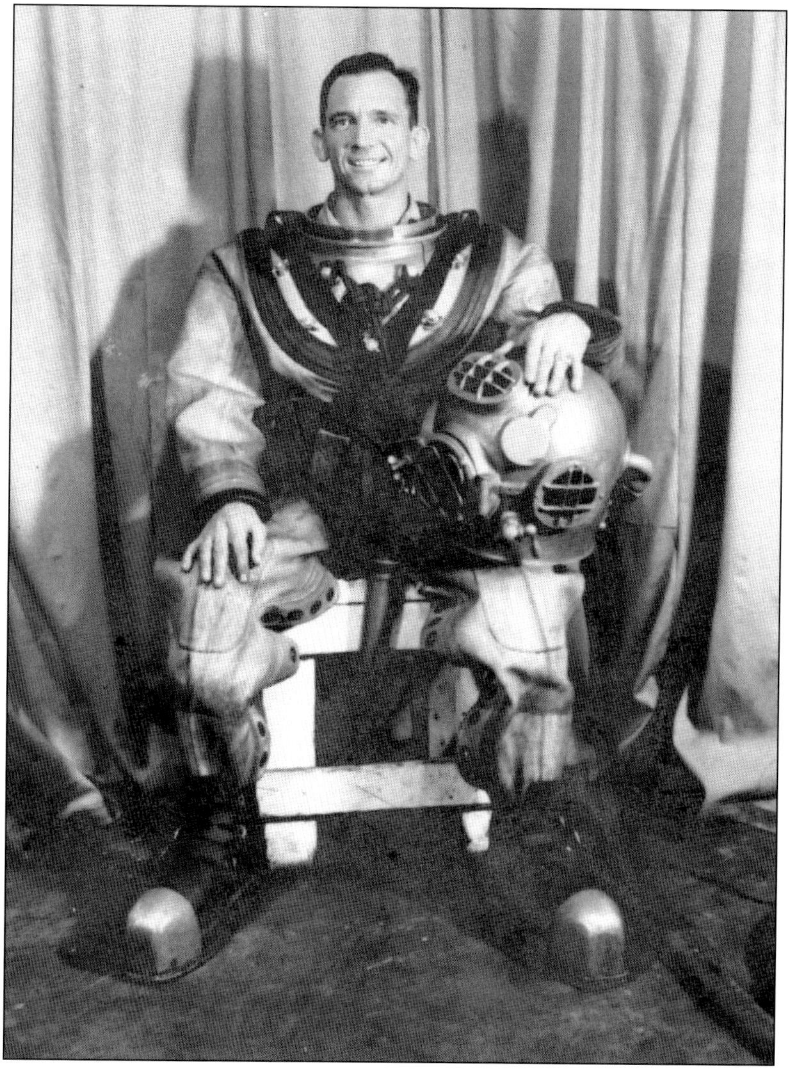

Thomas Otto Lambert was a diver for the Navy during World War II. He was part of the team that helped salvage ships that sank at Pearl Harbor on December 7, 1941. He and his wife, Lazell, built a home on Daisy Lane in 1950. (Lazell Lambert Banowsky.)

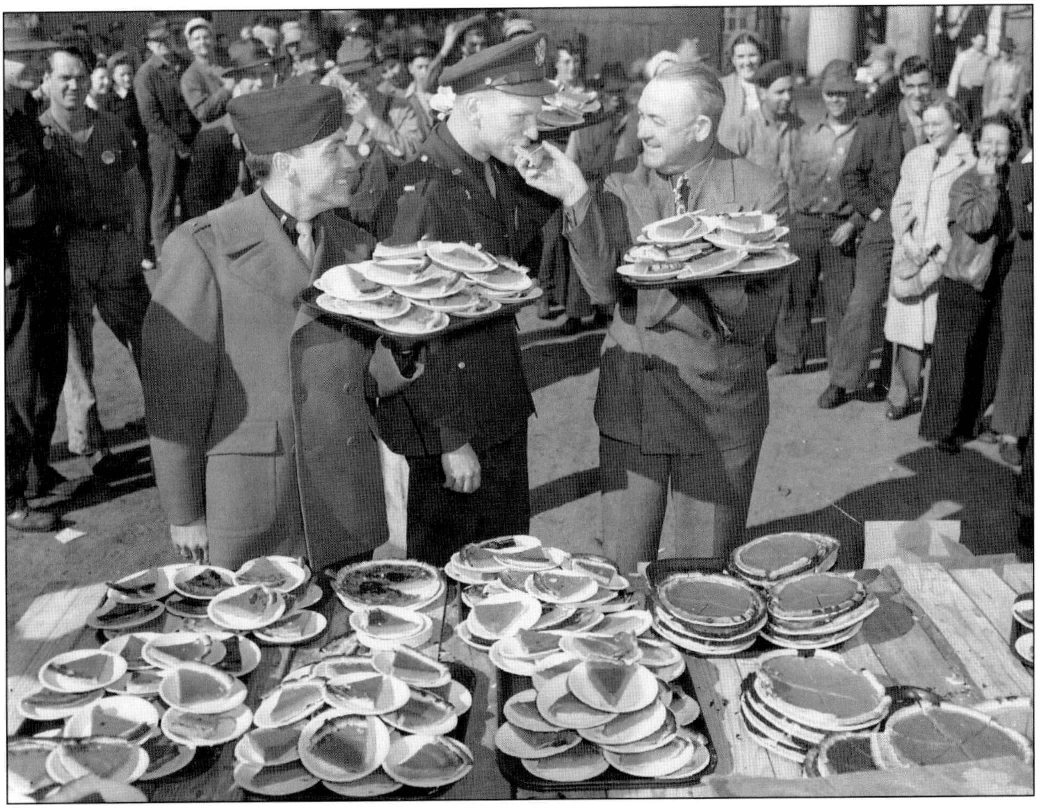

William J. Gourley (above, right), president of the American Manufacturing Company and a Wisteria Court resident, shares pie with Navy officer W.J. Cayotte (center). Cayotte was the liaison between American Manufacturing and the Navy at the company's North Sylvania Avenue plant during World War II. The company produced war materiel for the federal government and was, at the time, the largest employer in Fort Worth. (Frances Lott Turella/Wendy Vann Roach.)

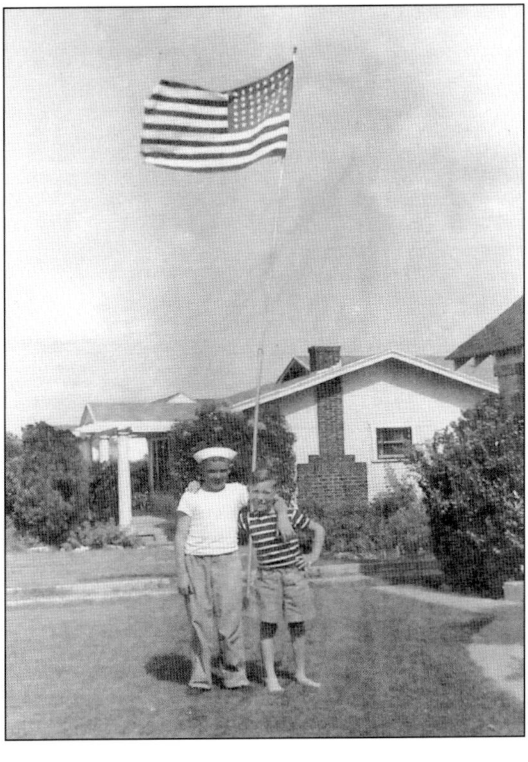

In June 1944, with the greatest amphibious assault in human history beginning the end of World War II on Omaha Beach in France, James Womack (left) and John Patterson Carver showed their patriotism with the US flag and a sailor's hat at 2508 Primrose Avenue. Everyone was thinking of the soldiers from Oakhurst who hit the beaches to drive back the Nazis and free Europe. (Delia Brelsford Shiflet.)

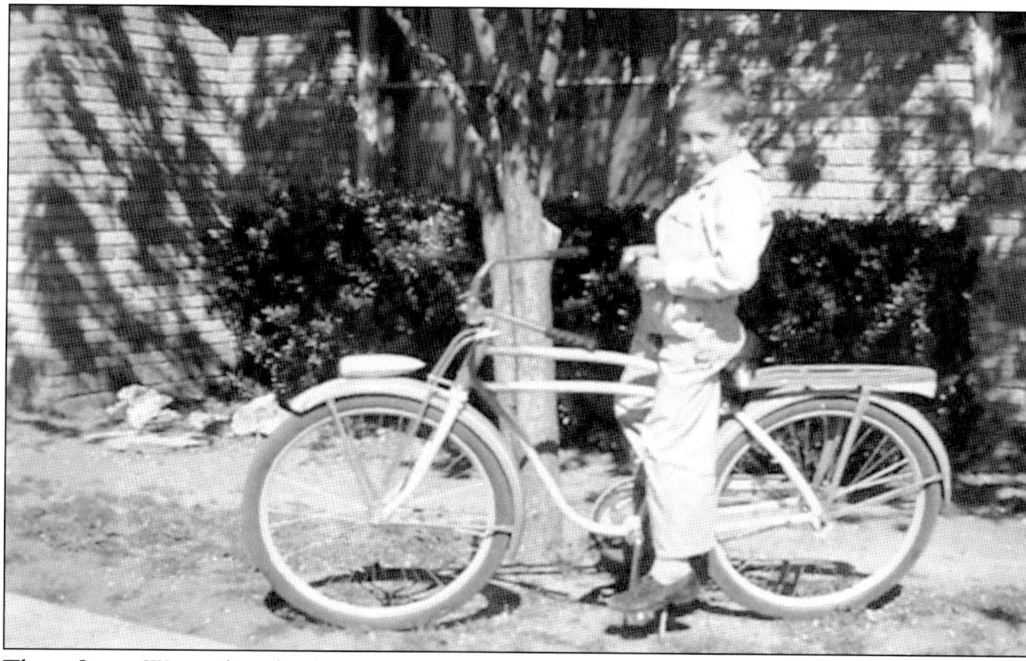

This is James Womack on his bike in 1941 in Oakhurst. David Martin wrote about metal shortages during the war: "An enterprising Oakhurst man began to collect old toy wagons and bicycles to rebuild and paint for resale. There was very little new merchandise available. I got one of his little bicycles for Christmas. Copper pennies were replaced with iron, cigarettes were no longer packaged with foil. Finally iron, too, was going to war." (Delia Brelsford Shiflet.)

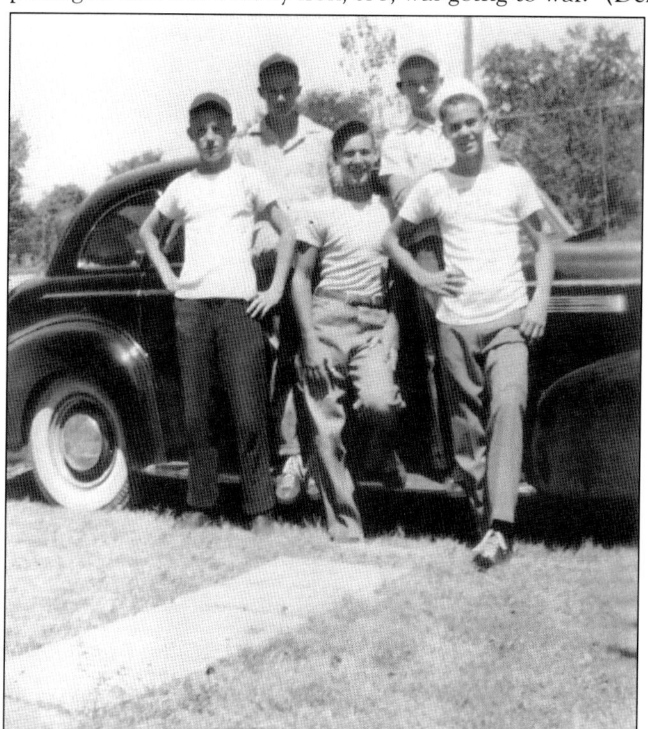

This is a 1945 photograph of Oakhurst teenagers in the backyard at 2501 Goldrenrod Avenue. They are, from left to right, (first row) Ray Jefferson, Johnny Freeman, and Donald Blankenship; (second row) brothers Earl and Joe Collins. Jefferson's father was an auto mechanic who sometimes worked on Oakhurst developer John P. King's cars. "Our house was built in 1928 and Dad bought it in 1930; his mortgage payment was $18 a month," Jefferson remembers. (Ray Jefferson.)

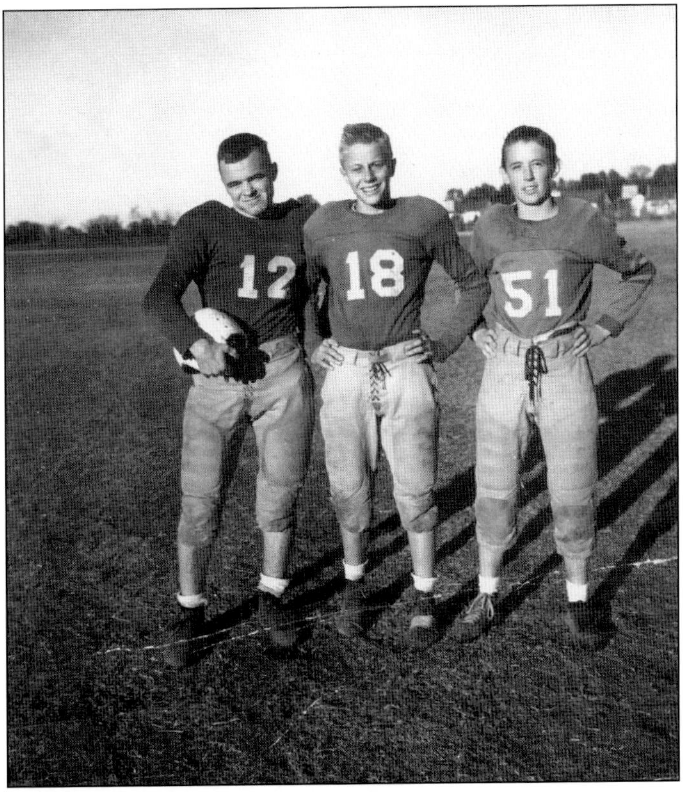

Oakhurst friends Perry Luckey (left), John Ellis (center), and Ray Jefferson pose in 1946 at Amon Carter Riverside High School. The three started together at Oakhurst Elementary and graduated from high school in 1948. Luckey, who lived on Primrose Avenue, became the chief financial officer of Mobil Oil. Ellis, from Yucca Avenue, became a judge in Dallas County. Jefferson became a PGA club golf professional and owned a golf business. They were all part of the Oakhurst Texan Theater gang. (Ray Jefferson.)

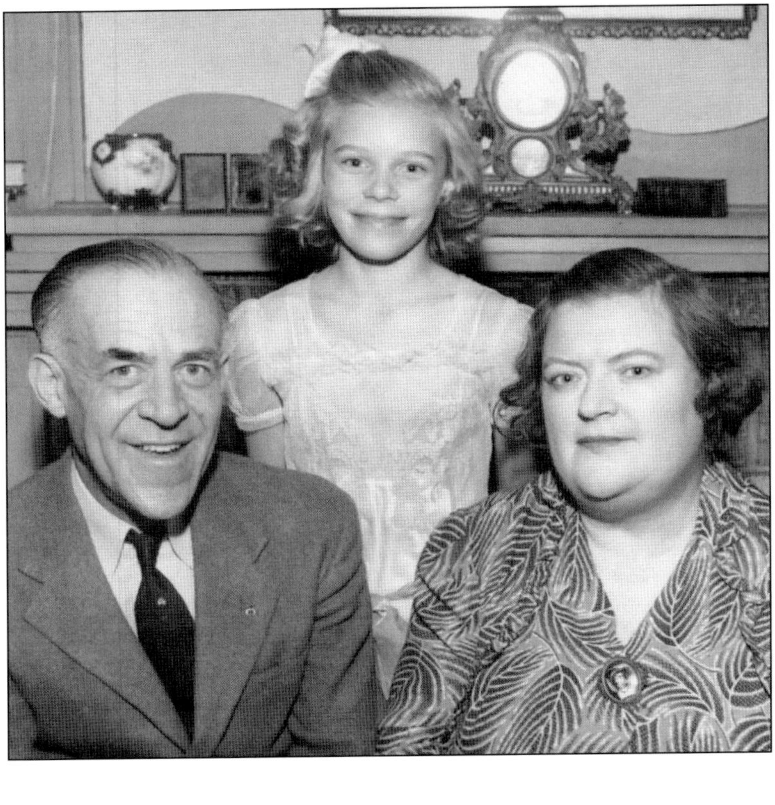

Fran Brown and her parents, Paul and Martha Brown, are shown in 1945 at their home at 2310 Primrose Avenue. As a youth, Paul was known as "The Boy Artist of Fort Worth." He painted longhorn steer heads on the transoms at the Exchange Building in the Fort Worth Stockyards. Fran became an organist and pianist and taught music at Riverside Middle School. She was the piano teacher of Oakhurst child music prodigy John Thomas Lenox. (Fran Brown Kerlin.)

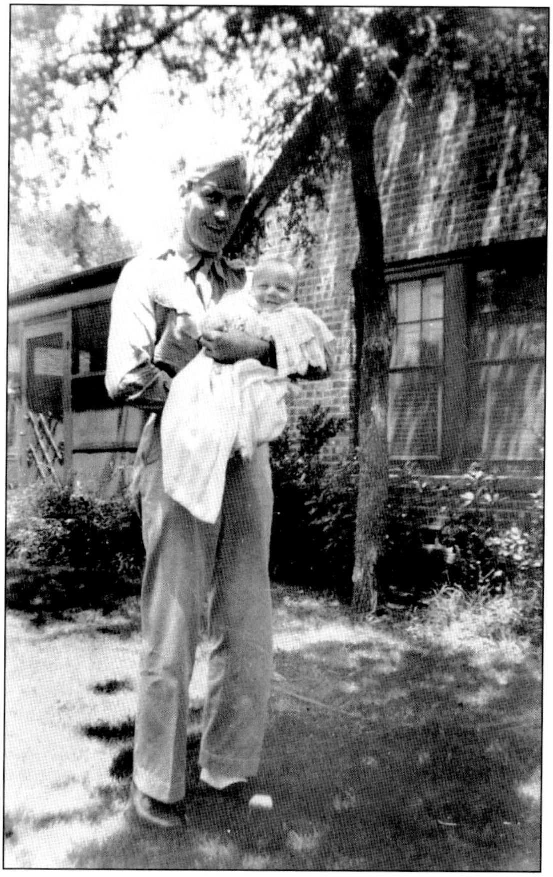

Lt. Francis H. Thompson stands with his infant son Paul in late 1945 at 2221 Primrose Avenue. Thompson was injured on Leyte, an island in the Philippines, and was awarded the Distinguished Service Cross during World War II. His daughter CeCe Thompson remembered, "General Douglas MacArthur said he would have given him the Medal of Honor, but he survived the Japanese attack and the general reserved the Medal of Honor for those soldiers who died. I am very satisfied with the DSC as he lived to become my wonderful Dad." (CeCe Thompson.)

Shown below are the Amon Carter Riverside High School District 7AA football champions of 1942. Many of the members were Oakhurst boys. This was the only time in the 1940s that the team won the district championship. (Ray Jefferson.)

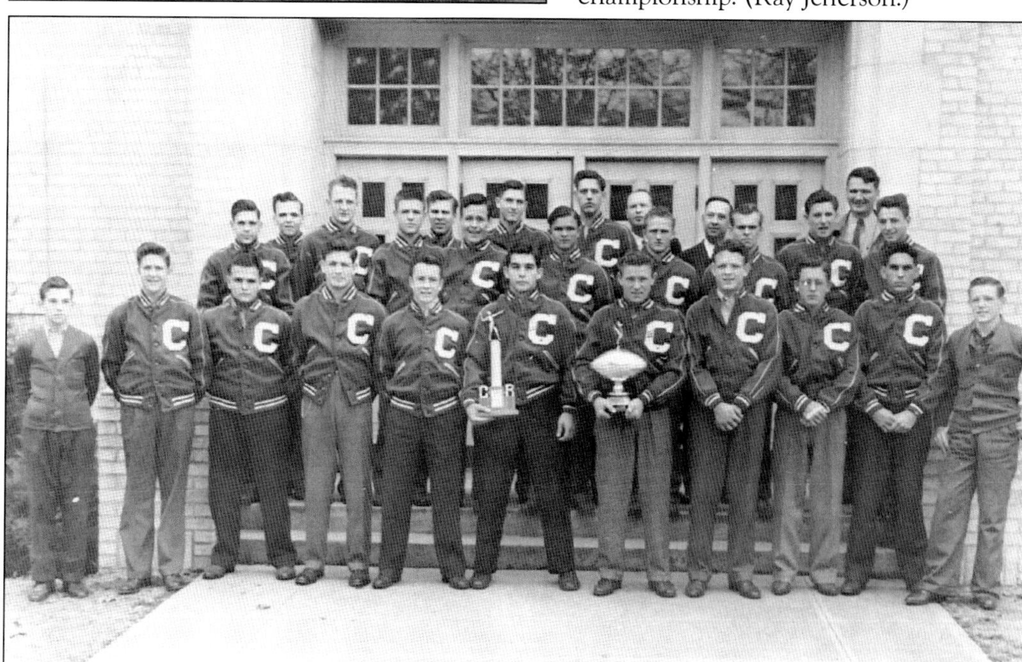

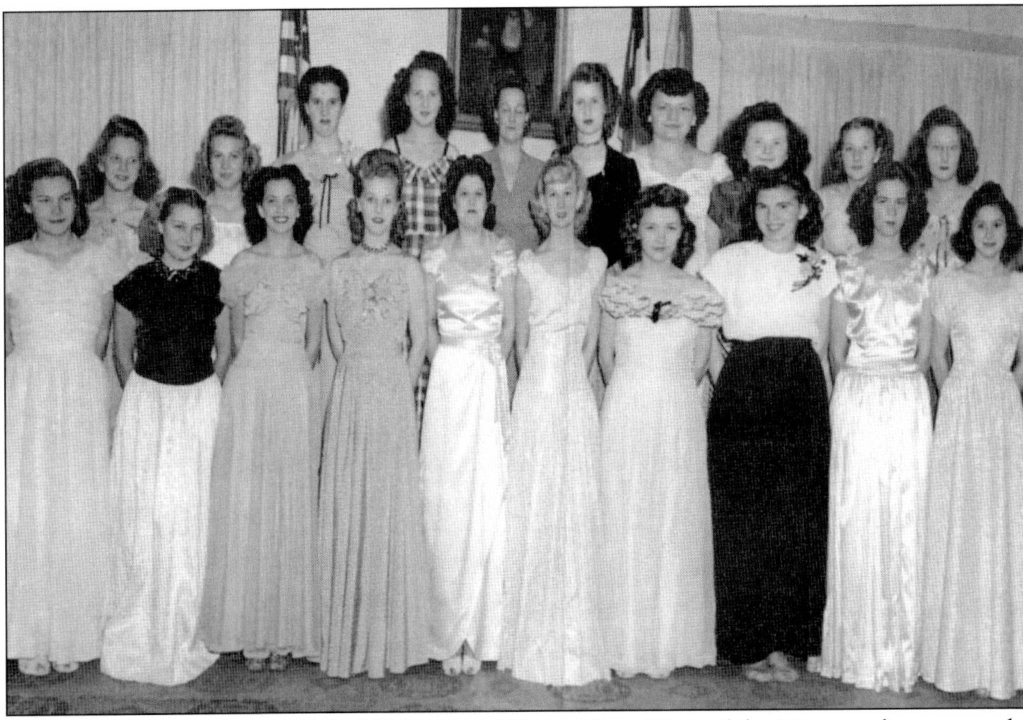

These are the "Rainbow Girls" of 1945–1946. The girls' auxiliary of the Masons, they met at the Masonic lodge at Six Points, on the corner of Belknap Street and Riverside Drive. There was a three-year span in their ages. (Beverly Sharp Germany.)

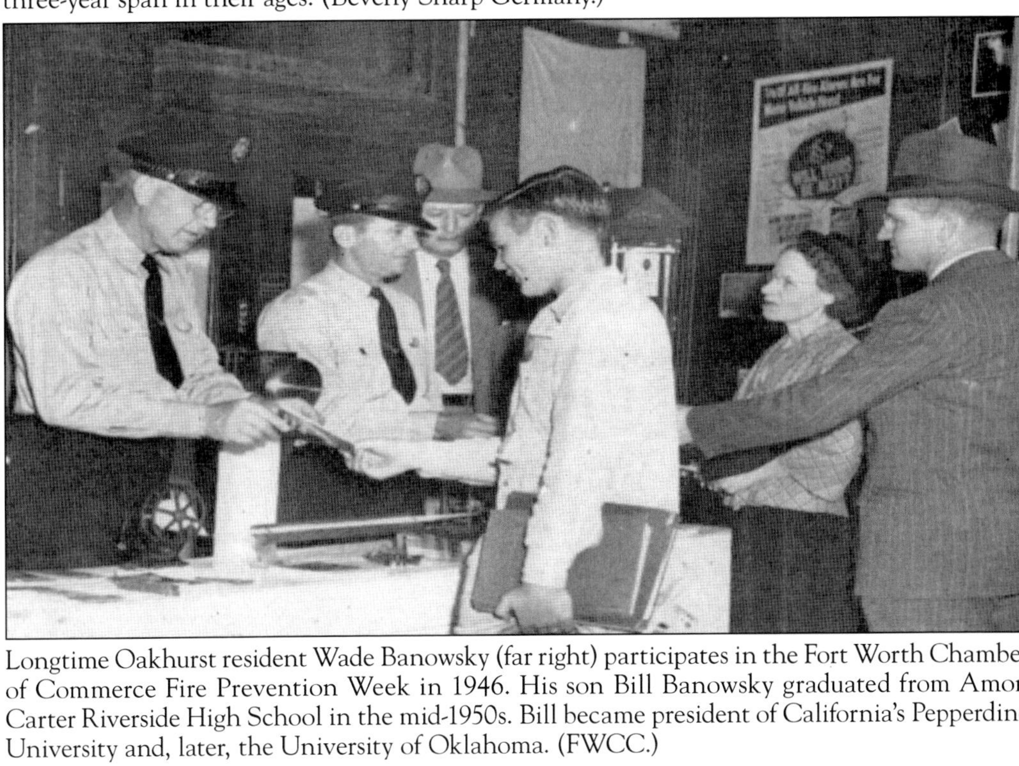

Longtime Oakhurst resident Wade Banowsky (far right) participates in the Fort Worth Chamber of Commerce Fire Prevention Week in 1946. His son Bill Banowsky graduated from Amon Carter Riverside High School in the mid-1950s. Bill became president of California's Pepperdine University and, later, the University of Oklahoma. (FWCC.)

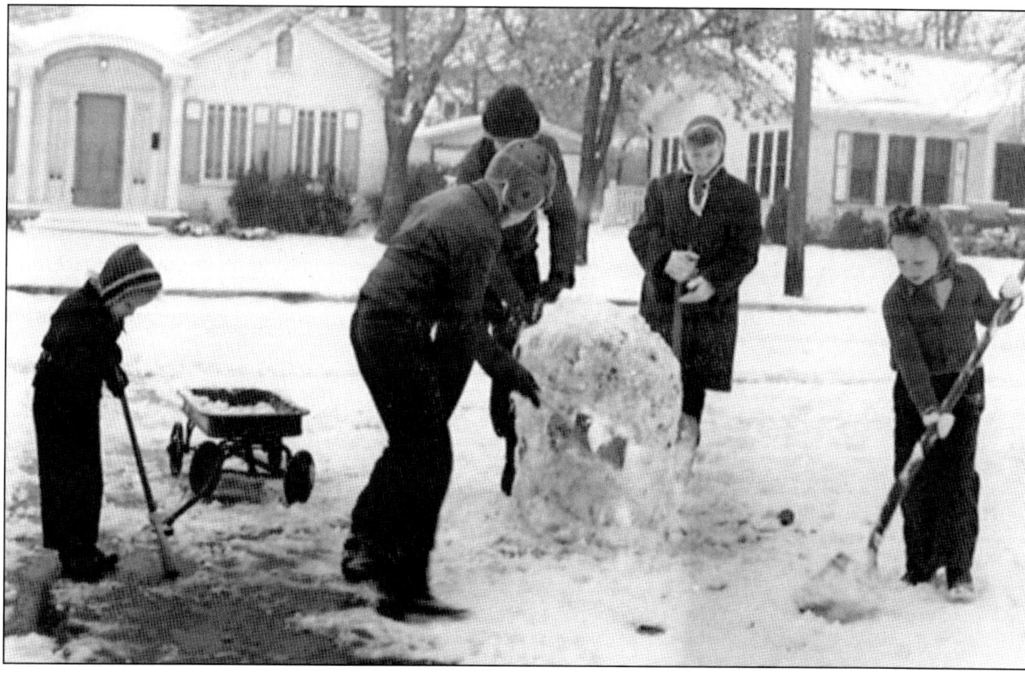

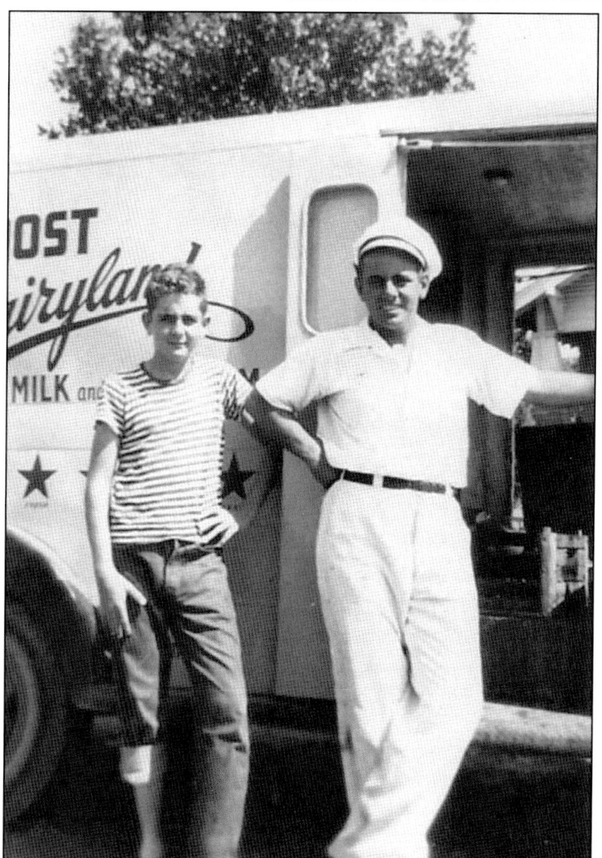

Above, the Wakefield girls of 2327 Marigold Avenue shovel snow in the late 1940s to help their neighbors build a snowman. Gloria is on the far right with the shovel, and Joyce is on the far left on the sidewalk. Every Oakhurst block had lots of kids, making for fast friends at school, in church, and in the neighborhood. (Kathryn Dunson Wicker.)

Like most neighborhoods of its era, Oakhurst was a deliveryman's haven. Here, James Womack (left) is on his first job delivering Foremost milk to residents of Oakhurst in the late 1940s. (Delia Brelsford Shiflet.)

The Riverside Lions Club sponsored a carnival in Sylvania Park in 1949. That year, Donna Hall was voted Miss Rey Bethea Florist. She is shown here with North Sylvania Avenue florist Rey Bethea Sr. after winning the title. (Rey Bethea Jr.)

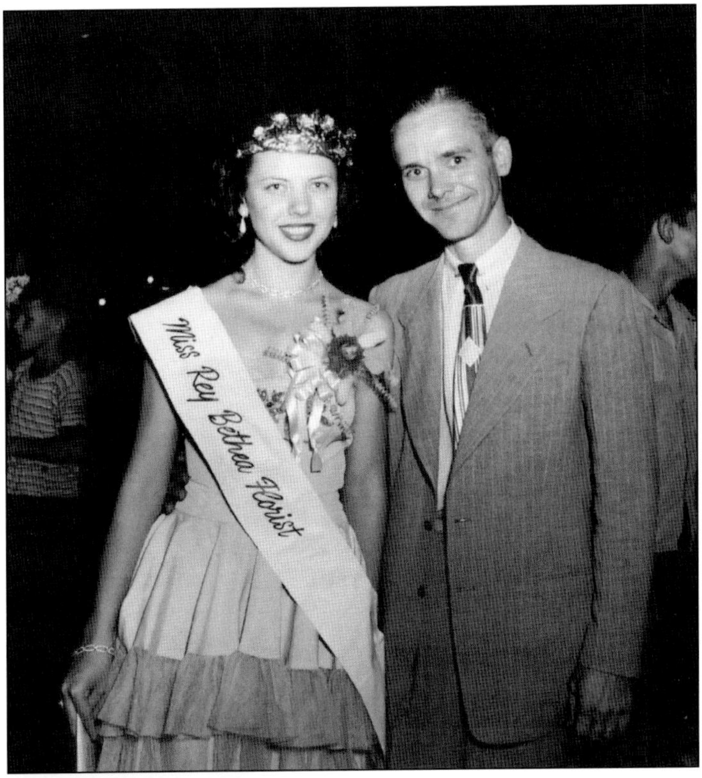

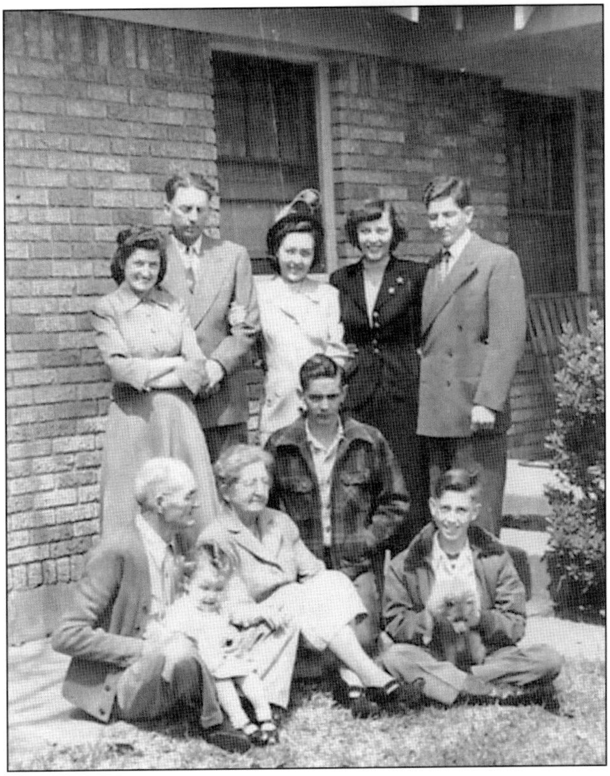

Oakhurst has always been a neighborhood where multiple generations of the same family live. In August 1949, the Womack family of 2508 Primrose Avenue posed for this three-generation picture. The family had survived the lean years of the Depression and World War II during its 22 years in Oakhurst. With the war over, the generation who grew up on Primrose Avenue began to marry and have children of their own. (Delia Brelsford Shiflet.)

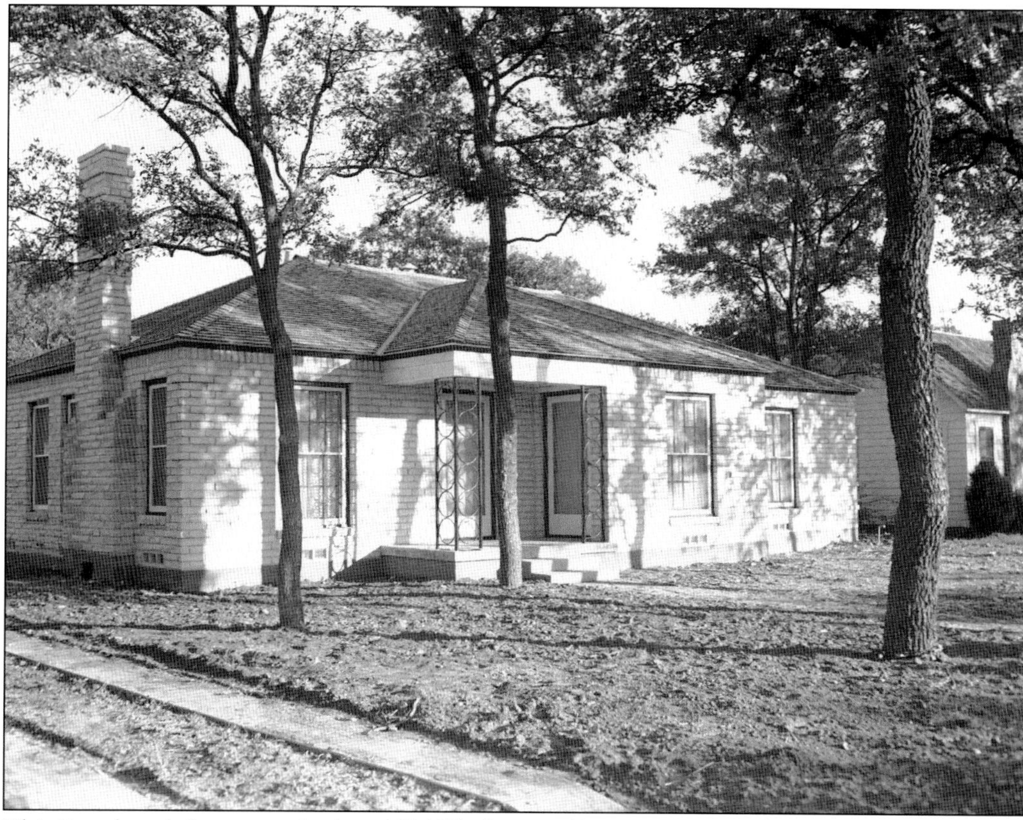

This Ranch-style home was built at 1604 Bluebonnet Drive in 1941. In that year, there were only two houses in the 1600 block of Bluebonnet Drive, and only 21 houses in all of the 1300–1900 blocks of the street. H.D. Connor owned this house. (FWSTC/SCUTA.)

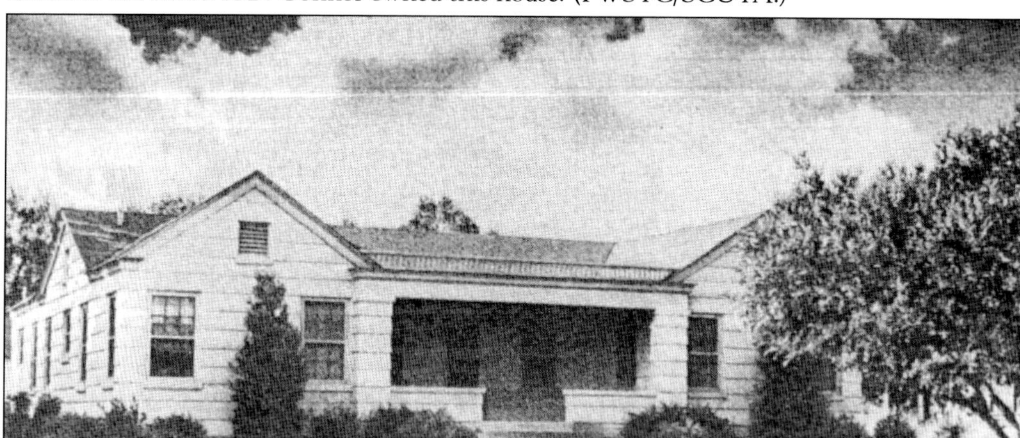

Builder and contractor Jim W. Clardy lived in this Colonial Revival house he built in 1947 at 2213 Yucca Avenue. The house is highly unusual because it is built entirely of concrete. The exterior is made to resemble drop siding. *Southwestern Home Builder* magazine described it as one of the most unusual homes ever built in the nation. (FWL.)

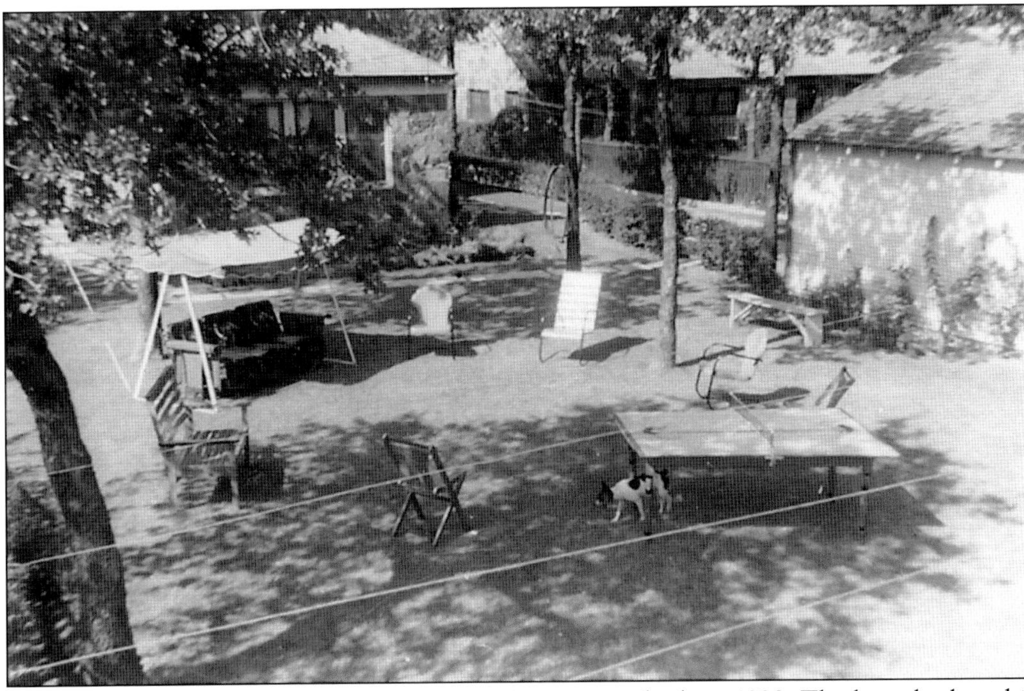

This stone-veneered house at 2332 Primrose Avenue was built in 1928. The large backyard is shown here in September 1940. Huge backyards in Oakhurst have always lent themselves to development as gardens or recreation areas. (Susie McKinzie.)

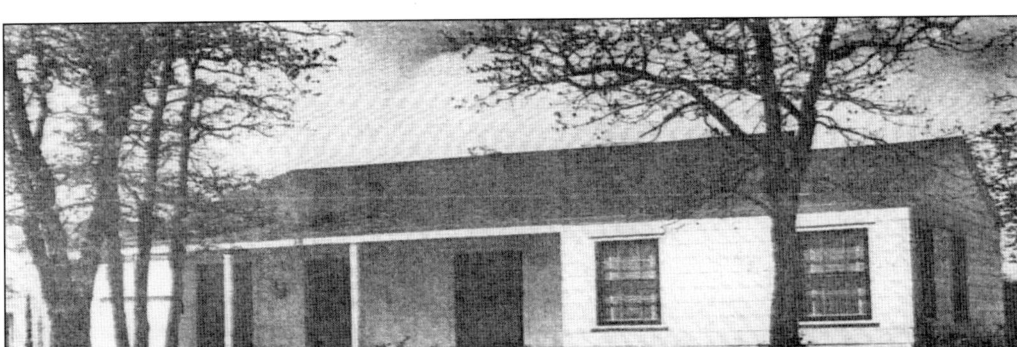

Paris E. Castleberry built this National Folk–style home at 2023 Daisy Lane in 1941. It was notable for its large, 80-foot-by-300-foot lot and for having two closets in each bedroom. (FWL.)

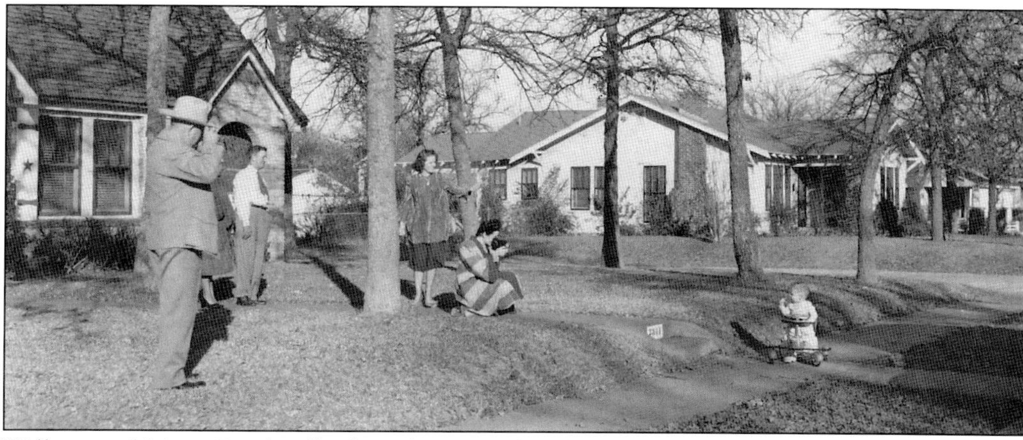

William and Mary Gourley (both with cameras) and their daughter Frances (center, standing) watch her son Hank Abernathy on his scooter at 2341 Goldenrod Avenue in the late 1940s. During the war, people began to work shifts at various defense-related firms, such as William Gourley's American Manufacturing Company. "It was common to see small signs on front doors which said 'Day Sleeper. Do not ring door bell,'" remembered David Martin. (Frances Lott Turella/ Wendy Vann Roach.)

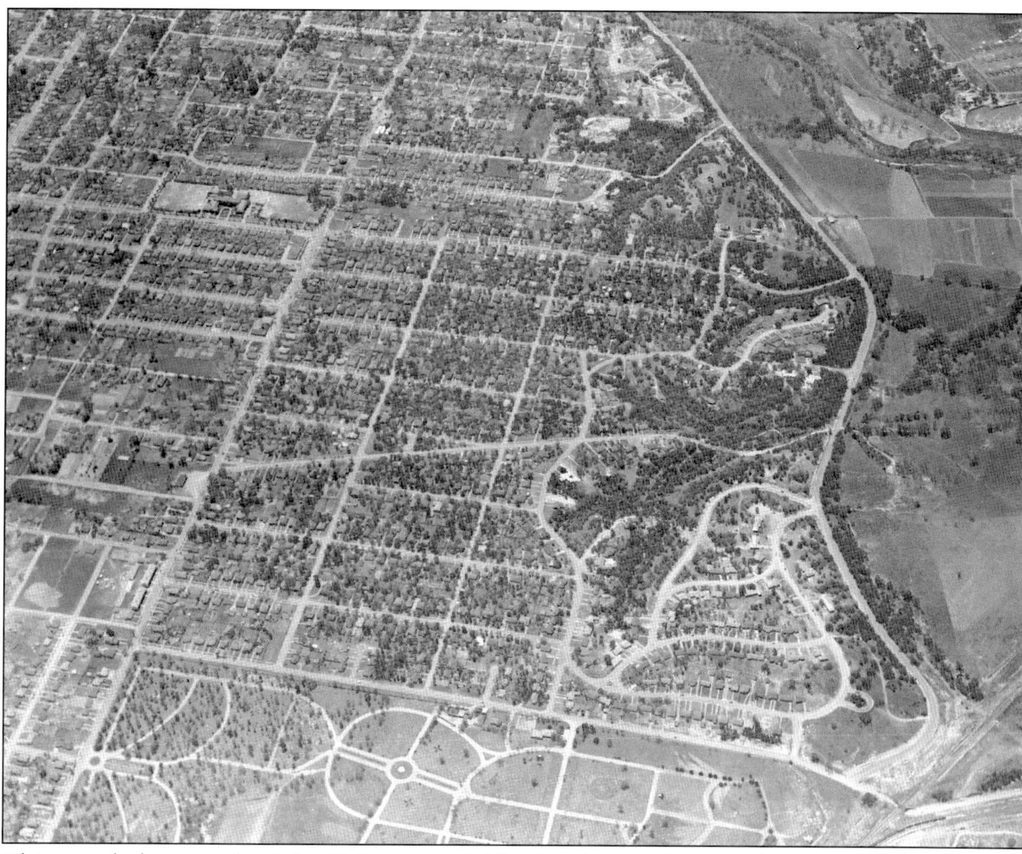

This aerial photograph of the Oakhurst neighborhood was taken on April 16, 1949. The view is to the southeast. Oakhurst Scenic Drive is the major curvilinear street on the right. Mount Olivet Cemetery is at the bottom of the image. (FWSTC/SCUTA.)

Five

Postwar Renaissance

All-American Neighborhood of the 1950s

There is no single neighborhood in Fort Worth other than Oakhurst that so clearly displays in its architecture what was happening in post–World War II American neighborhoods. In fact, Oakhurst is a visual encyclopedia of American residential buildings from the 1920s, 1930s, 1940s, and 1950s.

Even though the West Oakhurst Addition began to be platted in 1946, it was not until well after the war that most of the houses were built. Mostly Ranch-style houses built on big lots, they were light years away from the original Oakhurst, with period revival houses on smaller, deeper lots. The country was spreading out, and so was Oakhurst. Still, the houses and the lots fit into the neighborhood's initial parklike setting.

Oakhurst was the home of traditional moms and dads and kids. Dads usually worked, moms usually stayed home, and the kids went to school. But moms were branching out, and, in Oakhurst, that meant that they very likely belonged to a neighborhood garden club. The ladies of the Oakhurst and Oak Leaf Garden Clubs lunched once a month, heard programs, and made flower arrangements for the patients at the US Public Health Hospital at Carswell Air Force Base.

Meanwhile, kids could be found riding their bikes or learning to drive in Mount Olivet Cemetery, playing ball in a West Oakhurst cul-de-sac like Smilax Avenue, or exploring a ravine behind a friend's house. Truck farms and the Little League ball field were down on Oakhurst Scenic Drive. There were just a couple of swimming pools in the neighborhood, as well as a few bomb shelters, because, after all, 1957 was the height of the Cold War. Residents could do all they needed to do within close proximity to Oakhurst: go to school or church, bank at the Riverside State Bank, buy records at the Melody Shop at Six Points, and buy ice cream at Ashburn's.

These were the halcyon days of Oakhurst. The neighborhood was 30 years old and well established, and its residents were content with its beauty and calm and the order it brought to everyday life.

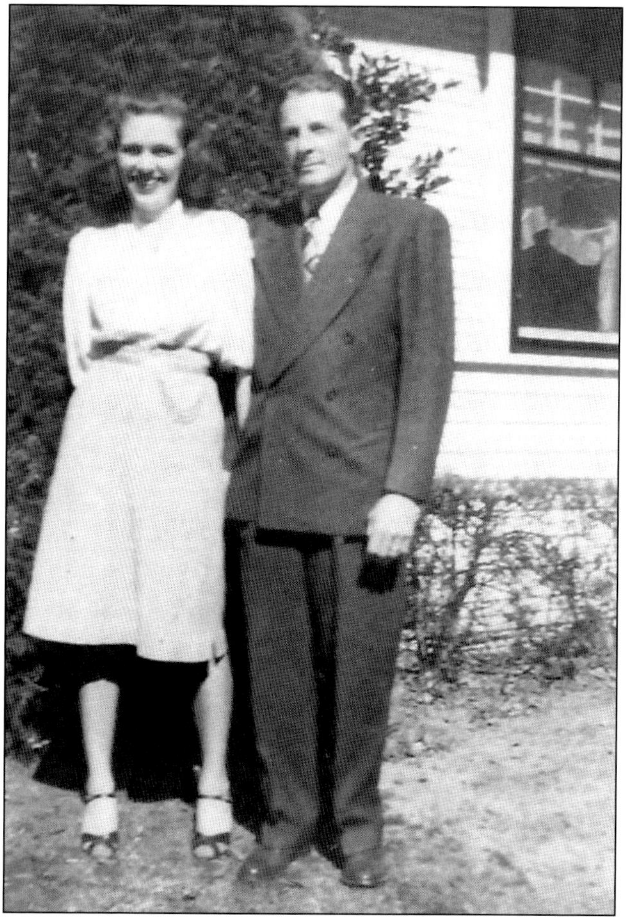

John and Vera James posed in 1947 just before purchasing 2011 Bluebird Avenue in West Oakhurst for $8,500. John was a window dresser for Leonard's Department Store in downtown Fort Worth. In later years, he was one of the stalwarts of the Oakhurst Citizens on Patrol and the Oakhurst Neighborhood Association. (Leslie James.)

The James's house, built in 1946 at 2011 Bluebird Avenue, is seen below around 1950. The frame house is typical of postwar construction in West Oakhurst and illustrates the difference in Oakhurst Addition and West Oakhurst Addition housing stock. Oakhurst Addition garages were usually detached and located toward the rear of the lot. In West Oakhurst, garages were more often attached to the house, indicating the growing importance of the automobile to postwar Oakhurst families. (Leslie James.)

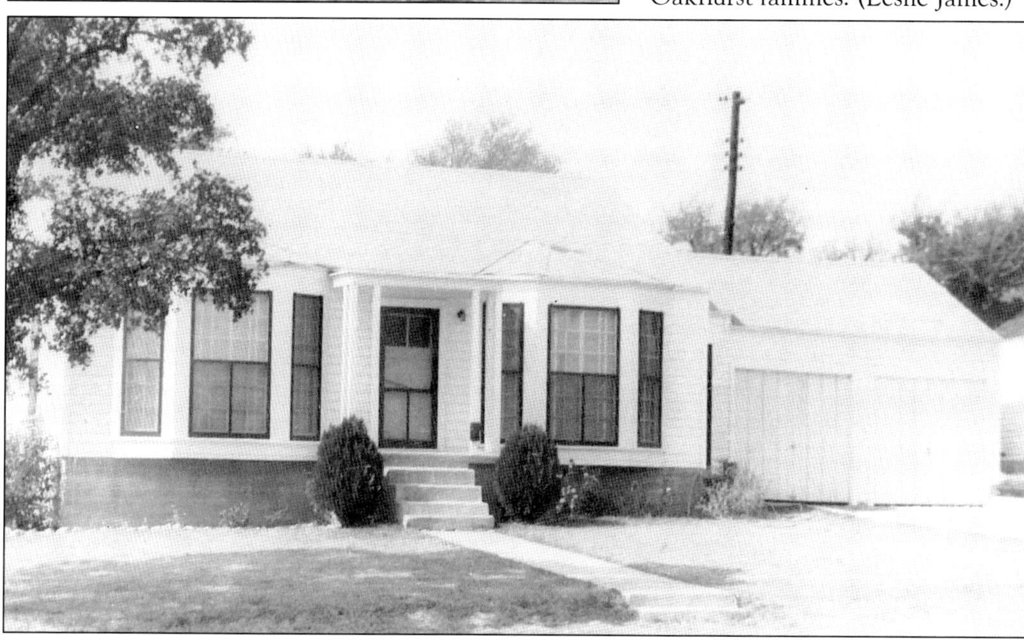

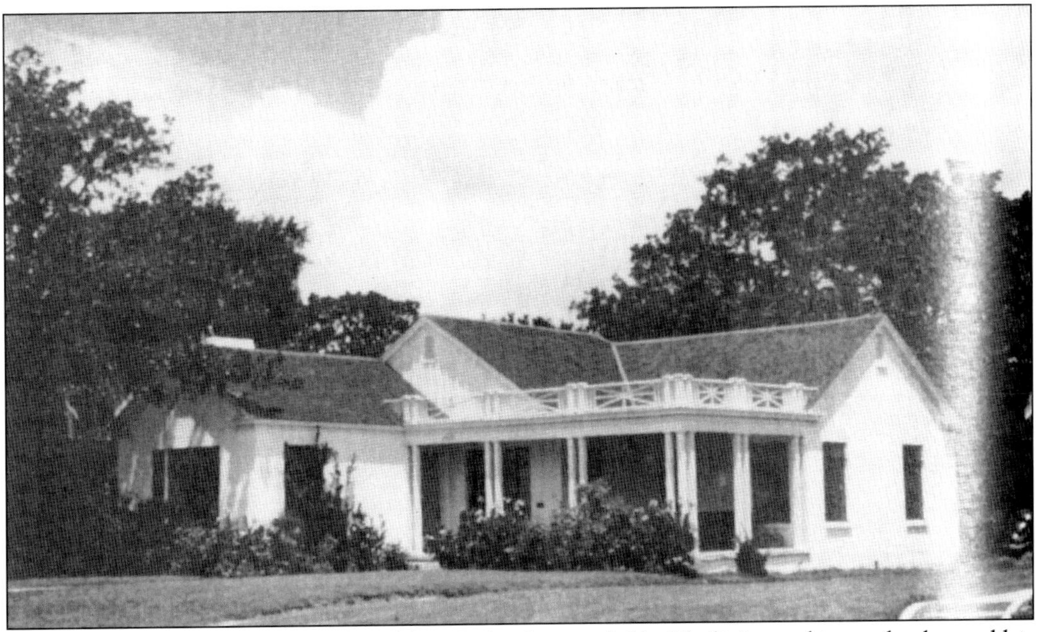

According to City of Fort Worth Public Works director Milo Thelin's autobiography, he and his wife bought 2517 Daisy Lane in 1938. The house is shown here in 1950. The couple lived here for 29 years before they built another home at 1805 Mapleleaf Street. Thelin worked for the city from 1928 until 1965 and designed the Henderson Street Bridge, the Lake Worth Bridge, and many other important structures and buildings throughout Fort Worth. (FWL.)

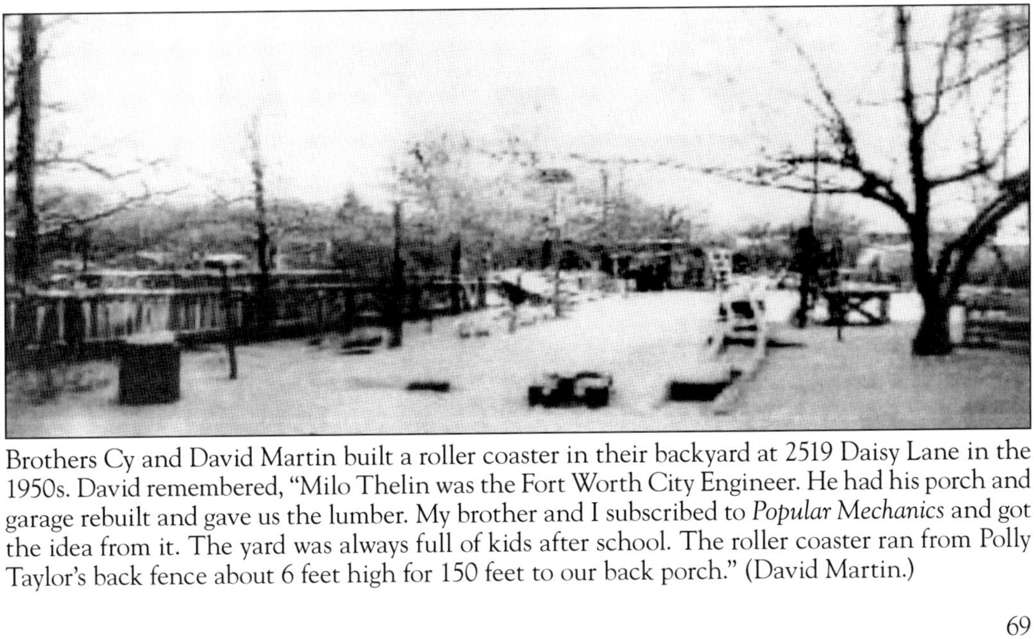

Brothers Cy and David Martin built a roller coaster in their backyard at 2519 Daisy Lane in the 1950s. David remembered, "Milo Thelin was the Fort Worth City Engineer. He had his porch and garage rebuilt and gave us the lumber. My brother and I subscribed to *Popular Mechanics* and got the idea from it. The yard was always full of kids after school. The roller coaster ran from Polly Taylor's back fence about 6 feet high for 150 feet to our back porch." (David Martin.)

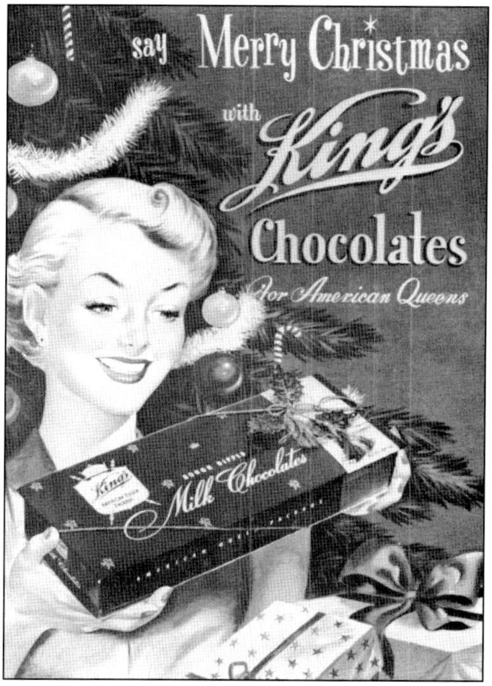

King Candy Company was still producing chocolates for American queens in 1952, as shown in this Christmas advertisement. Robert L. King, Oakhurst developer John P. King's son, was selling lots in West Oakhurst in the 1950s. (FWCC.)

Below, Lucia Johnson Alexander stands immediately to the left of her brother, US senator and future president Lyndon B. Johnson. Lucia and her husband, Birge Alexander, lived in Oakhurst with their daughter Rebekah (center of photograph, left of Lynda Bird Johnson) from 1944 to 1953 at 2319 Lotus Avenue. Lady Bird Johnson is on the far right. In 1943, Lucia and Birge had lived at 1316 Bluebonnet Drive for one year. Birge was chief of the construction unit at the Civil Aeronautics Administration at Meacham Field during their Oakhurst years. This is the family Christmas celebration in 1951 at the Johnson family ranch near Stonewall, Texas. (LBJ Library.)

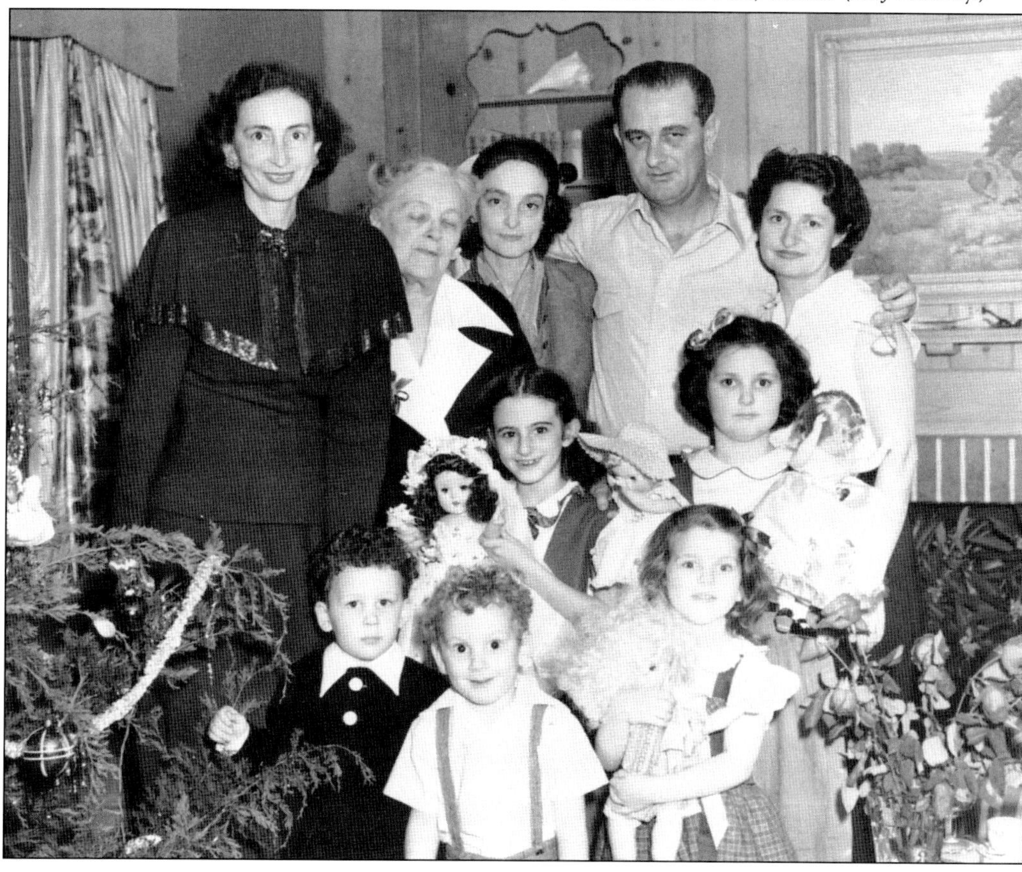

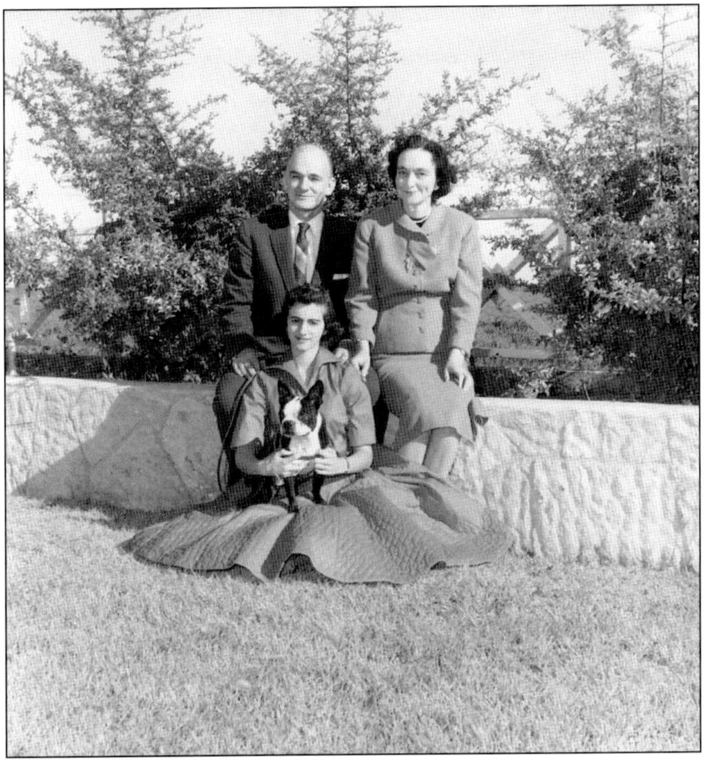

Lucia and Birge Alexander and their daughter Rebekah sat for this photograph at the Johnson ranch during Christmas in 1957, several years after they had moved from Oakhurst. Lucia's brother, Sen. Lyndon B. Johnson, was majority leader of the US Senate at the time. Birge, an engineer, later served as area manager for the southwest region of the Federal Aviation Administration. He told newsmen in later years that his wife "guards her privacy and refuses under any circumstances to discuss her brother, other members of her family, their private life or such that might be published." (Photograph by Art Kowert; LBJ Library.)

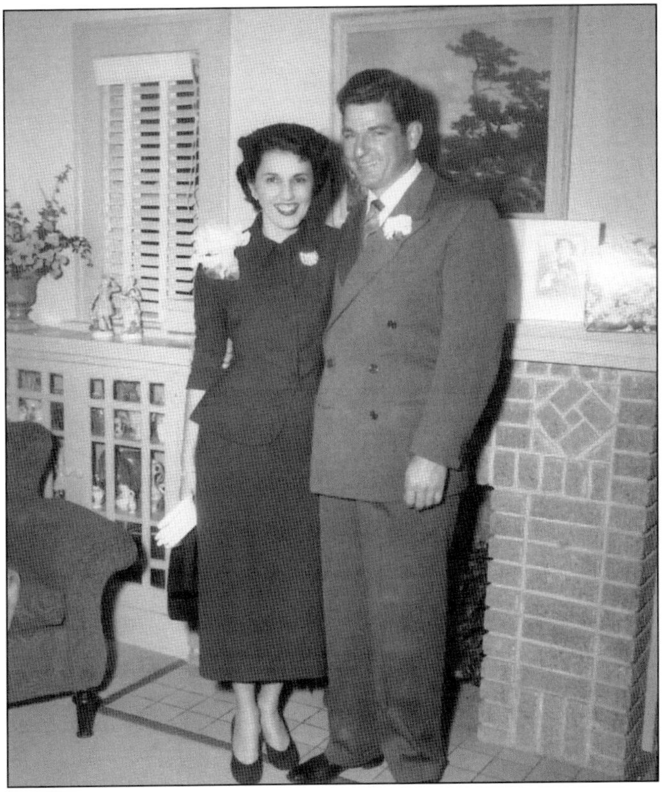

Newly married Char and Bill Womack pose in front of the mantel in the living room of his parents' home at 2508 Primrose Avenue in the early 1950s. Brick fireplaces and built-in curio and book cabinets were typical of Oakhurst homes, particularly those built from the 1920s to the 1940s. This fireplace had specialized inlaid brickwork that required craftsman skills. (Delia Brelsford Shiflet.)

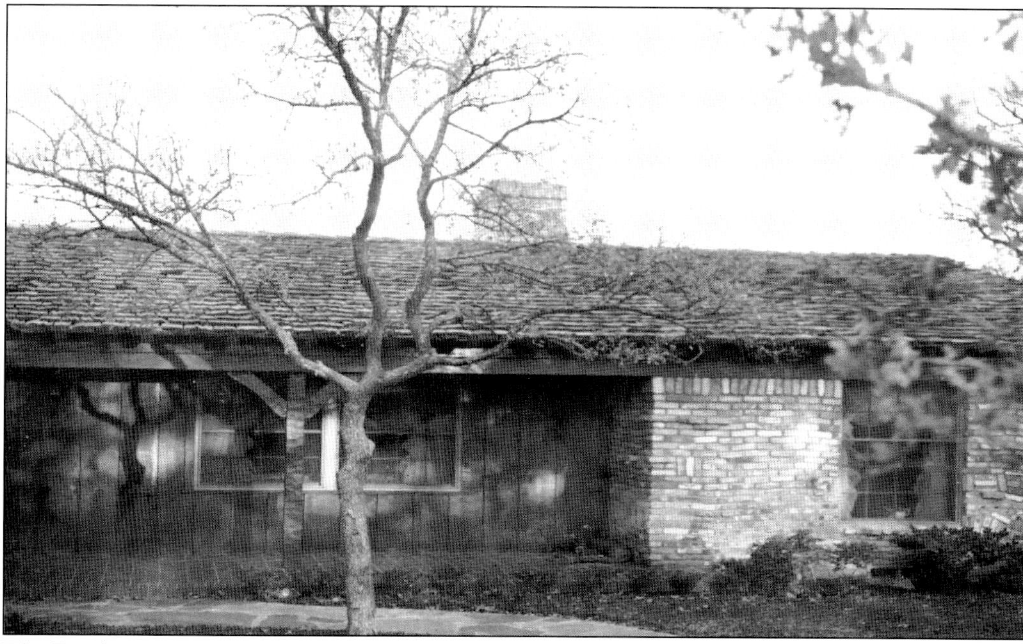

The Riscky House, at 1505 Smilax Avenue, is seen here in 1953. Ranch houses like this one are prevalent in West Oakhurst. The large lots lend themselves to the style, popular after World War II. From an architectural point of view, Oakhurst is a visual encyclopedia of house styles popular from the 1920s through the 1950s, in both the original Oakhurst Addition and the subsequent West Oakhurst Addition. (Dr. Ken Kirkham.)

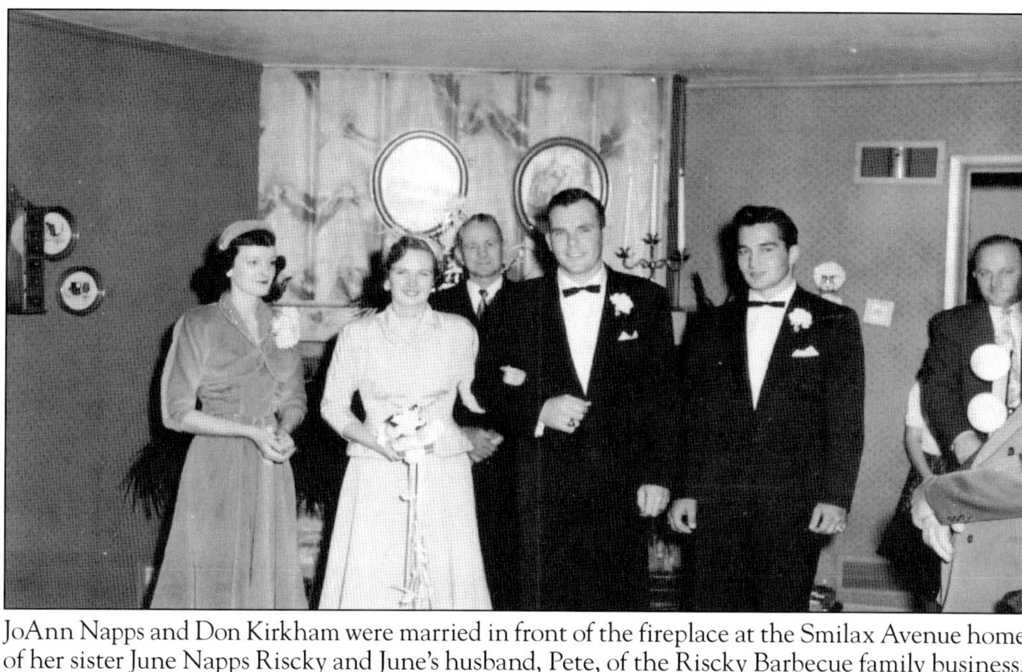

JoAnn Napps and Don Kirkham were married in front of the fireplace at the Smilax Avenue home of her sister June Napps Riscky and June's husband, Pete, of the Riscky Barbecue family business. The ceremony took place just after midnight on New Year's Day, 1954. Pictured here are, from left to right, Markey Shannon Hannigan, JoAnn Kirkham, Rev. A.K. Marney of the Boulevard Methodist Church, Don Kirkham, Bob Woody, and Pete Riscky. (Dr. Ken Kirkham.)

Shown here are Margaret Duke (left) and Kitty Brown, past and present presidents of the Oakhurst Garden Club, in 1955–1956. The club, established in 1942, often made flower arrangements for the hospital at Carswell Air Force Base on Fort Worth's West Side. (AC.)

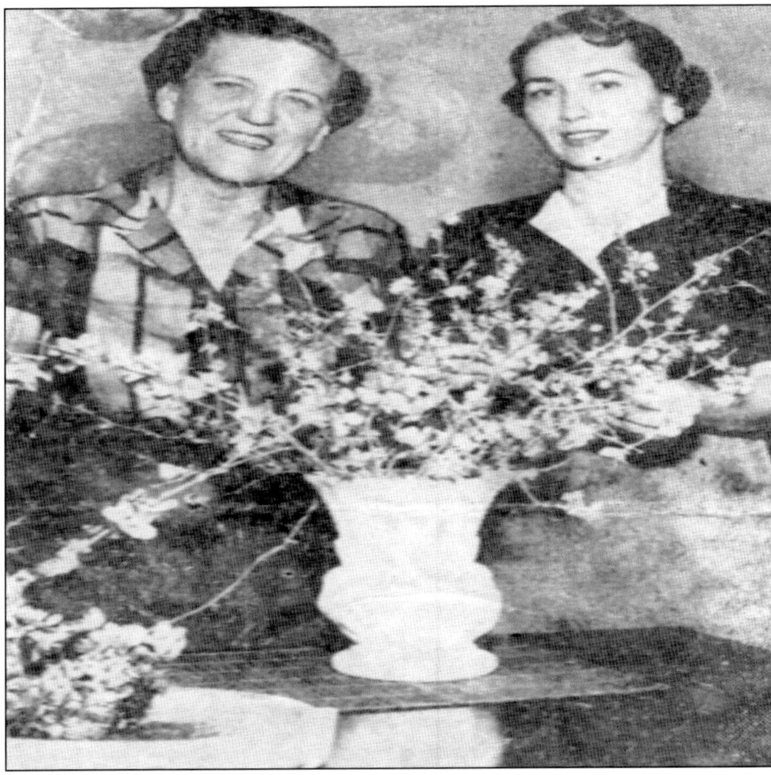

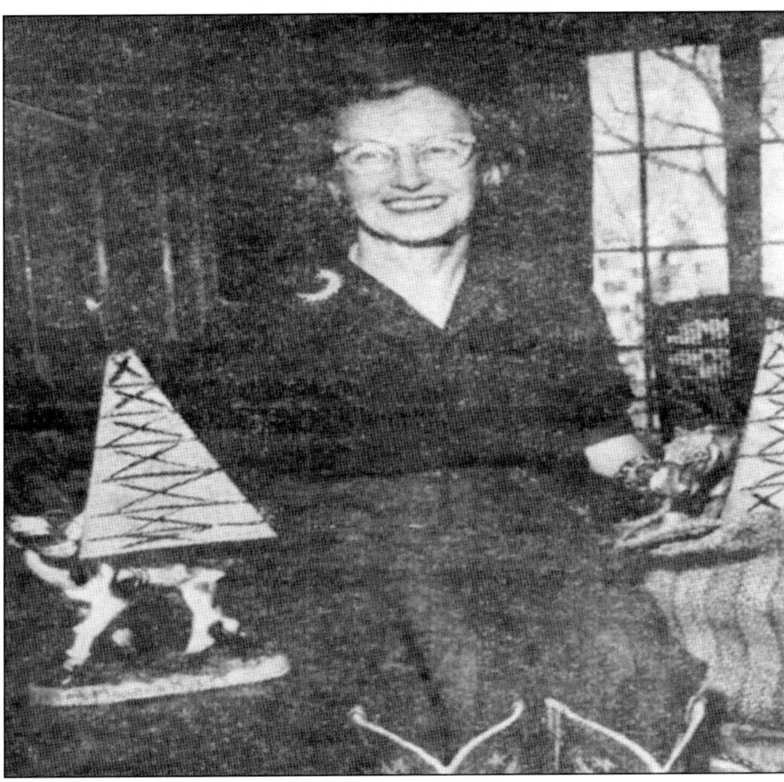

Wearing a 10-gallon hat, Jean Cox played Santa Claus in the 1955 Christmas program for Oakhurst Garden Club members. The favors were "oil well totin' Santas." The ladies luncheon took place at the Riverside Lions Club on Race Street. Club members sent gifts to children at the All Church Home. (AC.)

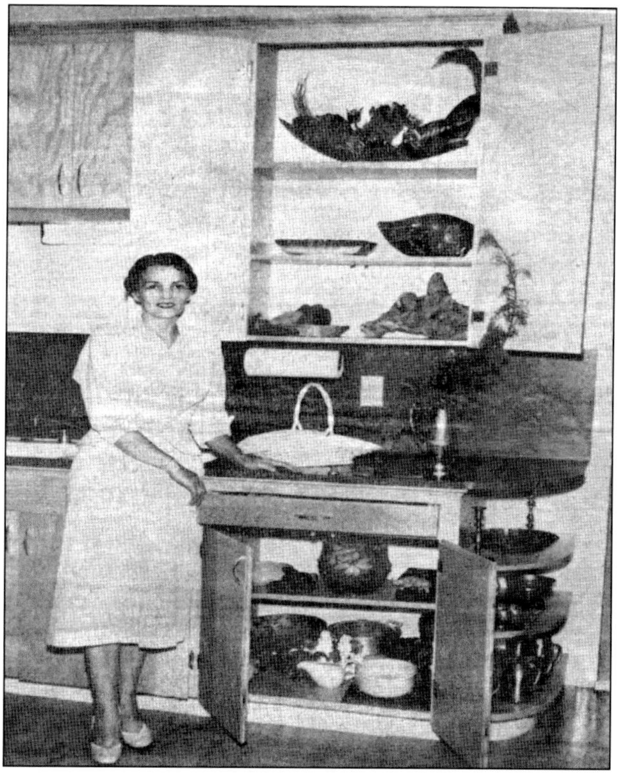

Dr. and Mrs. C.E. Dickey bought and enlarged the Ranch-style home at 1900 Bluebird Avenue in 1951, providing flower-arranging space for Vivian Dickey, shown here. She was a member of the Oakhurst Garden Club. (AC.)

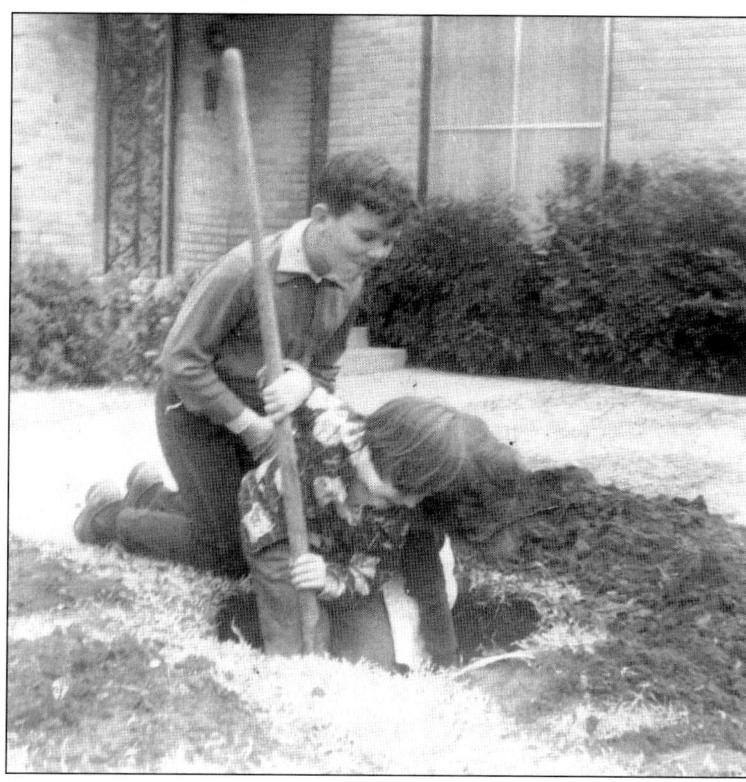

These are the Thompson children at 2221 Primrose Avenue in May 1956, digging a hole to plant a mulberry tree. According to CeCe Thompson, "it was a fun project, as Daddy always loved trees. That is probably why he loved Oakhurst so much." (CeCe Thompson.)

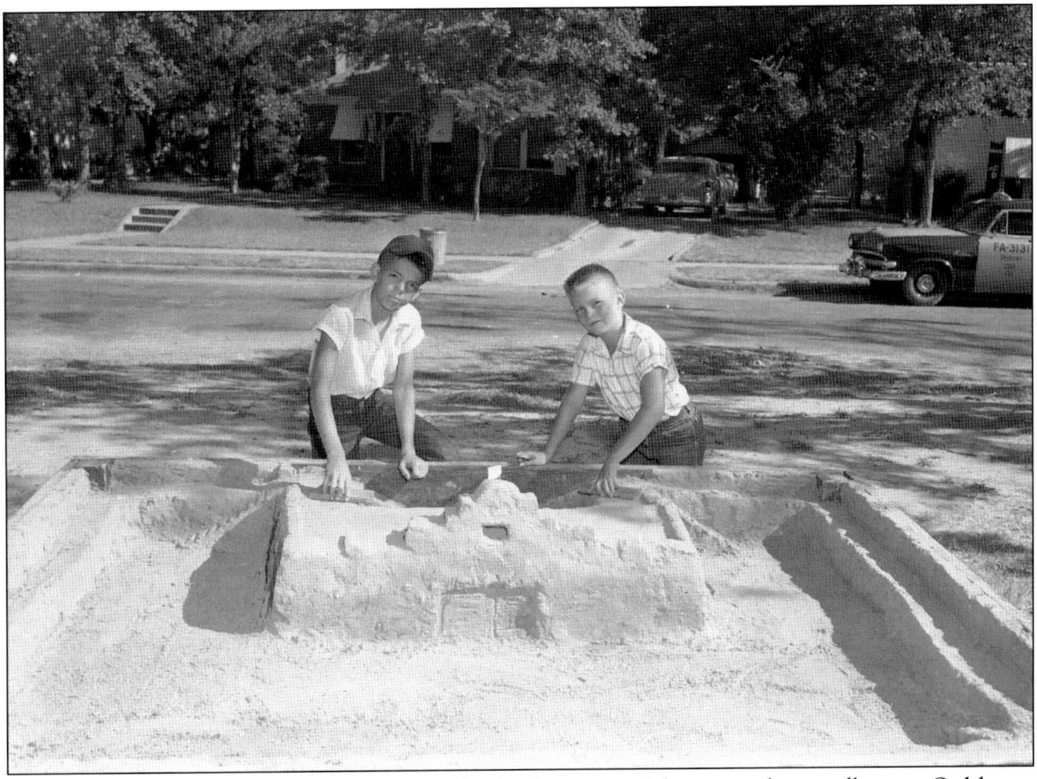

Freddy Drysdale (left) and Sparky Jones built their own Alamo in the sandbox at Oakhurst Triangle Park in July 1955 as part of a citywide recreation department competition. The boys had evidently seen the 1955 Walt Disney film *Davy Crockett*, which started a craze across the nation for all things related to the Alamo. (FWSTC/SCUTA.)

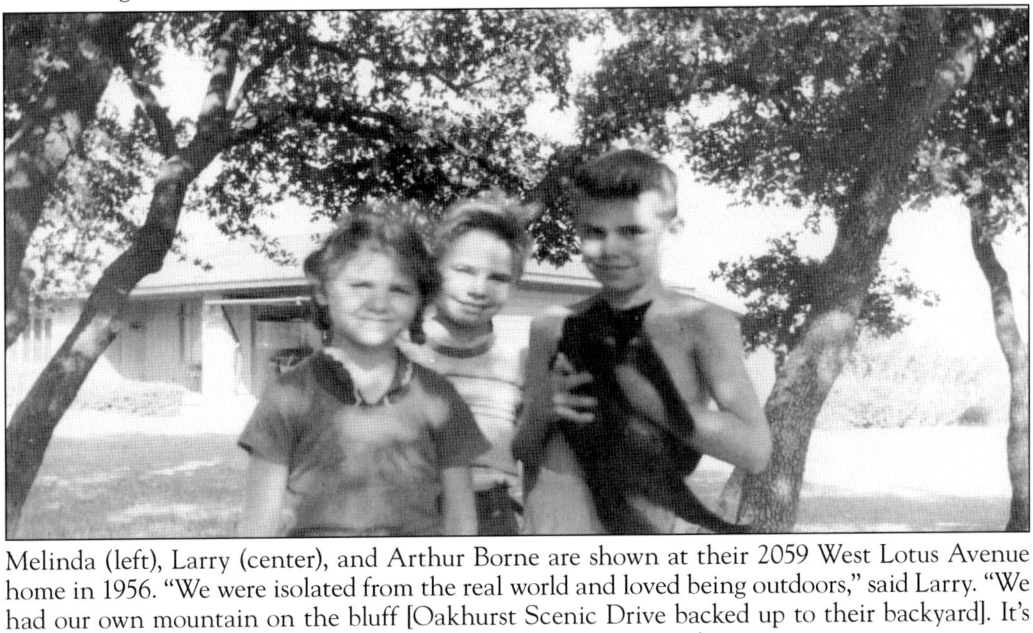

Melinda (left), Larry (center), and Arthur Borne are shown at their 2059 West Lotus Avenue home in 1956. "We were isolated from the real world and loved being outdoors," said Larry. "We had our own mountain on the bluff [Oakhurst Scenic Drive backed up to their backyard]. It's probably where my interest in archeology started." (Larry Borne.)

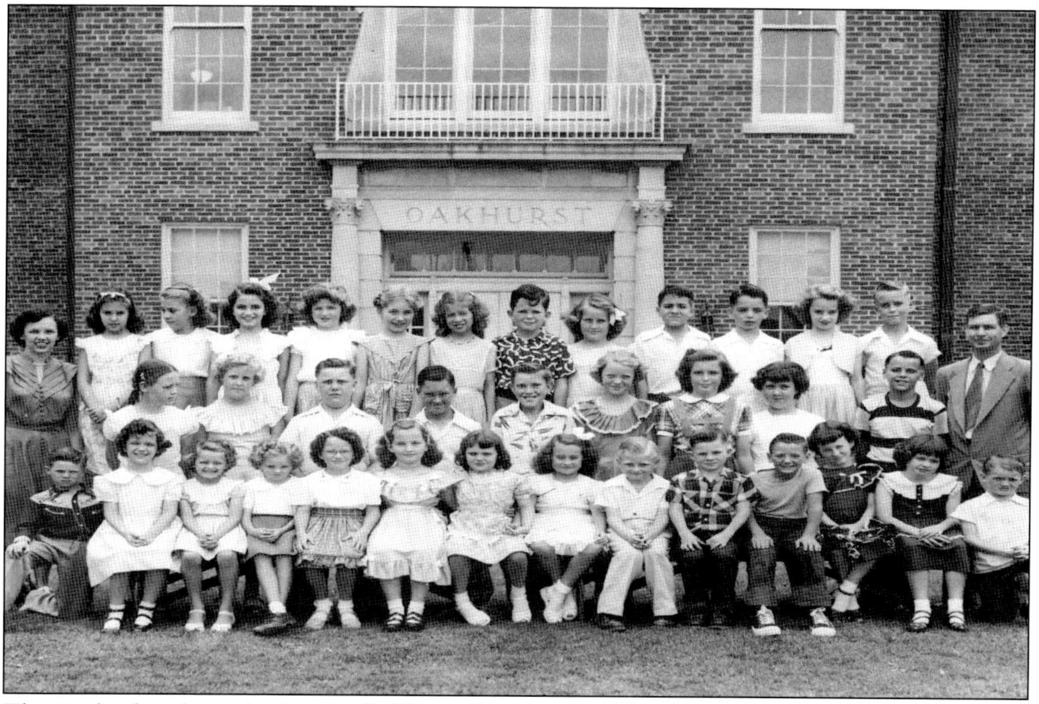

This is the fourth-grade class at Oakhurst Elementary School in May 1950. Nancy Anderson Thurmond (standing, far left) was the teacher, and Noble Norman (standing, far right) was the principal. Note the bumper crop of 35 students. The 1950s saw many large classes like this at Oakhurst. (Nancy Thurmond.)

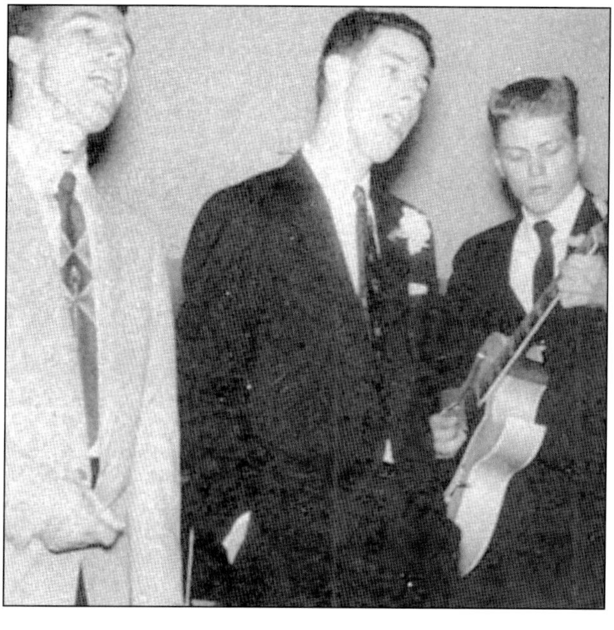

Amon Carter Riverside High School senior Johnny Simons (center) sang at the 1957 school football banquet, with Jerry Fuller (left) and Jim Powell. At age 16, Simons was already directing at Fort Worth's Casa Mañana Theatre. Simons, who grew up on Smilax Avenue, became an actor and director and founded Fort Worth's acclaimed Hip Pocket Theater with his wife, Diane Simons, and Doug Balentine. Simons has written an Oakhurst-like setting into some of his plays; his *Old River High* is a lightly disguised version of Carter Riverside High. Longtime Tandy Corporation CEO John Roach was a fellow member of the class of 1957. (NGB.)

John Thomas Lenox grew up at 1901 West Lotus Avenue in the 1950s. He is seen here (plaid shirt, center) with his Amon Carter Riverside High School Music Appreciation Club in 1964. With an SMU degree in cinematography, Lenox moved to Hollywood. He produced Ron Howard's 1984 film *Splash*, starring Tom Hanks, and was known for television direction on *The Odd Couple*, *Happy Days*, and *Laverne & Shirley*. Lenox was a cofounder of UCLA's Making the Short Fiction Film program. He died on his 50th birthday, in 1996. (AC.)

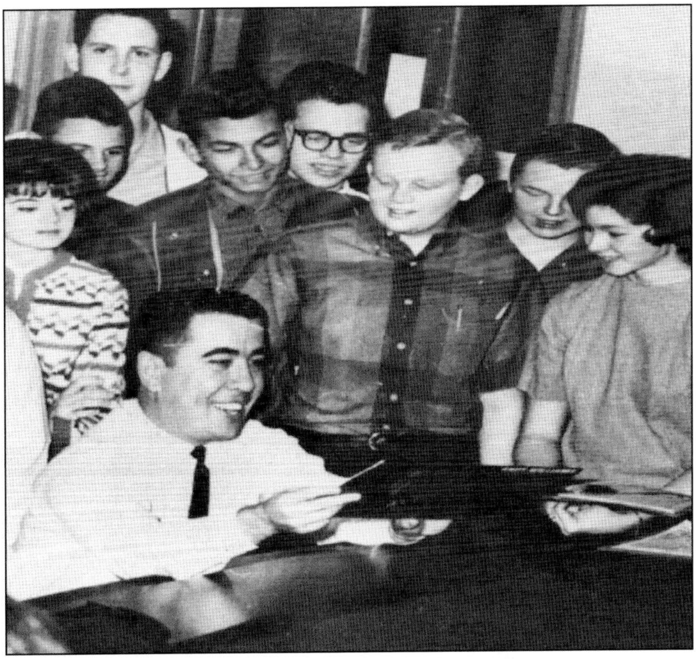

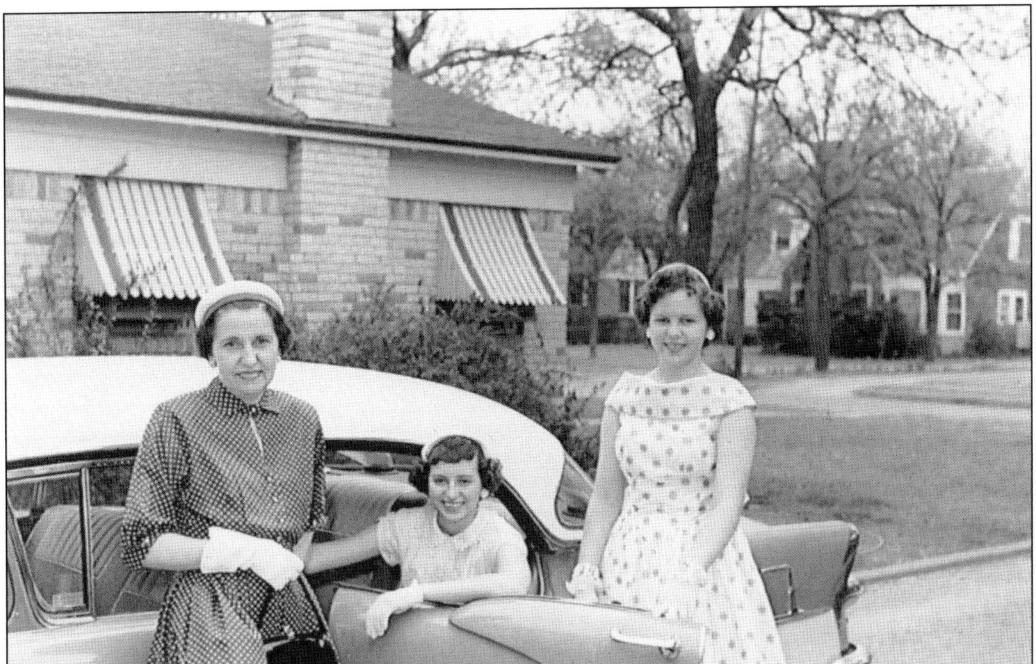

Fay Wakefield (left) and her daughters Gloria (center) and Joyce, of 2337 Marigold Avenue, are shown around 1959 "all dressed up," perhaps for church. Their home, a bungalow built in 1927, is a contributing structure in the Oakhurst National Register Historic District. It is considered to have a high degree of architectural integrity. (Kathryn Dunson Wicker.)

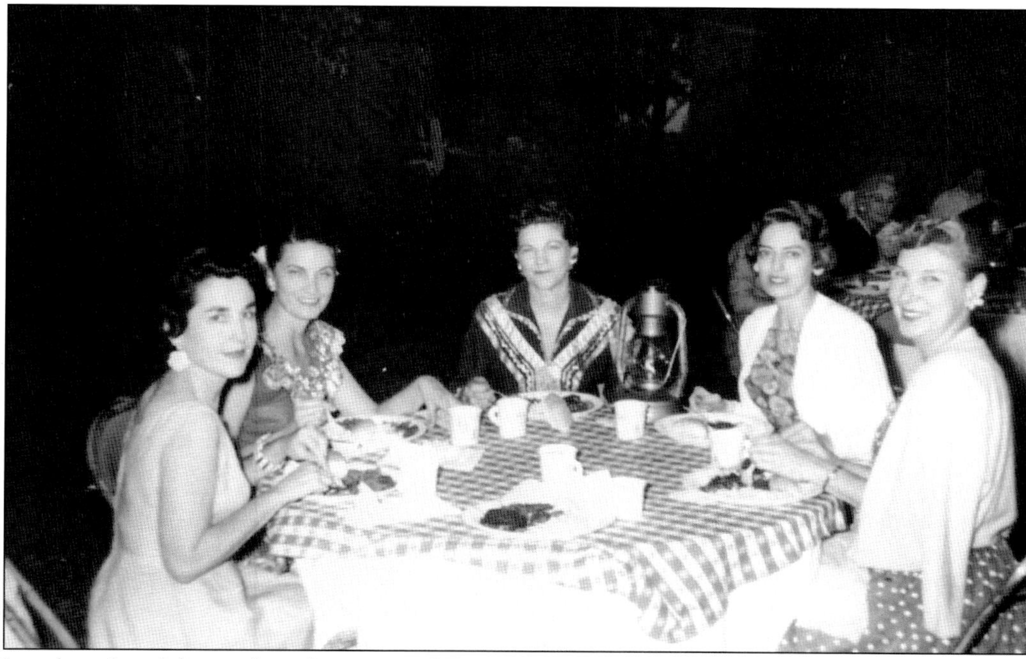

Local garden club members from around Texas met in Fort Worth for the Texas Garden Clubs, Inc., convention in April 1958. Here, members of Oakhurst's Oak Leaf Garden Club, established in 1950, gather at the convention's Chuck Wagon Dinner. They are, from left to right, Frances Taylor, Frances Abernathy, Gerry Jennings, Eunice Buse, and Mary Ellen Atkinson. (AC.)

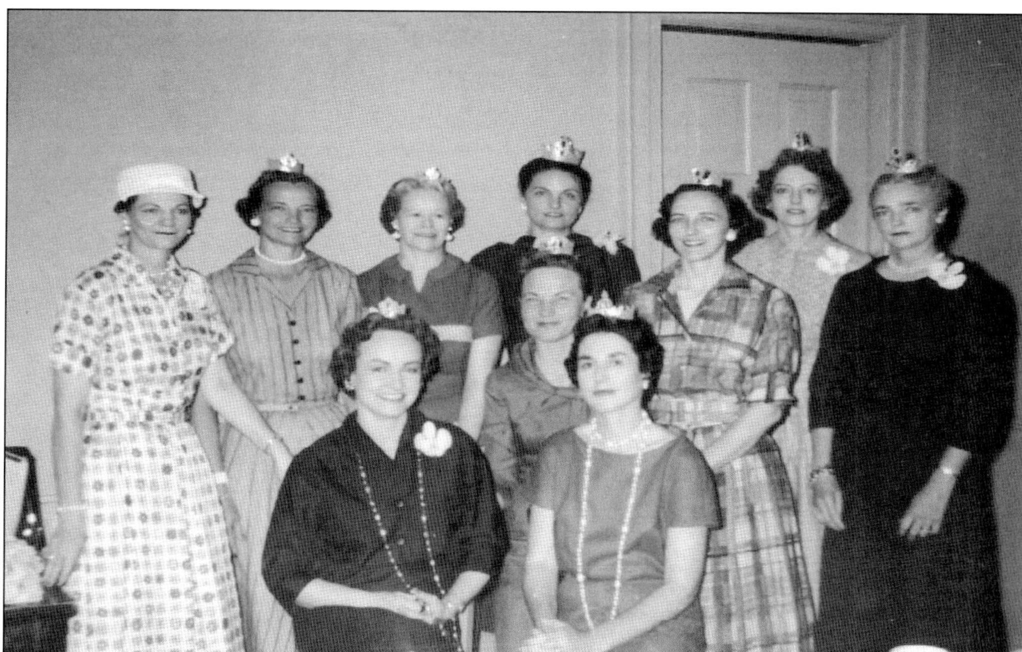

These are the officers for the 1958–1959 Oak Leaf Garden Club. Seated are club president Peggy Selcer (left) and Frances Taylor. Once an Oakhurst garden club's membership hit 50, a new club was started. Oakhurst had as many as three active garden clubs at one time. (AC.)

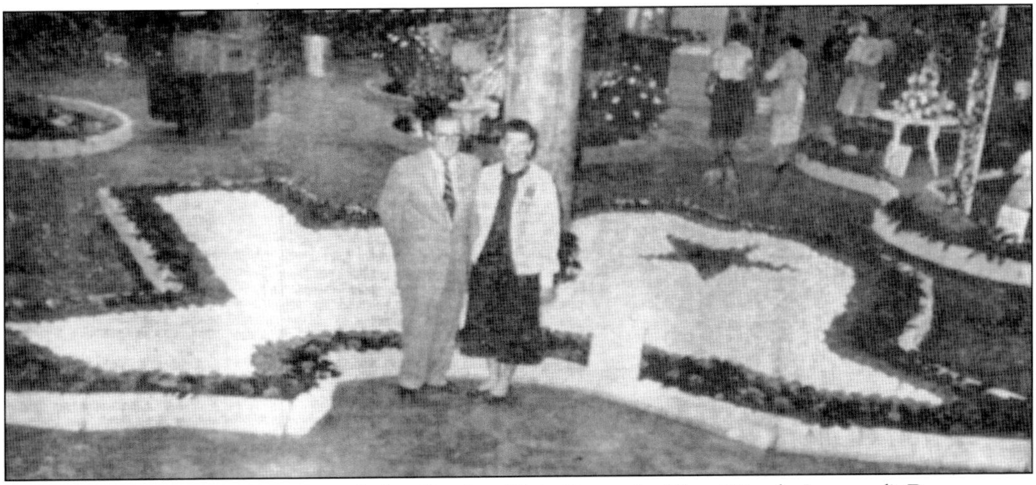

In March 1958, in cooperation with the Garden Club Council of Fort Worth, Leonard's Department Store in downtown Fort Worth staged its fifth annual Flowercade, using a Texas Under Six Flags Theme. Garden clubs from throughout the city, including the Oak Leaf and Oakhurst Garden Clubs, entered the flower show. Oakhurst resident John James (left) staged the show for the store. With him is Garden Club Council president Mrs. Robert Denney. James used over 4,000 red and white carnations to create the map of Texas. The star represents Fort Worth. (AC.)

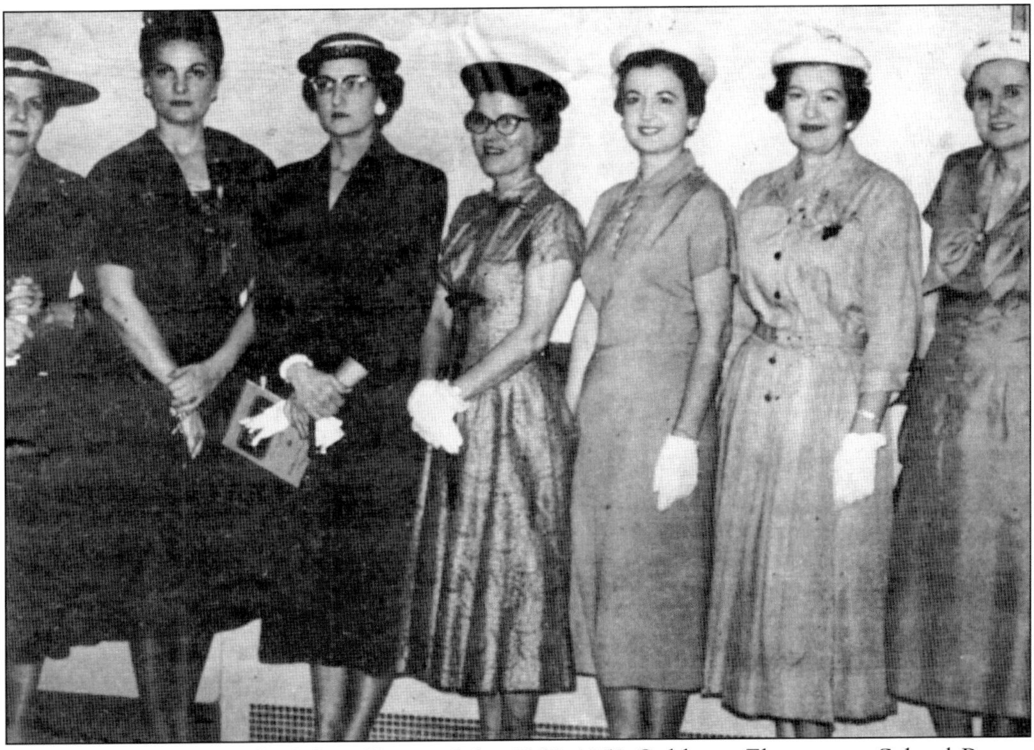

In May 1958, almost all of the officers of the 1958–1959 Oakhurst Elementary School Parent Teacher Association lived in Oakhurst. These included, from left to right, Mrs. Carey Snyder, Mrs. Frances Abernathy, Mrs. Carl Paxton, Mrs. John Adkins, Mrs. Harold Coon, Mrs. T.G. Ledel, and Mrs. Eugene A. Heike. (AC.)

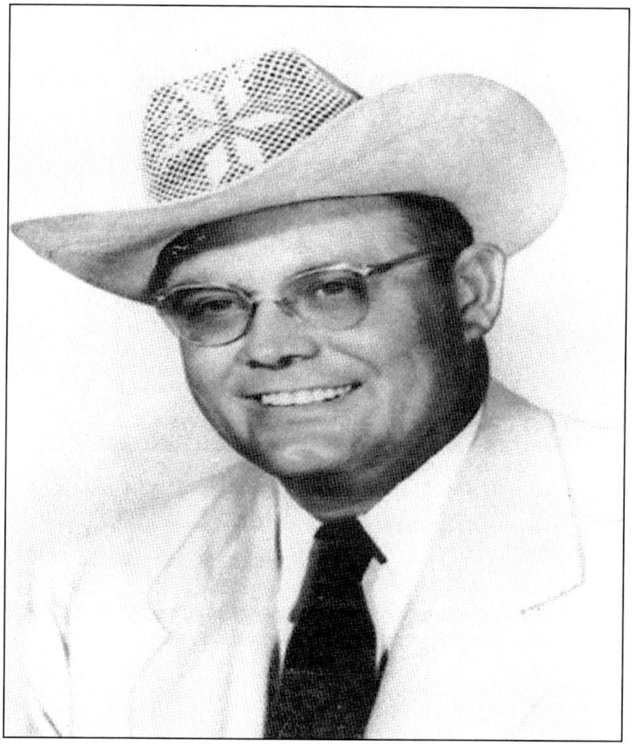

Harlan O. Wright was Tarrant County sheriff from 1953 to 1961. He and his wife, Truma, and their family lived at 2055 West Lotus Avenue in West Oakhurst during that period. In 1953, after a notorious jailbreak by three inmates, Wright put it "bluntly" to county commissioners that they would have to give him more guards or expect more bloody jailbreaks. Wright was a captain of Oakhurst Baptist Church's bond-selling drive in 1959, when the church was raising funds to pay for and remodel the former home of Oakhurst Methodist Church, at 1516 North Sylvania Avenue. (James Jennings.)

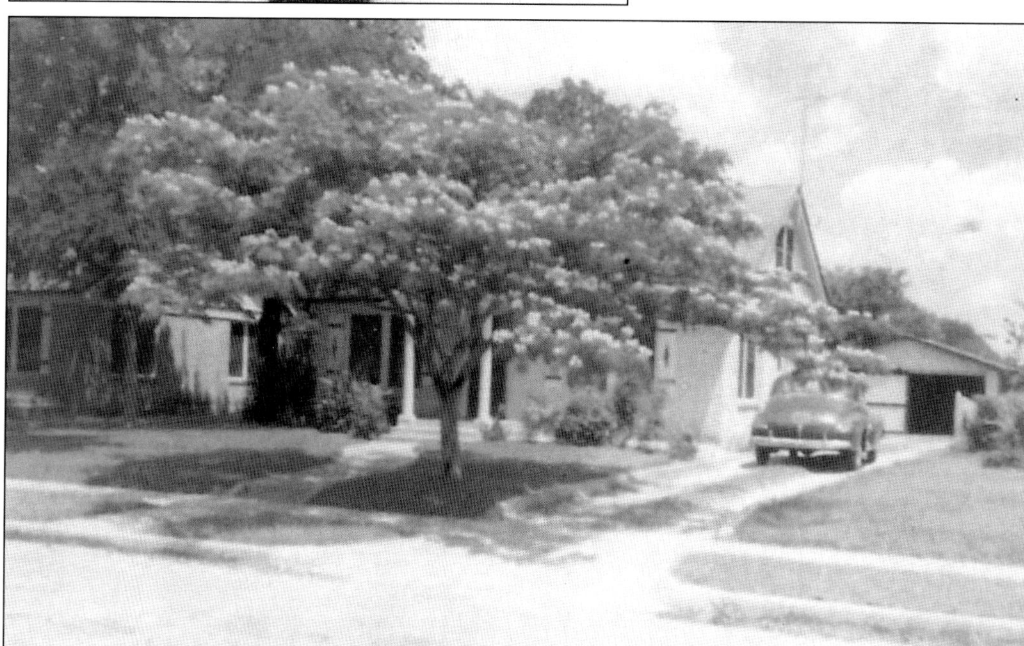

This is 2337 Lotus Avenue in June 1951. The Tudor-style house was built in 1930. Zula Flynn, a retail store proprietor, and her niece Ethel Collins were the original occupants. They bought it for $3,500. Henry and Vera Belle Moelk bought the house in 1949. It was a convenient location for Henry, who owned Moelk's Radio Service, fairly close to Oakhurst at 150A North Sylvania Avenue. (Leslie James.)

The experience of Frances Taylor, seen here, and her family at 1504 Smilax Avenue is one for Texas music history. Oakhurst friend and Fort Worth historian Dr. Rick Selcer wrote that Frances's son Tim "vividly remembers" Willie Nelson coming to their home as a door-to-door encyclopedia salesman "sometime between 1956 and 1960." Nelson came inside to make his pitch and sat down at the Taylor piano, "playing a little bit before he left." The Taylors did not buy any encyclopedias. (AC.)

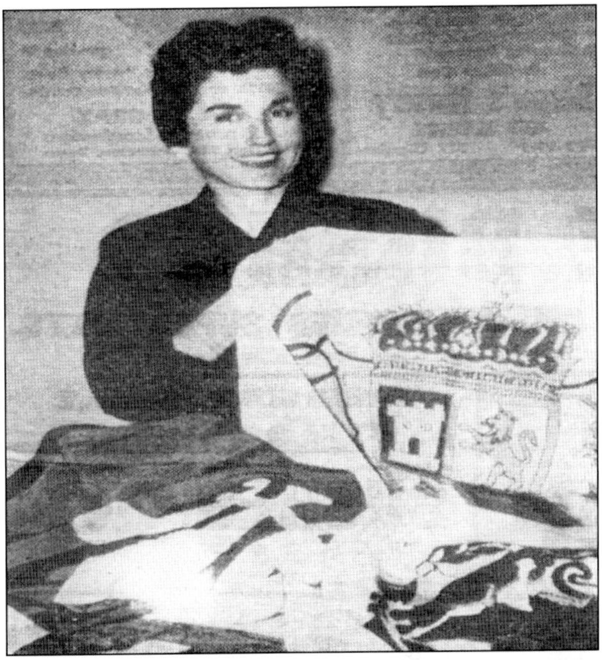

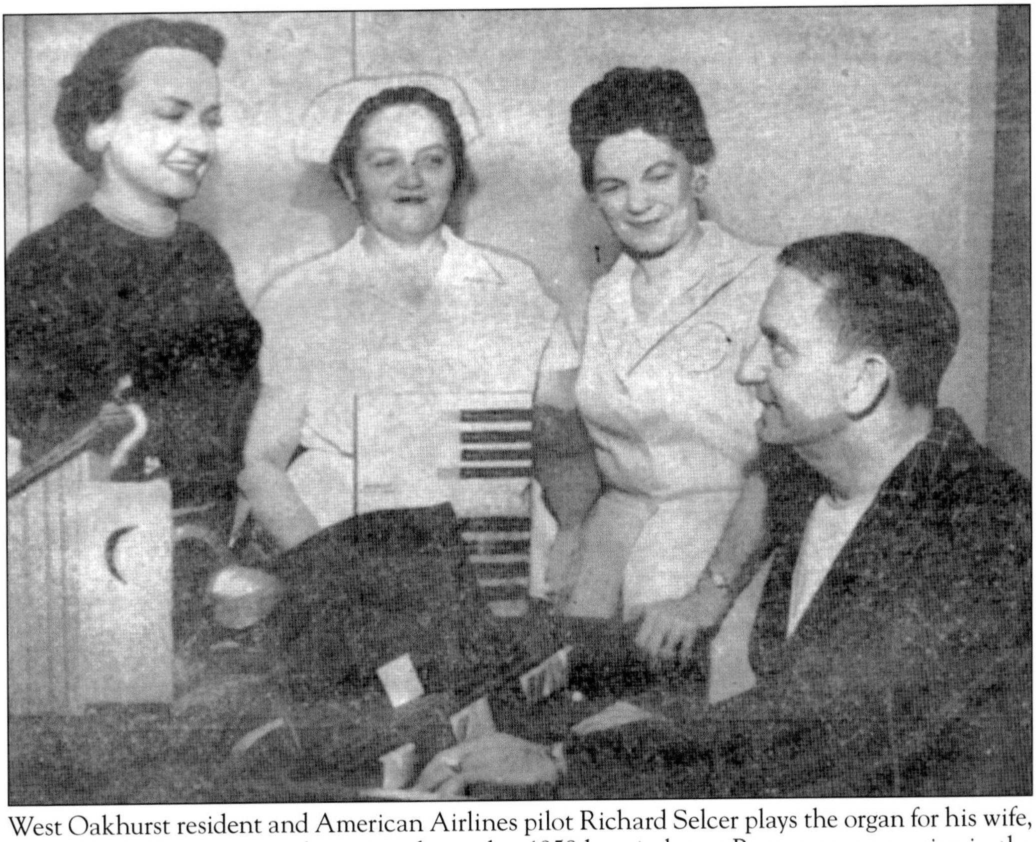

West Oakhurst resident and American Airlines pilot Richard Selcer plays the organ for his wife, Peggy (far left), a nurse, and a visitor during his 1958 hospital stay. Peggy was very active in the Fort Worth Garden Club Council. (AC.)

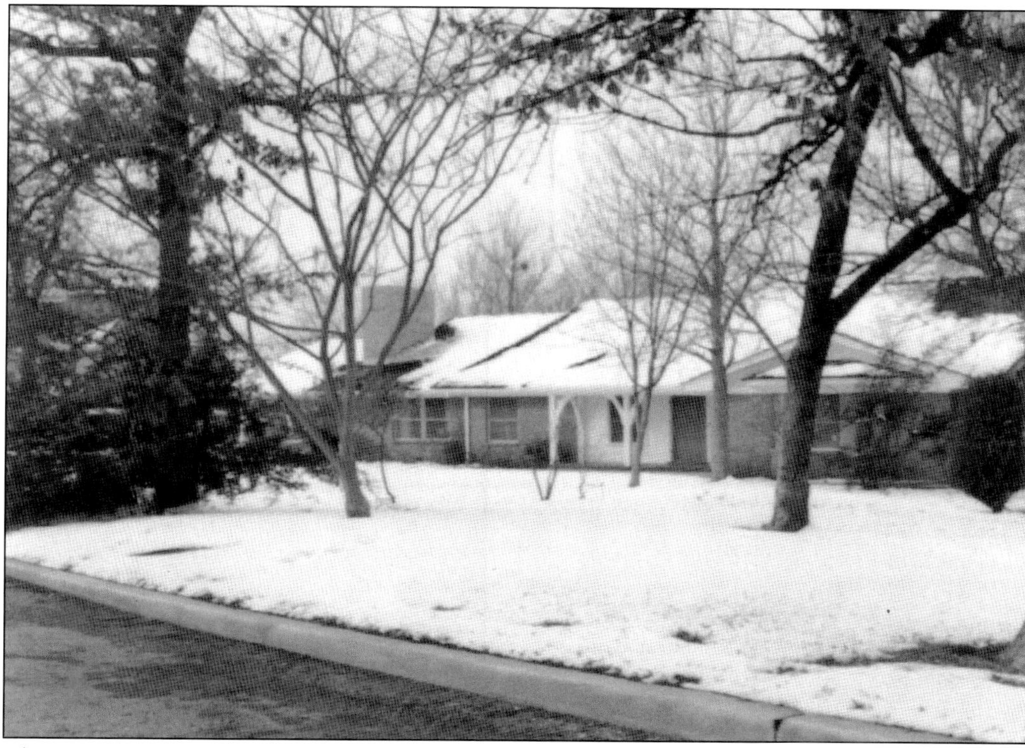

This is a 1956 shot of 1809 Wisteria Court, built in the mid-1950s for Frances Gourley Abernathy by her parents, Mary and William Gourley, who lived at 1800 Wisteria Court. The cul-de-sac where the houses are built backs up to a ravine, creating a kind of compound that is now a recognized wildlife habitat. (Frances Lott Turella/Wendy Vann Roach.)

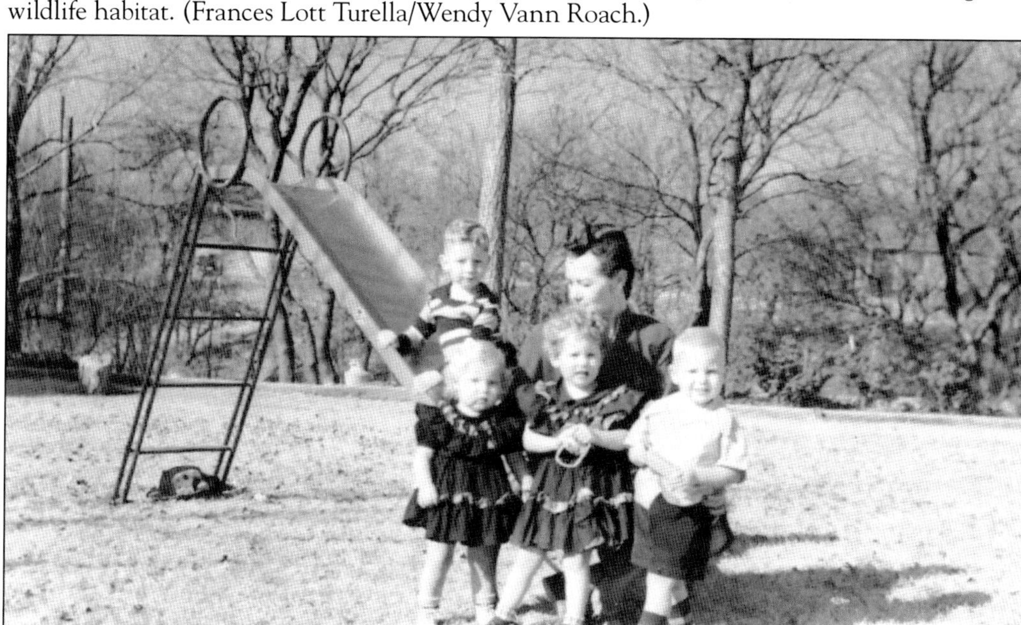

"Mama" Mary Gourley poses with her grandchildren in 1951 near her home on Wisteria Court. There was a victory garden here during World War II. (Frances Lott Turella/Wendy Vann Roach.)

Lazell and Thomas O. Lambert built this house at 2105 Daisy Lane in 1950. Seen here under construction, it was part of a large postwar development boom in Oakhurst. (Lazell Lambert Banowsky.)

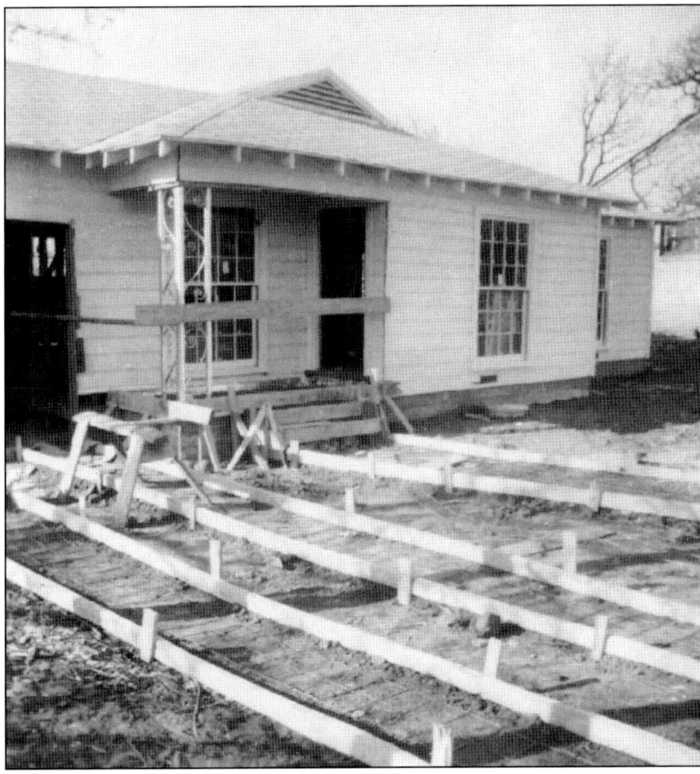

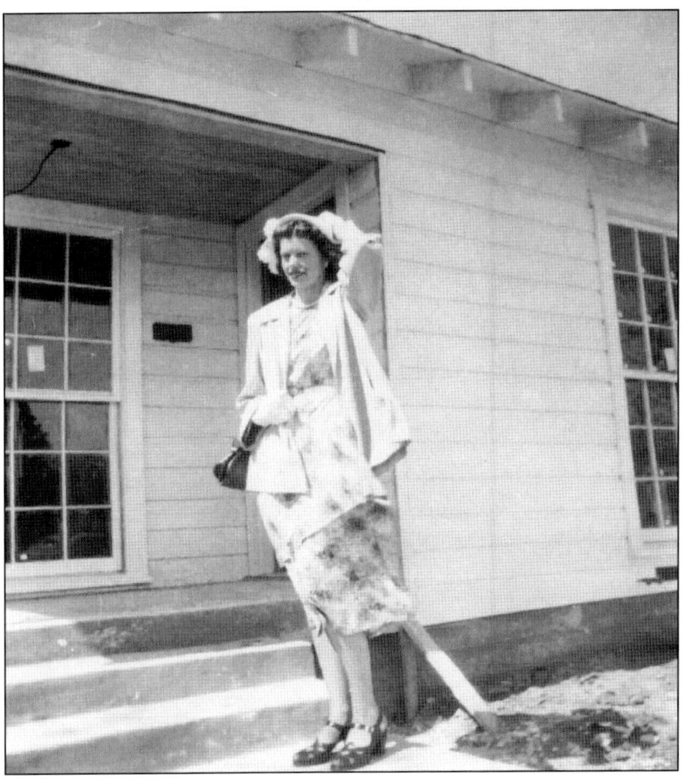

Lazell Lambert is about to inspect her new home on Daisy Lane in June 1950. The house was built in just three months. The Ranch-style house is now a contributing structure in the Oakhurst National Register Historic District. (Lazell Lambert Banowsky.)

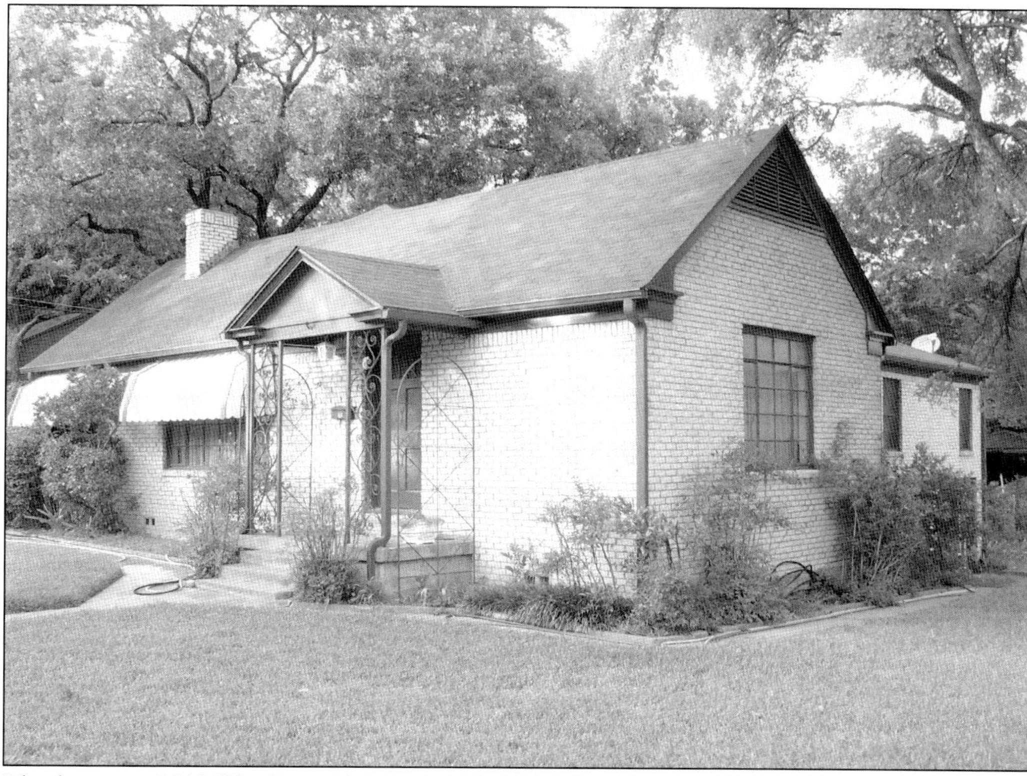

This house, at 2000 West Lotus Avenue, was built by the Kithas family in 1949 in the Minimalist Traditional style. The Kithas family, of Greek heritage, has been prominent in Oakhurst and Fort Worth for many years. (Doyle Willis Jr.)

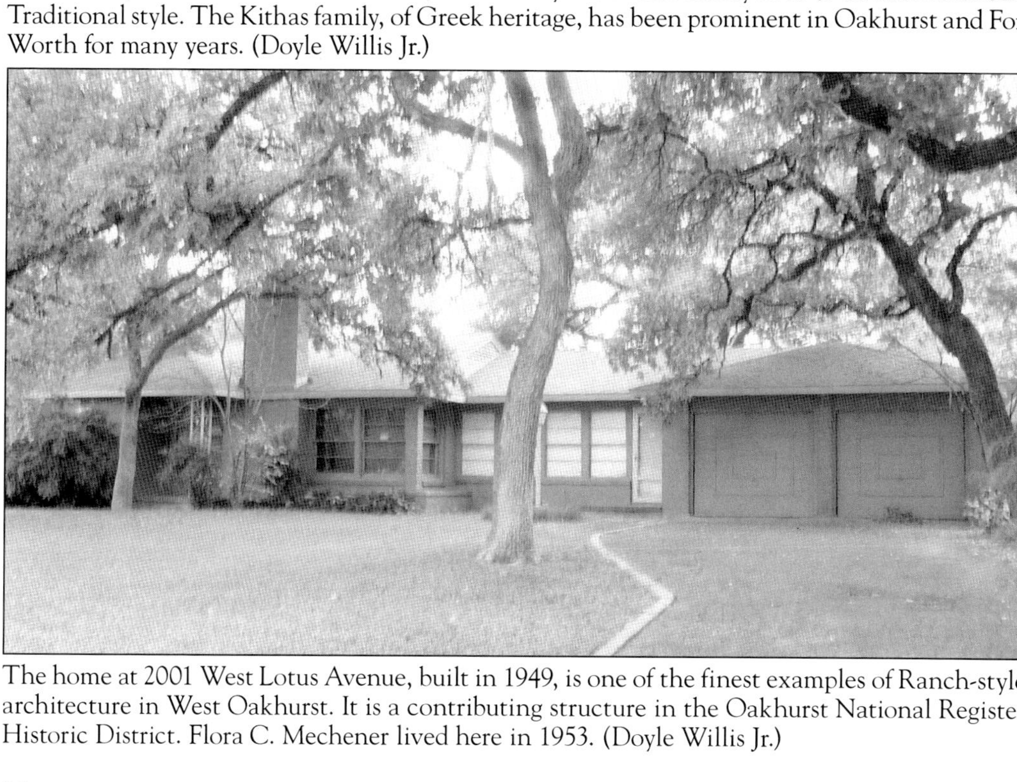

The home at 2001 West Lotus Avenue, built in 1949, is one of the finest examples of Ranch-style architecture in West Oakhurst. It is a contributing structure in the Oakhurst National Register Historic District. Flora C. Mechener lived here in 1953. (Doyle Willis Jr.)

Six

One Big Park

Living in Green Space

Riverside's original name was Sylvania, hence the name of the major street that is the easternmost border of Oakhurst. Mature trees nurtured by their close proximity to the Trinity River are the dominant feature of the area. From the early truck farms of Riverside to the development of Daggett's Woods as West Oakhurst, the area has benefited from development sensitive to its landscape.

Mount Olivet, carved out of Daggett's Woods and patterned after a Nashville cemetery of the same name, was developed in 1907 as a cemetery in a "park-like setting." Nationally renowned landscape architects Sidney Hare and S. Herbert Hare's work in designing Mount Olivet, Oakhurst, Oakhurst Scenic Drive, and other projects help make the Riverside collection one of their most important in Fort Worth. Riverside's importance in Fort Worth's landscape history has only grown with the recognition of just how much Hare & Hare designed in the area.

In both his 1930 and 1957 Park Master Plans for the Fort Worth Board of Park Commissioners, S. Herbert Hare envisioned a connected series of major parks throughout the city. Working with the raw green space of Riverside, he designed Oakhurst Scenic Drive in 1936–1937 as one of those connecting park roads. He designed landscape plans for Oakhurst and West Oakhurst, recommended the creation of Riverside Park (and more parks along his park road that were never realized), facilitated John P. King's donation of land for Oakhurst Park in the middle of the neighborhood, worked with the board of park commissioners and the trustees of the Fort Worth Independent School District on landscaping for Riverside High School and the esplanade on Bonnie Brae Avenue, and contributed to the landscape design for Oakhurst Elementary School's 1935 addition.

Early recognition of the value of Riverside (and thus Oakhurst's qualities as a big park) and a vision for developing high-quality neighborhoods and public institutions have been extremely important to the area for more than 100 years. Hare saw the natural beauty of Oakhurst and Riverside as integral to a good life. His design excellence and the commitment of developer John P. King and elected officials of bygone days to build what Hare envisioned explains why Oakhurst is still a viable place so many years later.

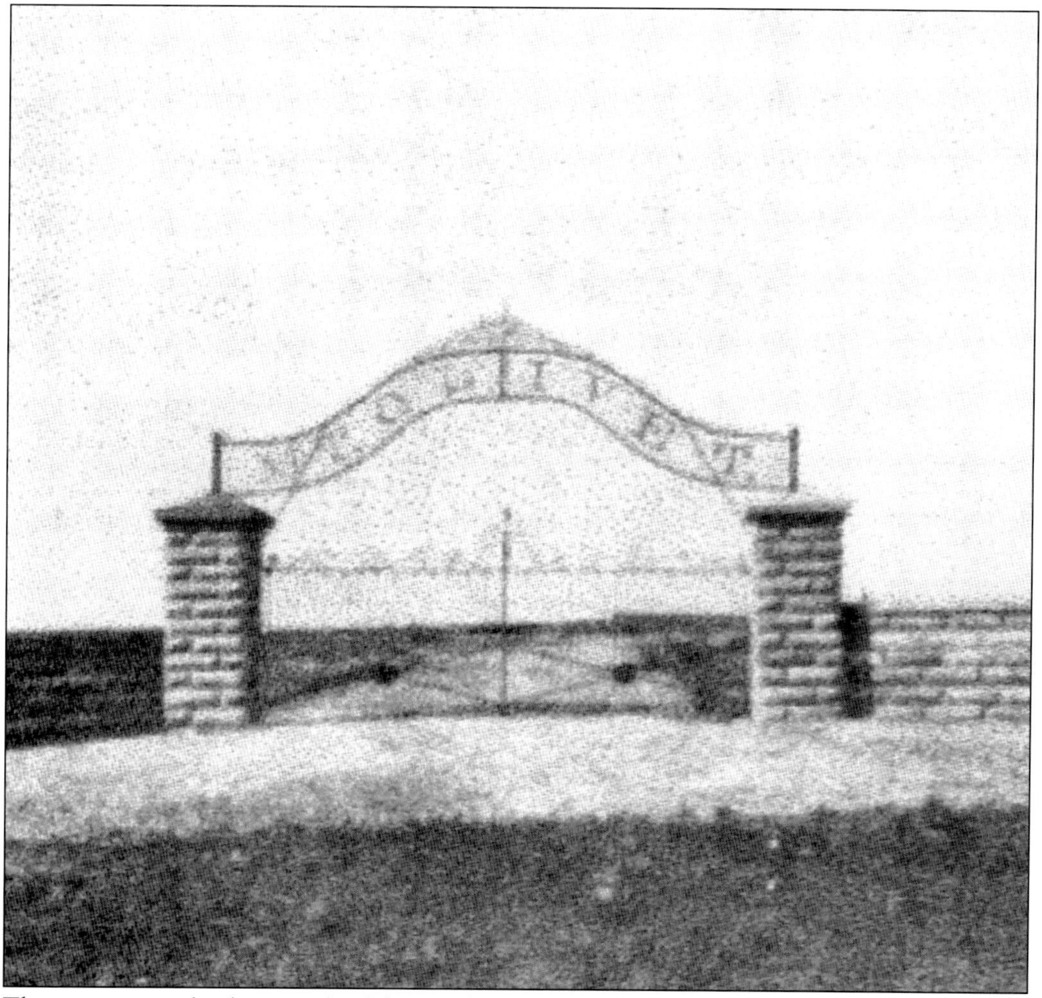

This is a very early photograph of the north entrance to Mount Olivet Cemetery, designed in part by the landscape architecture firm of Hare & Hare. Established as one of the first perpetual care cemeteries in Texas, it was built by F.G. McPeak in 1907 after he visited Nashville's Mount Olivet Cemetery. (AC.)

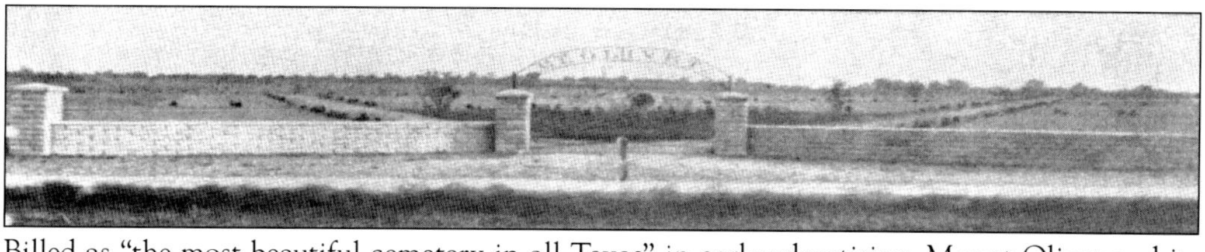

Billed as "the most beautiful cemetery in all Texas" in early advertising, Mount Olivet and its north entrance are seen here after 1907. Its "pleasing landscape effects and beautiful curved drives" were repeated in Oakhurst's layout. (AC.)

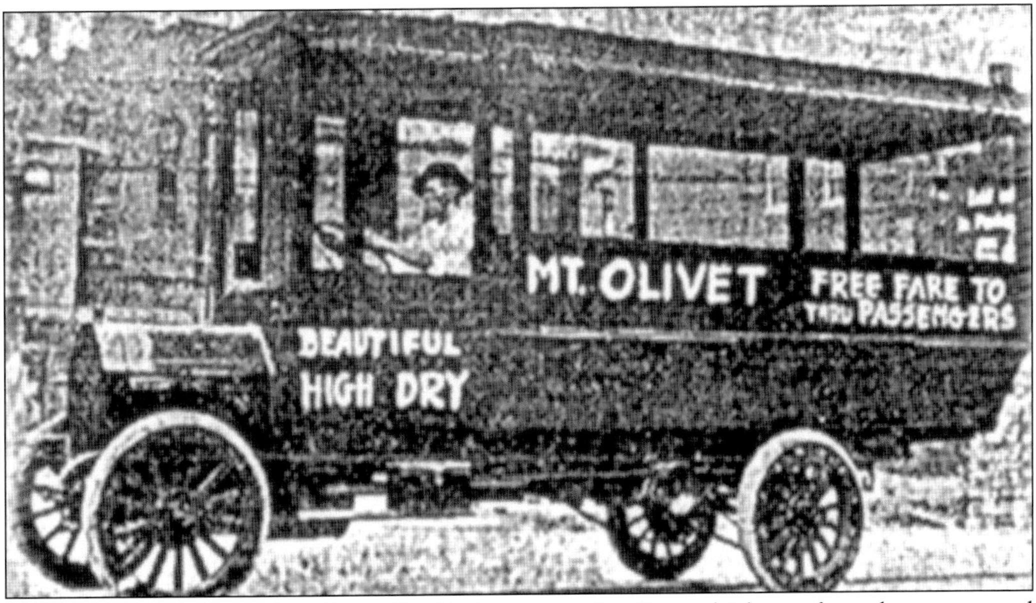

This is a 1914 photograph of Fort Worth's first motor bus line, which ran from downtown and Mount Olivet via Ninth Street to Main Street, the courthouse, Samuels Avenue, Niles City, and Diamond Hill. Mount Olivet ordered the 18-passenger truck especially for the service, and it ran seven days a week. (AC.)

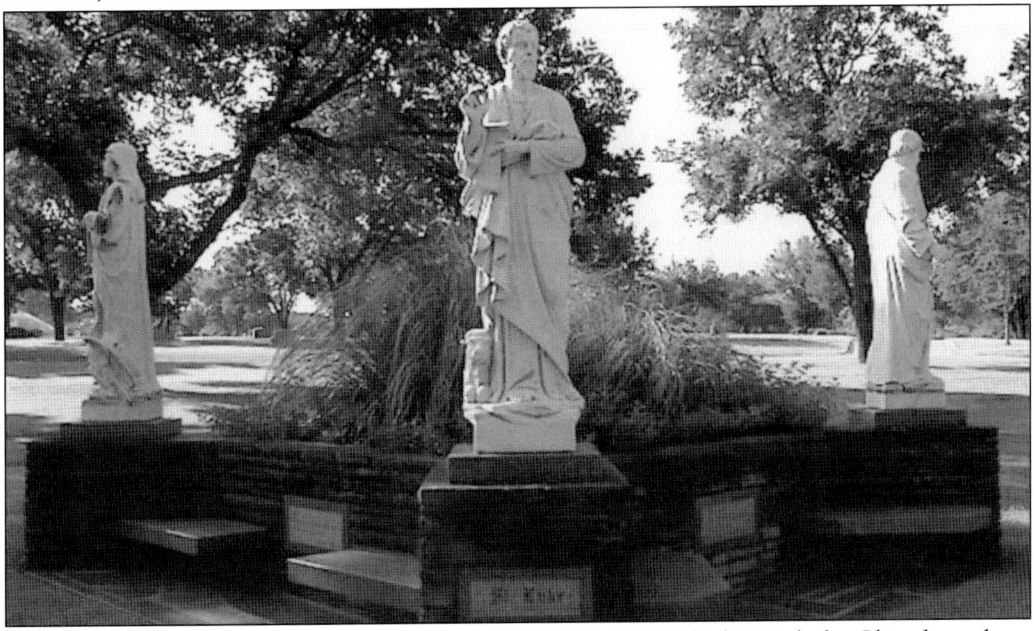

In 1929, Mount Olivet Cemetery entered into an agreement with the Catholic Church, making a portion of the land the official Catholic cemetery in Fort Worth. At Calvary Circle, priests are buried on the west side and nuns are buried on the east side. Among the well-known people buried at Mount Olivet are B.B. Paddock, Fort Worth mayor (1892–1900); US congressman William Pinkney McLean; 1930s film actress Catherine M. Singleton; and Doyle Willis, who served Tarrant County for 42 years in the Texas Legislature, the second-longest tenure in Texas history. (Doyle Willis Jr.)

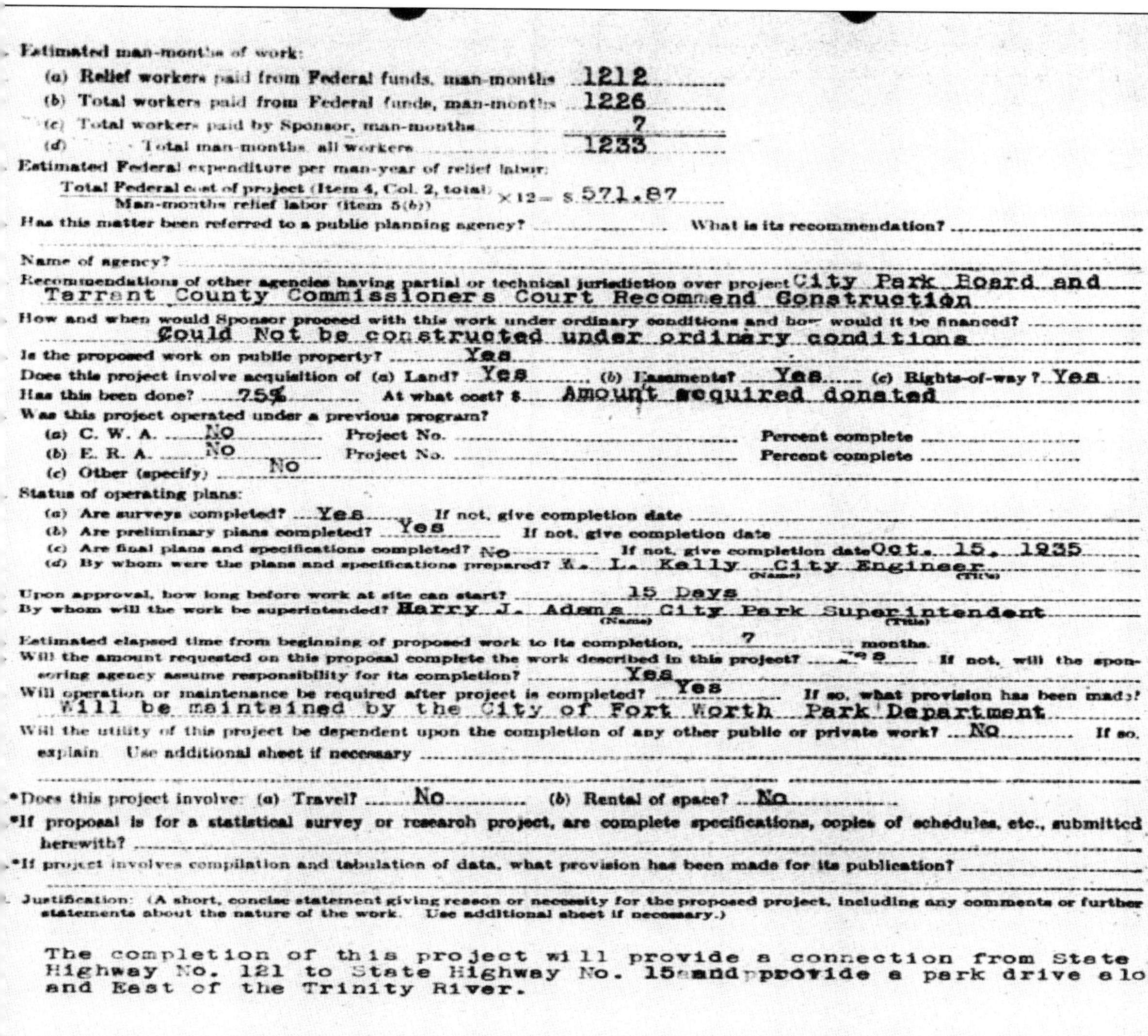

Estimated man-months of work:

(a) Relief workers paid from Federal funds, man-months 1212

(b) Total workers paid from Federal funds, man-months 1226

(c) Total workers paid by Sponsor, man-months 7

(d) Total man-months all workers 1233

Estimated Federal expenditure per man-year of relief labor:

Total Federal cost of project (Item 4, Col. 2, total) / Man-months relief labor (Item 5(b)) × 12 = $ 571.87

Has this matter been referred to a public planning agency? .... What is its recommendation? ....

Name of agency? ....

Recommendations of other agencies having partial or technical jurisdiction over project City Park Board and Tarrant County Commissioners Court Recommend Construction

How and when would Sponsor proceed with this work under ordinary conditions and how would it be financed? Could Not be constructed under ordinary conditions

Is the proposed work on public property? Yes

Does this project involve acquisition of (a) Land? Yes (b) Easements? Yes (c) Rights-of-way? Yes

Has this been done? 75% At what cost? $ Amount acquired donated

Was this project operated under a previous program?

(a) C. W. A. No Project No. .... Percent complete ....

(b) E. R. A. No Project No. .... Percent complete ....

(c) Other (specify) No

Status of operating plans:

(a) Are surveys completed? Yes If not, give completion date ....

(b) Are preliminary plans completed? Yes If not, give completion date ....

(c) Are final plans and specifications completed? No If not, give completion date Oct. 15, 1935

(d) By whom were the plans and specifications prepared? E. L. Kelly (Name) City Engineer (Title)

Upon approval, how long before work at site can start? 15 Days

By whom will the work be superintended? Harry J. Adams (Name) City Park Superintendent (Title)

Estimated elapsed time from beginning of proposed work to its completion, 7 months.

Will the amount requested on this proposal complete the work described in this project? Yes If not, will the sponsoring agency assume responsibility for its completion? Yes

Will operation or maintenance be required after project is completed? Yes If so, what provision has been made? Will be maintained by the City of Fort Worth Park Department

Will the utility of this project be dependent upon the completion of any other public or private work? No If so, explain. Use additional sheet if necessary ....

*Does this project involve: (a) Travel? No (b) Rental of space? No

*If proposal is for a statistical survey or research project, are complete specifications, copies of schedules, etc., submitted herewith? ....

*If project involves compilation and tabulation of data, what provision has been made for its publication? ....

Justification: (A short, concise statement giving reason or necessity for the proposed project, including any comments or further statements about the nature of the work. Use additional sheet if necessary.)

The completion of this project will provide a connection from State Highway No. 121 to State Highway No. 15 and provide a park drive alo[ng] and East of the Trinity River.

This is the Fort Worth Park Department's application to the Works Progress Administration (WPA) in 1935 for federal funds to build a park road, Oakhurst Scenic Drive. (AC.)

This is a 1937 photograph of Oakhurst Scenic Drive, built as a park road in 1936–1937 by the WPA. The federal government invested almost $55,000 in the road, and the City of Fort Worth Board of Park Commissioners contributed over $10,000. A Park Department summary of road construction between 1931 and 1936, during the height of the Depression, showed that Oakhurst Scenic Drive was 35 feet wide and 2.25 miles long and was oil-treated. (FWL.)

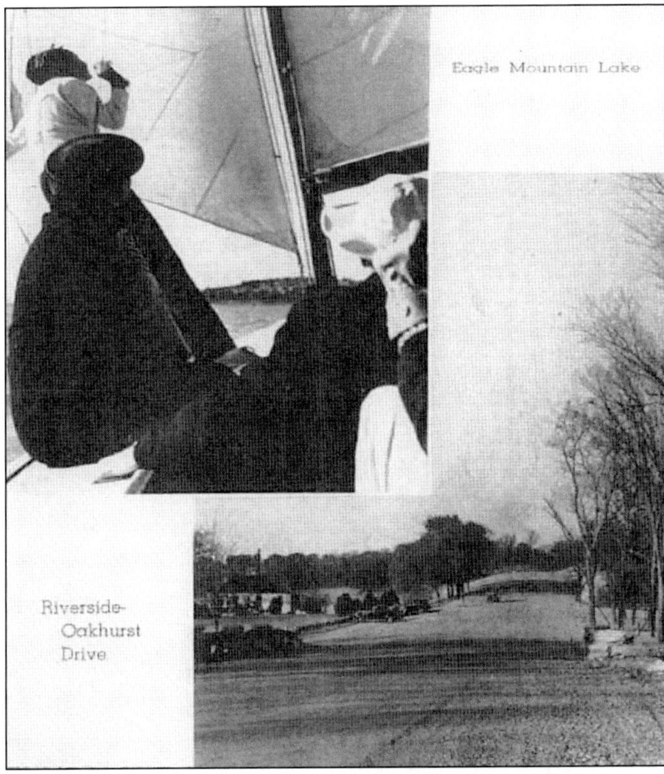

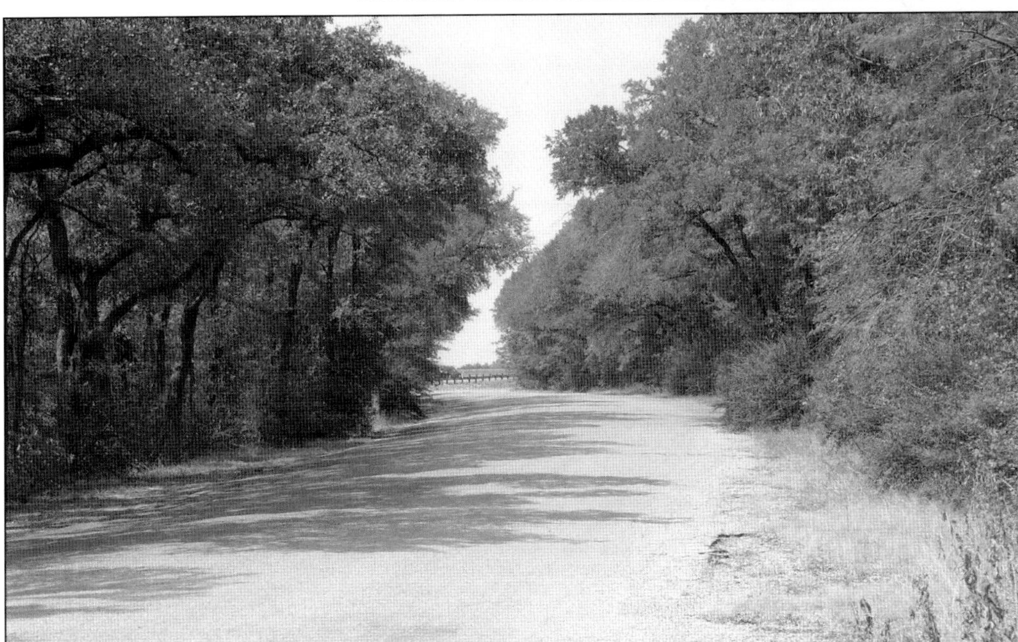

This is Oakhurst Scenic Drive today. It is still a "bit of the country in the city" and is a treasured cultural and historical scenic drive just 2.8 miles from downtown Fort Worth. The City of Fort Worth designated it as an official scenic corridor in 1995, and it is included as the westernmost boundary of the Oakhurst National Register Historic District. (Doyle Willis Jr.)

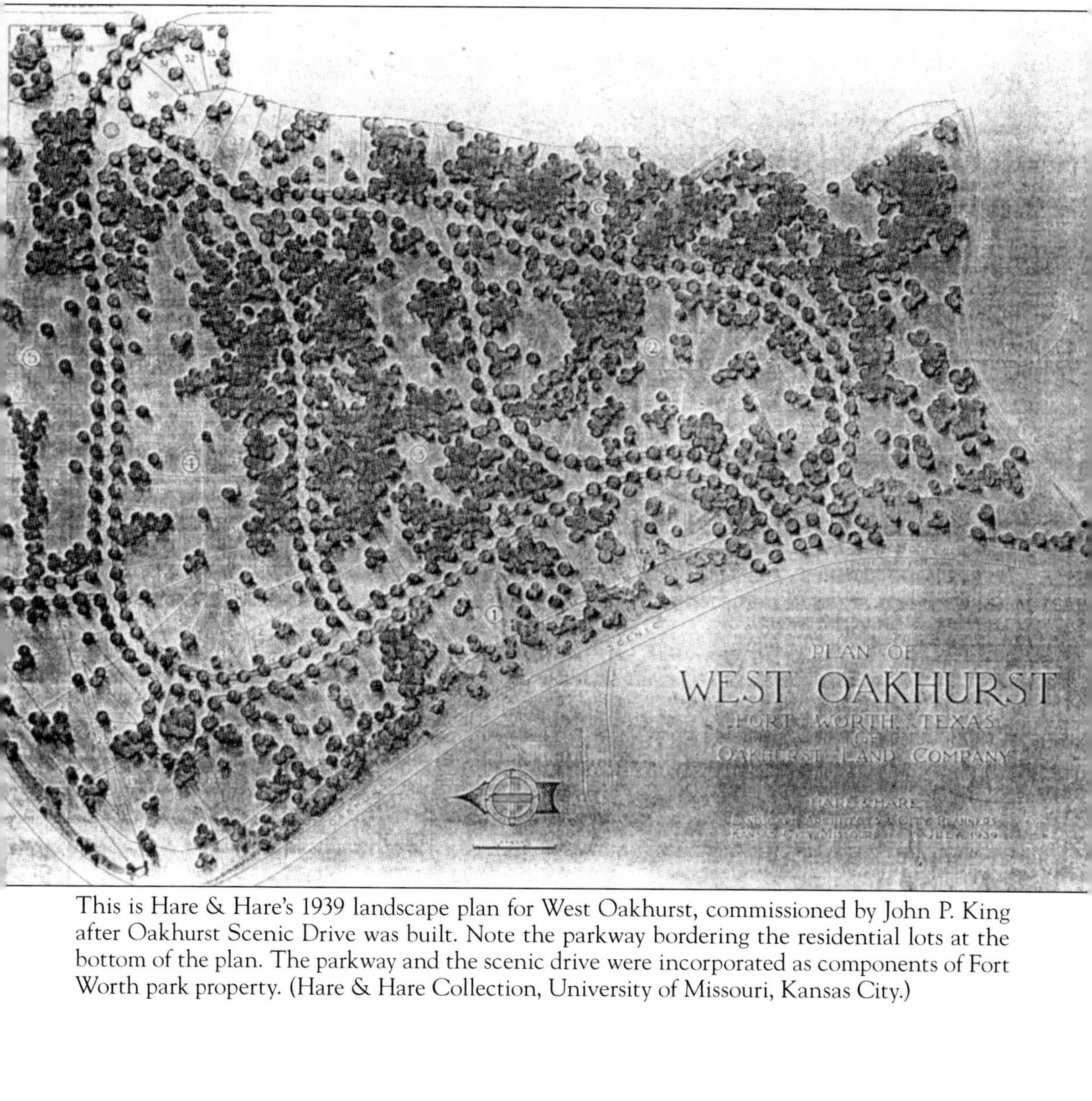

This is Hare & Hare's 1939 landscape plan for West Oakhurst, commissioned by John P. King after Oakhurst Scenic Drive was built. Note the parkway bordering the residential lots at the bottom of the plan. The parkway and the scenic drive were incorporated as components of Fort Worth park property. (Hare & Hare Collection, University of Missouri, Kansas City.)

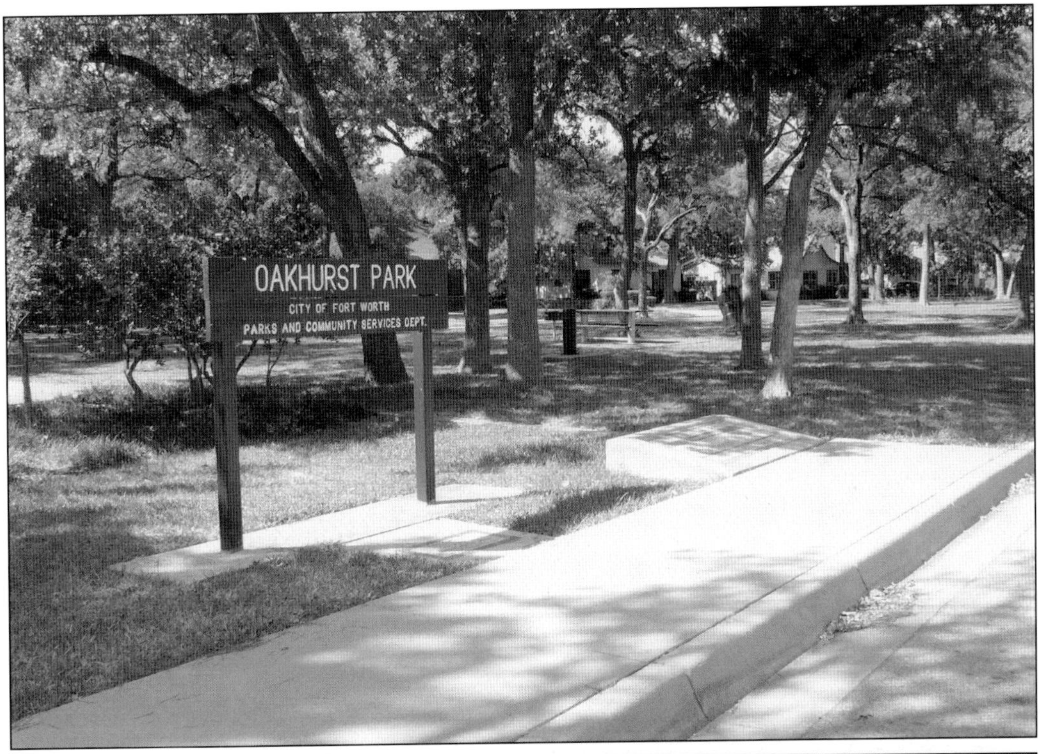

In 1944, John P. King decided to donate Daisy Lane Park, sometimes known as Triangle Park, to the City of Fort Worth as Oakhurst Park (above). Park superintendent Harry Adams reported that S. Herbert Hare "felt this area would make a useful and ornamental park." The park, situated in the middle of the neighborhood, is a frequent location for Oakhurst Neighborhood Association events. (Doyle Willis Jr.)

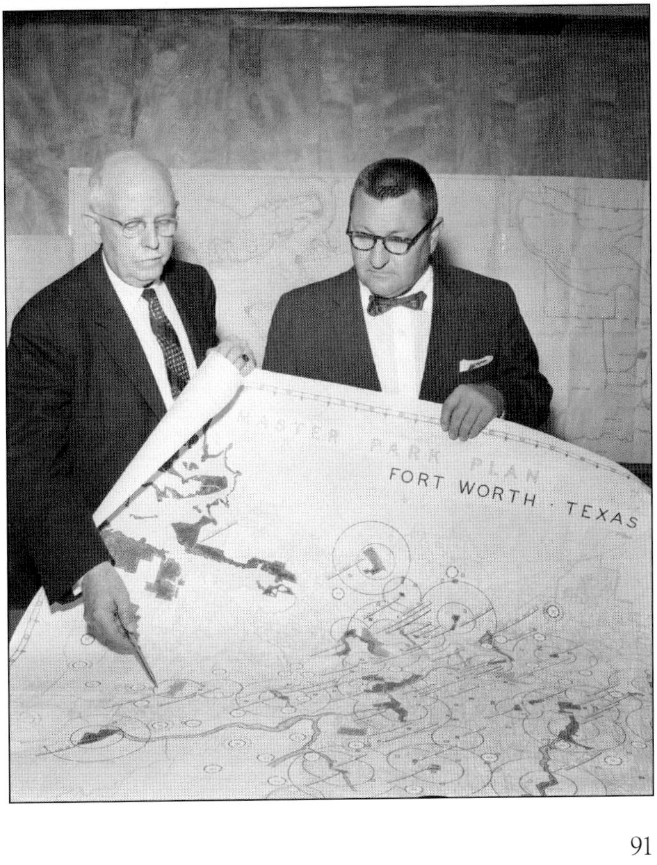

S. Herbert Hare (left) and Hamilton Hittson, Fort Worth park director, review the map of the 1957 Park Master Plan, which Hare prepared. The plan and map identified Oakhurst Scenic Drive as a 41-acre park and recommended that the city purchase property just west of the drive and north of Yucca Avenue as parkland. (FWSTC/SCUTA.)

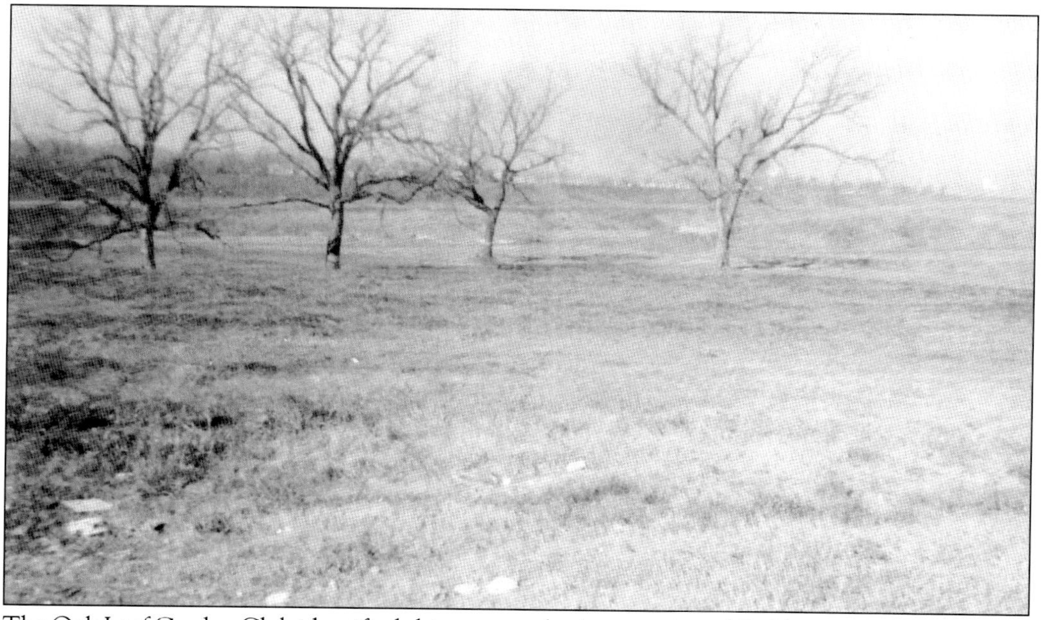

The Oak Leaf Garden Club identified this area, at the intersection of Oakhurst Scenic Drive and Belknap Street, as a beautification project in 1959. It was called Scenic Drive Park. Downtown Fort Worth is visible in the distance. In 1974, the city added the property west of the drive from Belknap almost to Yucca Avenue as Riverside Park. (AC.)

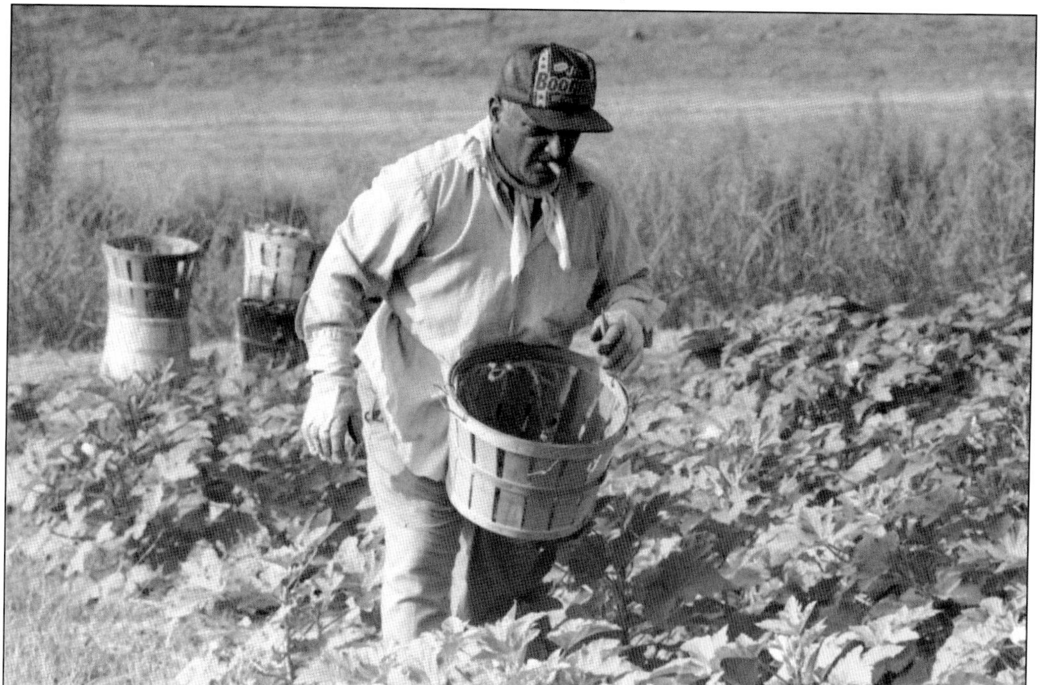

James Sparto picks okra on Sparto family land off of Oakhurst Scenic Drive near the Trinity River. The Sparto family has long been prominent in Riverside. James was an early graduate of Amon Carter Riverside High School and a longtime member of the Riverside Lions Club. (FWSTC/SCUTA.)

Seven

Beyond Oakhurst

Businesses, Schools, and Churches

Oakhurst was designed as a residential neighborhood that was simply a neighborhood. The original development contained only homes, and that is still the case today. But Oakhurst's proximity to nearby commercial areas made shopping and access to schools and churches easy. Permanently protected on the north by the presence of Mount Olivet Cemetery, residents have not had to deal with commercial encroachment.

The bustling North Sylvania thoroughfare put Oakhurst close to small shops and services from the beginning of its existence. Over a mile's worth of shops along North Sylvania Avenue, as well as those on Race Street and Six Points, have traditionally been Oakhurst residents' stomping grounds. Markets, restaurants, cleaners, hairdressers, furniture stores, dress shops, and many more small businesses were especially important to Oakhurst from the 1920s through their gradual decline after the 1950s.

Schools have also traditionally been nearby. Just three years after Oakhurst was established, the Fort Worth Independent School District built Oakhurst Elementary School on Yucca Avenue for the neighborhood's children. Until the district added on to the building in 1935, however, elementary school students attended Oakhurst Elementary only through the third grade, after which they went to Riverside Elementary. Also in 1935, the district built Riverside High School to serve Oakhurst and surrounding Riverside neighborhoods. Just six blocks from Oakhurst, the high school became Amon Carter Riverside High School after a 1941 name change. In 1953, the district added Riverside Middle School to the high school campus. Oakhurst's schools were always within walking distance of the neighborhood.

And while Riverside has always been a religious community, with many well-established churches, the advent of Oakhurst spawned even more congregations. Large numbers of members from the neighborhood acted as founders and "pillar" members for decades. Oakhurst Presbyterian Church, Oakhurst Methodist Church, a one-time Oakhurst Baptist Church, Midtown Church of Christ, and others, such as St. George Catholic Church, thrived with Oakhurst residents' participation. Residents also became staunch members of other Riverside churches, and many of these institutions incorporated "Oakhurst" into their names. Even though they were located outside of the boundaries of the neighborhood, they saw it as the most important residential development in Riverside and wanted to be considered part of the "Oakhurst orbit."

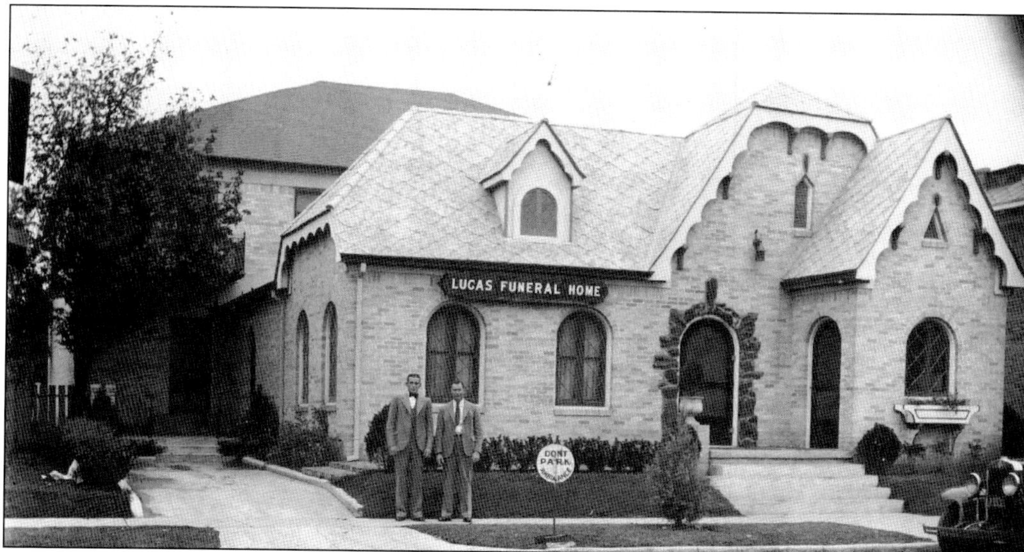

In 1929, the Lucas family established its funeral home in Riverside at 617 North Sylvania Avenue. Pictured here are Harry "Fuzzy" Wiggins and Zippy Lucas, Bob Lucas's younger brother. After World War II, Mildred and Bobby Joe Lucas came back to Fort Worth and lived at the funeral home. "Mr. Bob thought everyone should live at the funeral home," said Mildred, who later became a licensed mortician. (Mildred Lucas/Lucas Funeral Home.)

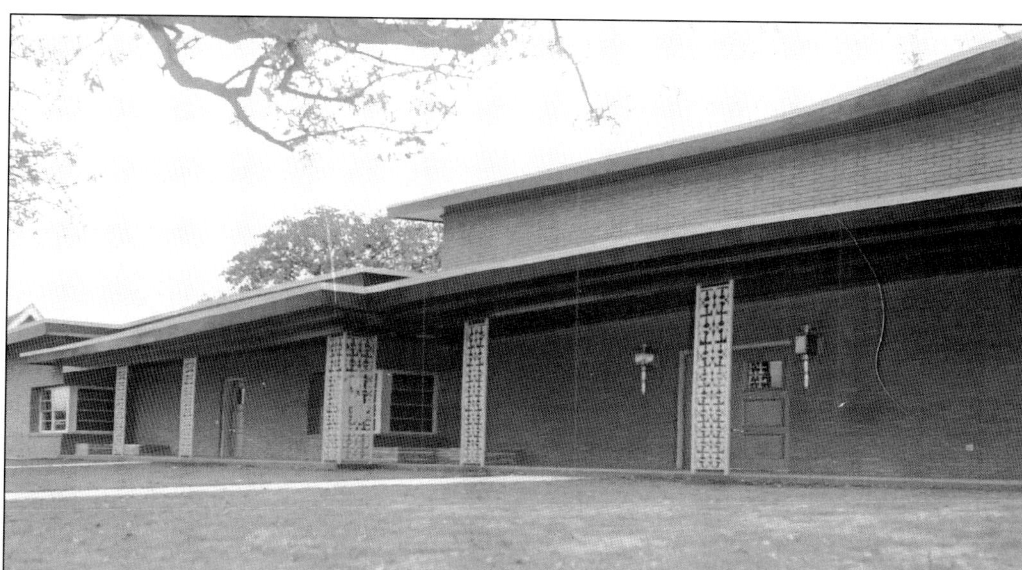

The 1950s-era Lucas Funeral Home, at 517 North Sylvania Avenue, was constructed one block from the original 1920s location. The business has been a mainstay in Riverside for 85 years and has often provided space for community meetings. (Mildred Lucas/Lucas Funeral Home.)

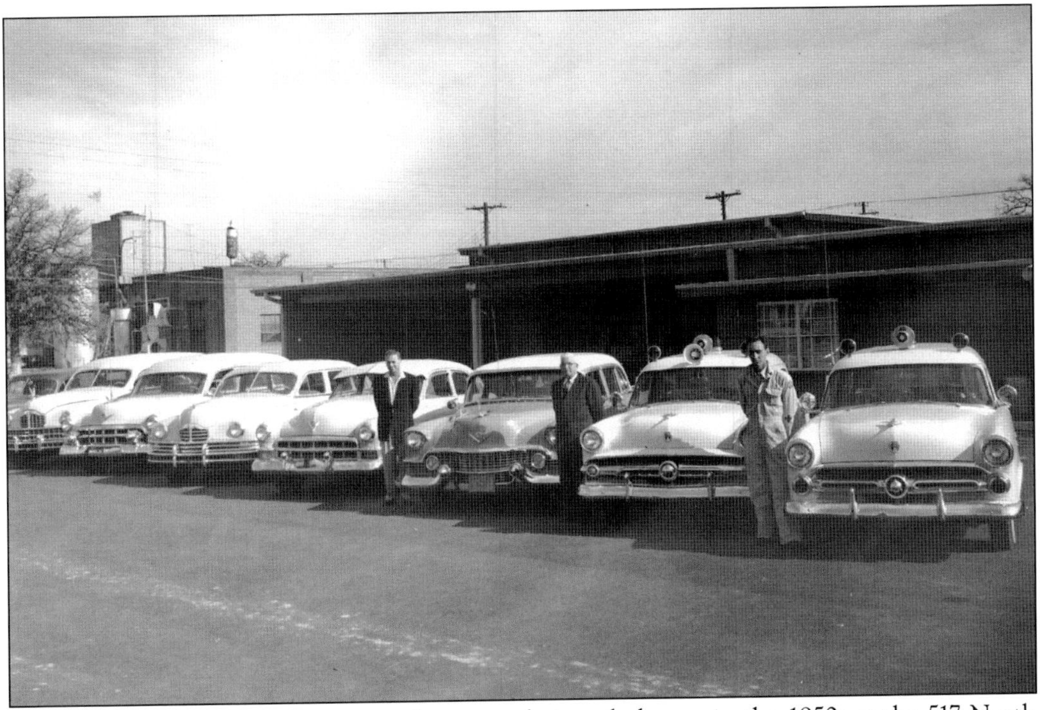

Lucas Funeral Home employees stand next to their ambulances in the 1950s at the 517 North Sylvania Avenue location. At the time, ambulances worked from funeral homes. (Mildred Lucas/ Lucas Funeral Home.)

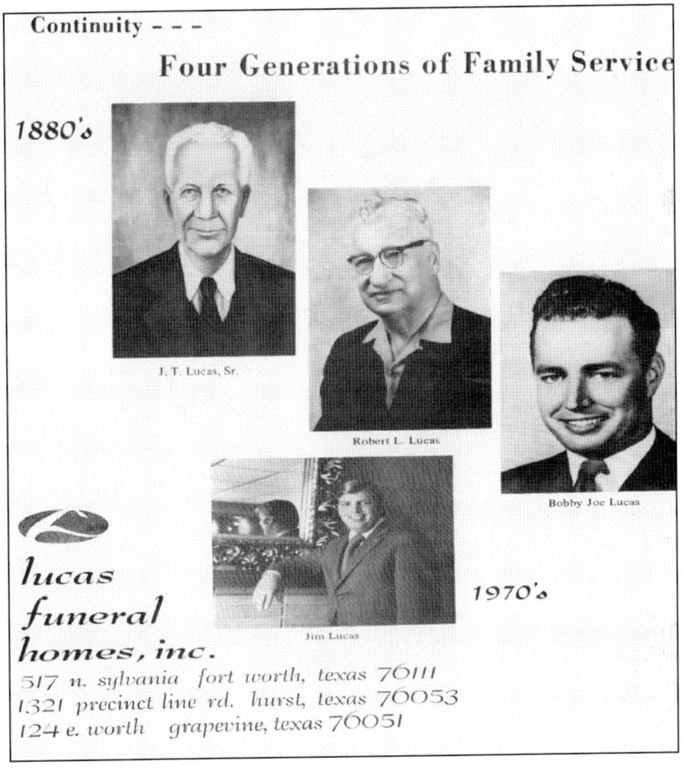

This 1970s advertisement shows the four generations of the Lucas family who have operated Lucas Funeral Homes in Riverside and in other North Texas locations. J.T. Lucas began the family's business in Grapevine. The fifth generation of Lucases are now serving as funeral directors. (Mildred Lucas/ Lucas Funeral Home.)

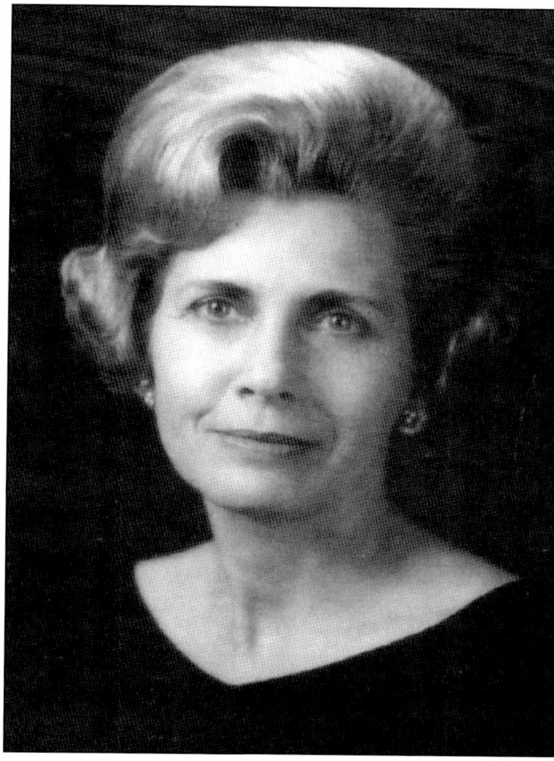

Mildred Nimmo Lucas received her certification as a licensed mortician in 1967. She was one of the first women in Texas to hold that distinction. A beloved Riverside leader, she was in the first graduating class at Amon Carter Riverside High School. (Mildred Lucas/Lucas Funeral Home.)

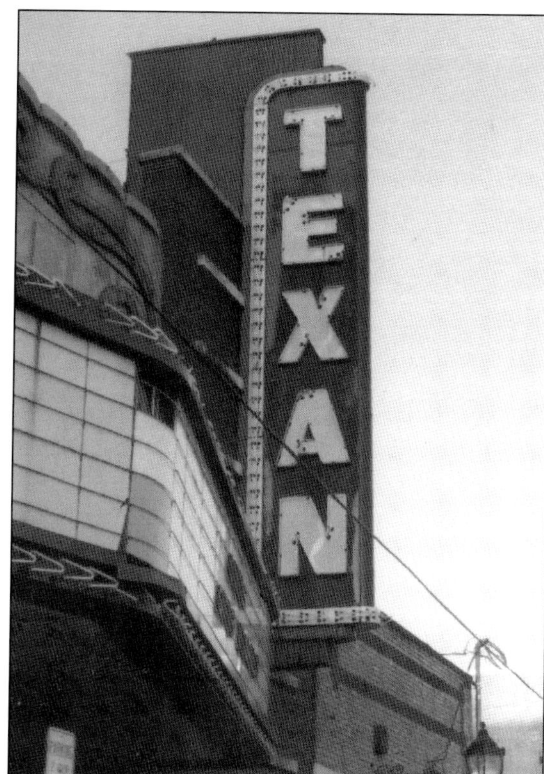

The Texan Theater, on North Sylvania Avenue, was the only movie theater in Riverside during the 1930s and early 1940s. From 1936 to 1942, "Three or four of us would meet at Sylvania and Goldenrod," said Ray Jefferson, "and walk to the movie, picking up more boys at Honeysuckle, Marigold, Primrose, and Yucca. We would watch the movie and serial and then walk back home." (Ray Jefferson.)

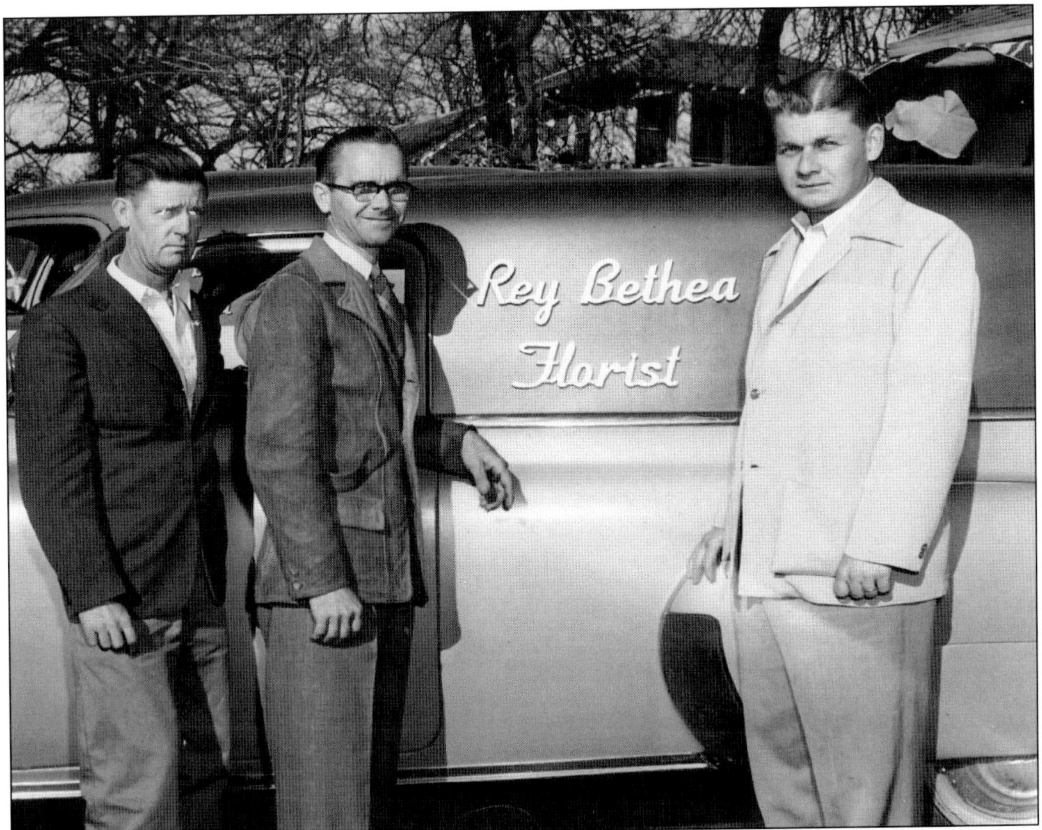

Rey Bethea (center) and his employees pose at his florist shop on North Sylvania Avenue. The street has been home to many florists over the years because of its proximity to Mount Olivet Cemetery. (Rey Bethea Jr.)

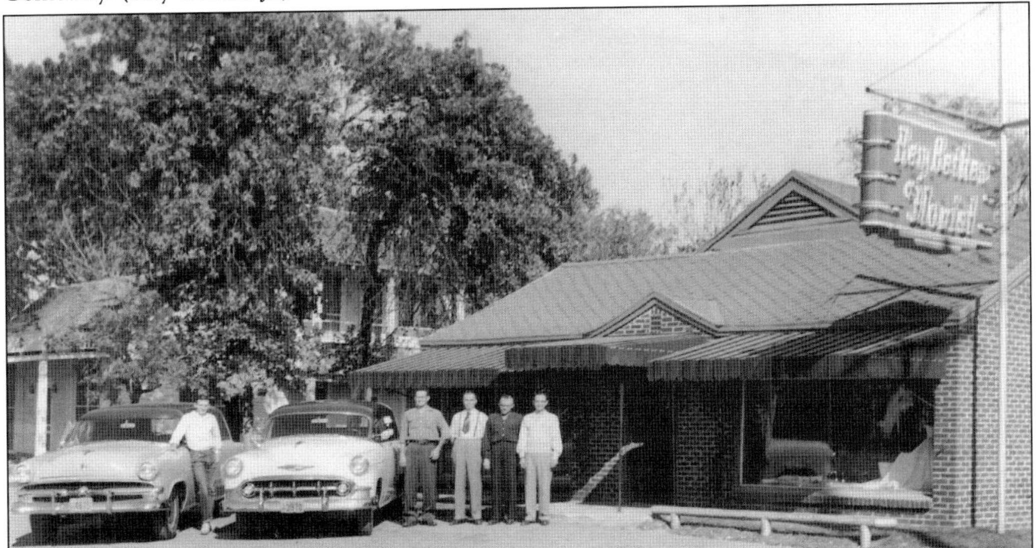

The Rey Bethea Florist shop on North Sylvania Avenue is seen here in 1953. Rey Bethea Sr. started the business in 1945. (Rey Bethea Jr.)

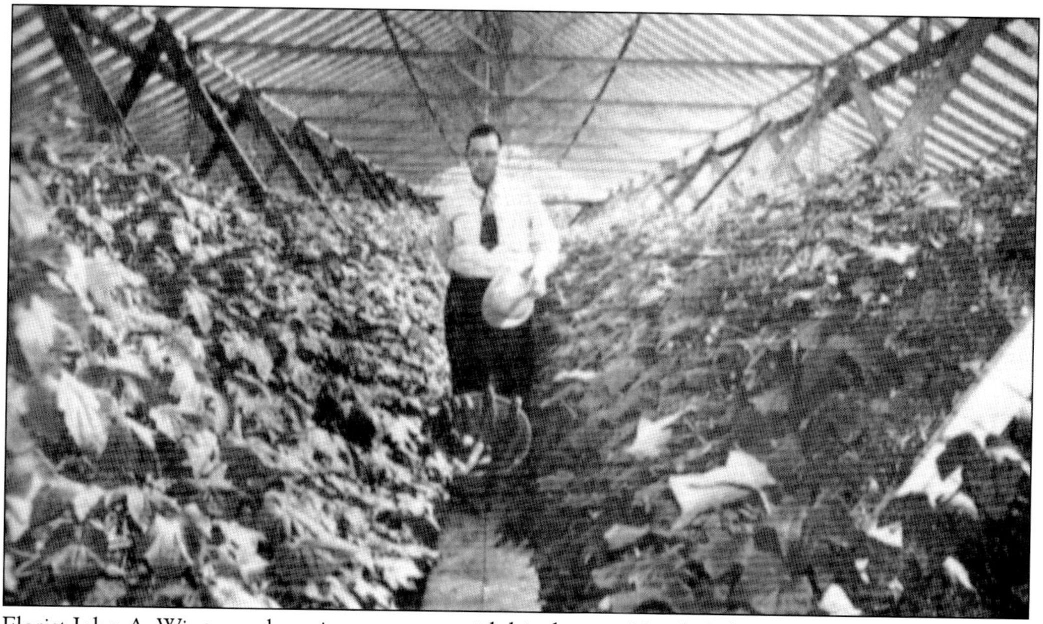

Florist John A. Winters, a longtime presence with his shop on North Sylvania Avenue, experimented in 1946 with growing cucumbers in his Riverside greenhouse. Soon, Winters was harvesting 100 pounds of cucumbers every other day during the growing season. His was one of several florist shops located on North Sylvania Avenue. (FWCC.)

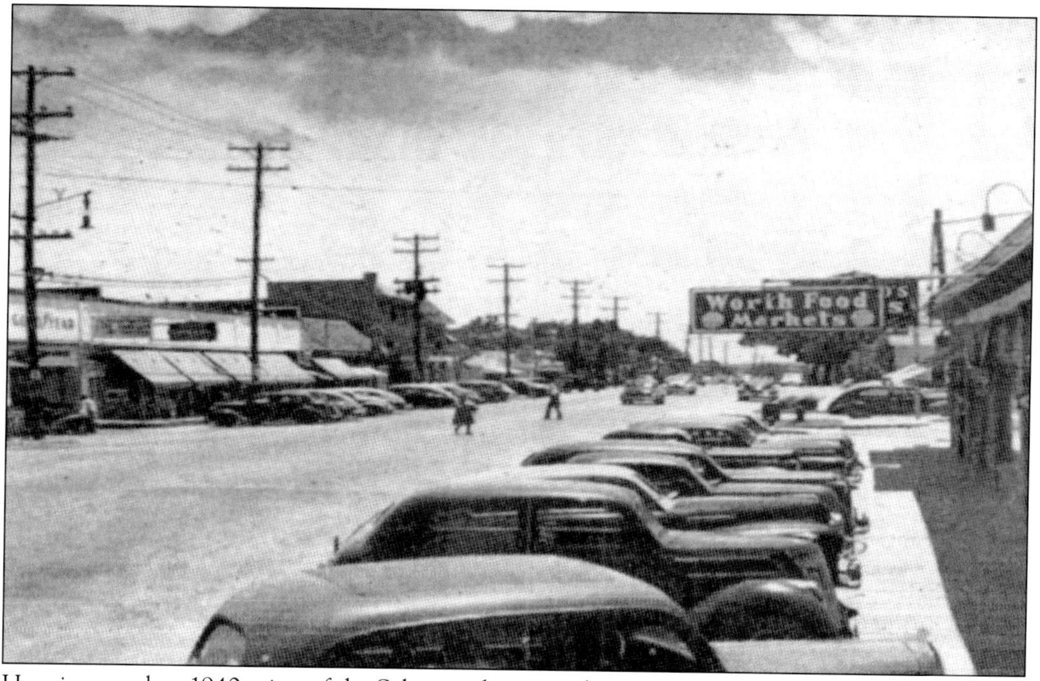

Here is a rare late-1940s view of the Sylvania shopping district, frequented by Oakhurst residents. Just past the intersection with Race Street is the Worth Food Market (right). Across the street, midway down the block, is the two-story building that was the original home of the Fort Worth Community Theater (1957–1966) and then the home of the Prayer of Faith Temple. (FWCC.)

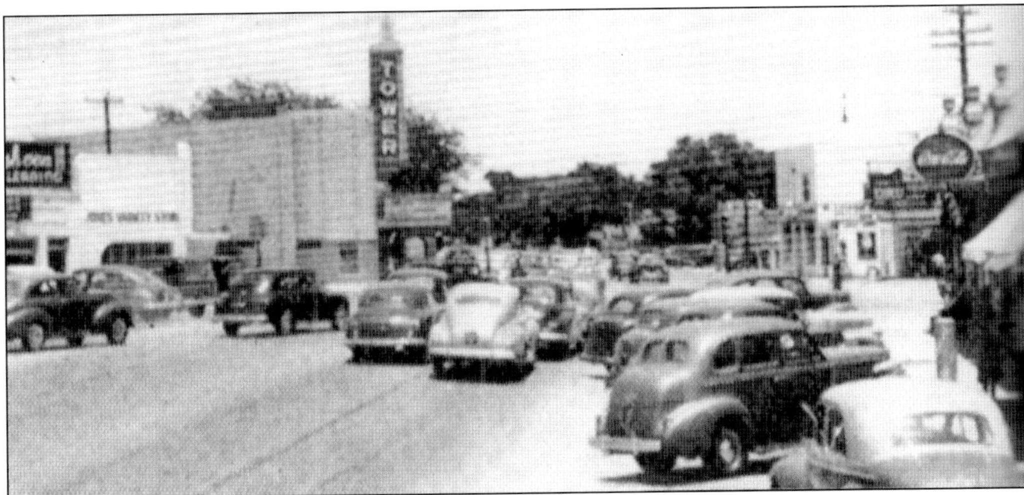

Riverside's Six Points, where Belknap Street, Race Street, and Riverside Drive intersect, is shown here in 1948. The area was the hub of commercial activity for residents of Oakhurst and Riverside for decades. This photograph offers a rare view of the Tower Theater, which operated from at least 1941 until the late 1960s. Paramount Pictures operated it through their subsidiary, Hoblitzelle & O'Donnell. "It was named for Mr. Hightower, the manager of the Texan Theater, who built it," according to Ray Jefferson. (FWCC.)

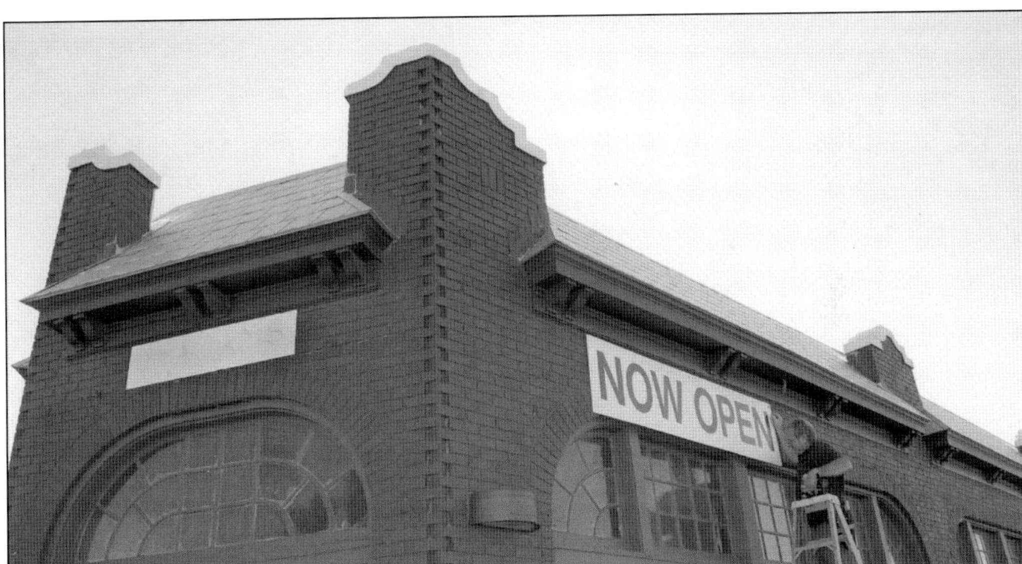

This is a photograph of the 1931 McAdams Building, which housed Scott's Drug Store, a popular hangout for Amon Carter Riverside High School students for many decades. In 2004, the building and site were threatened with being demolished and replaced by a used-car lot. Instead, entrepreneur and Haltom City native Robert Bell purchased the building and recruited Mamma Mia's Restaurant to make the site a favorite Riverside establishment once again. (Doyle Willis Jr.)

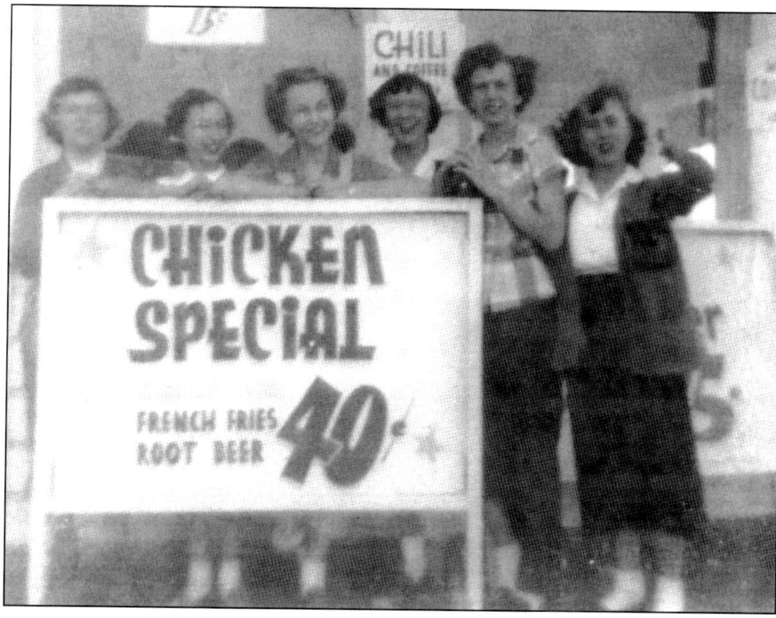

"The Root Beer Stand" was a hangout on 28th Street where Amon Carter Riverside High School coeds went for root beer floats. "We were all learning to drive and sometimes got to go up there after school," remembered Sue Shugart Drautz. (Sue Shugart Drautz.)

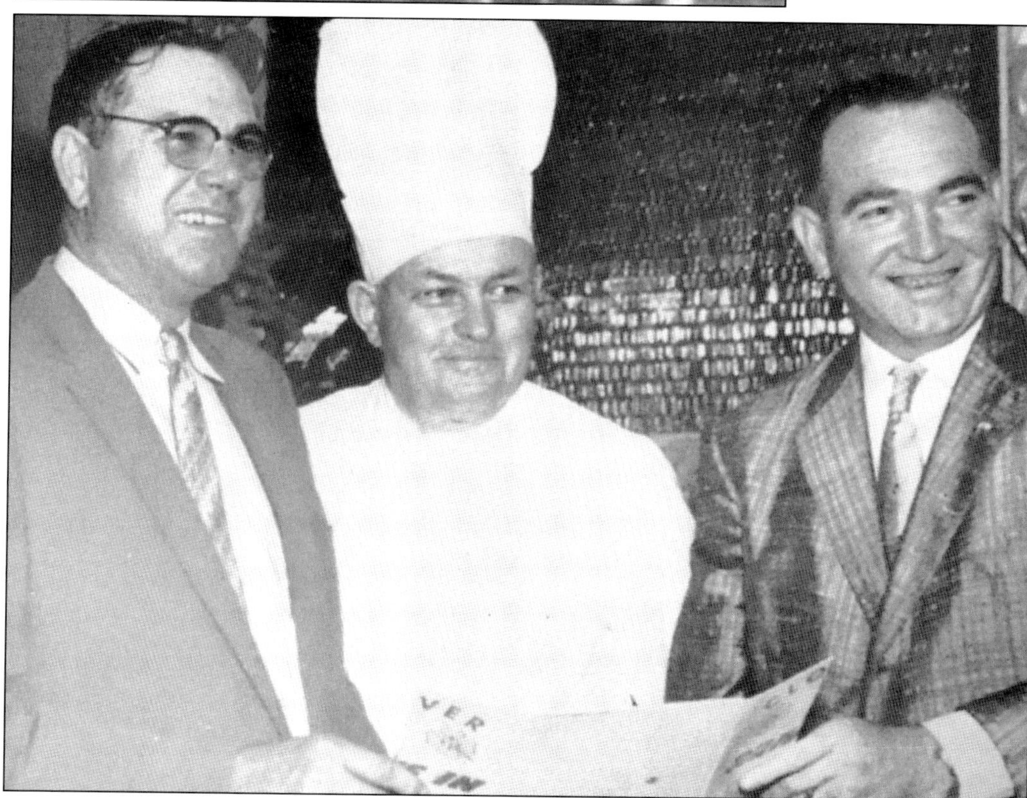

In 1959, Odell Allen (left) opened his Clover Drive-In No. 3 at the corner of 28th Street and North Sylvania Avenue, on the edge of Oakhurst. Chef William McDaniel is in the center and Herman Allen is on the right. The new restaurant included a coffee shop and rooms for private parties, as well as awnings on two sides for drive-in visitors. Allen had also developed the Allendale Apartments, across from Oakhurst, in 1949. (FWL.)

These advertisements in an early-1960s Oakhurst Elementary School class play program illustrate the bustling commercial activity around Six Points, Race Street, and North Sylvania Avenue. A drugstore, several beauty shops, and a supermarket were immediately across from the neighborhood. In 1943, Oakhurst Barber Shop, Oakhurst Beauty Shop, and Oakhurst Cleaners existed in the 600 and 700 blocks of North Sylvania Avenue, about a mile from Oakhurst. (BWSCA/FWISD.)

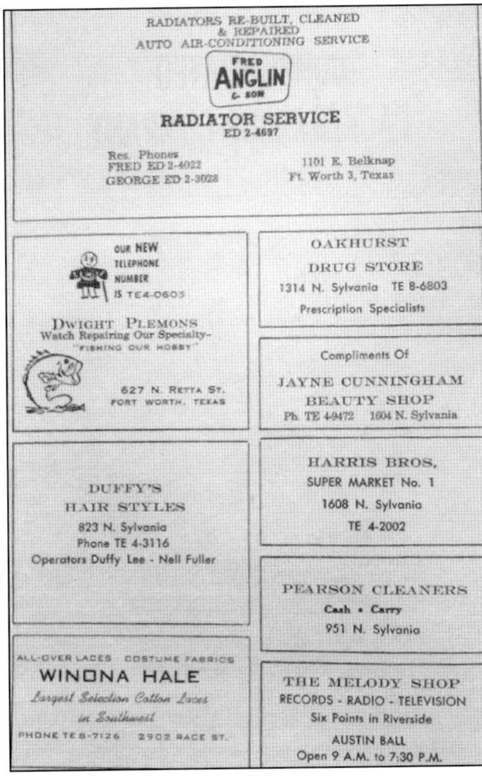

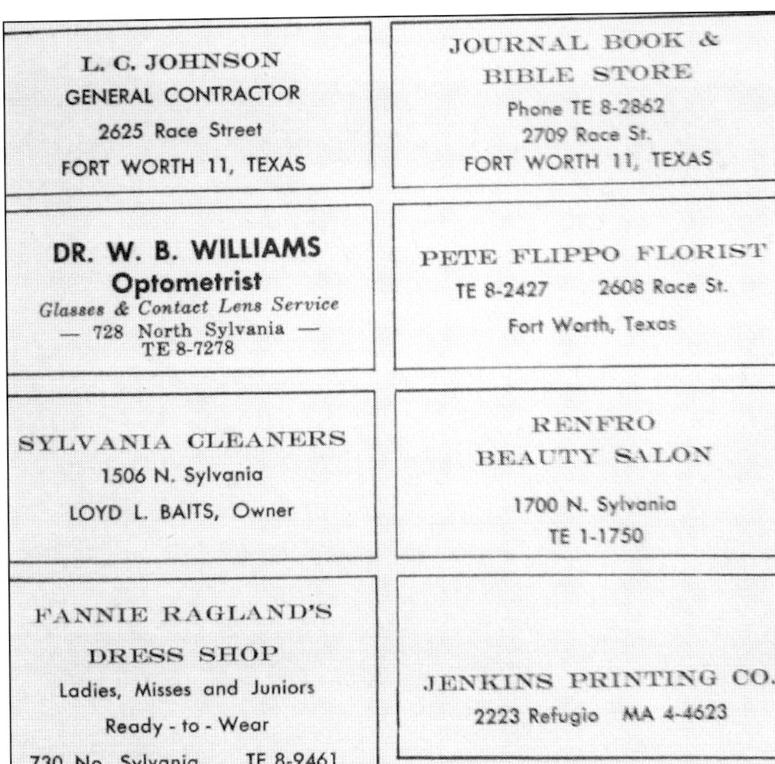

Here, from the same Oakhurst Elementary School class play program, is a partial listing of neighborhood businesses, including Sylvania Cleaners and Renfro Beauty Salon, immediately across from Oakhurst. Their location made it easy for Oakhurst residents to walk to the shops. (BWSCA/FWISD.)

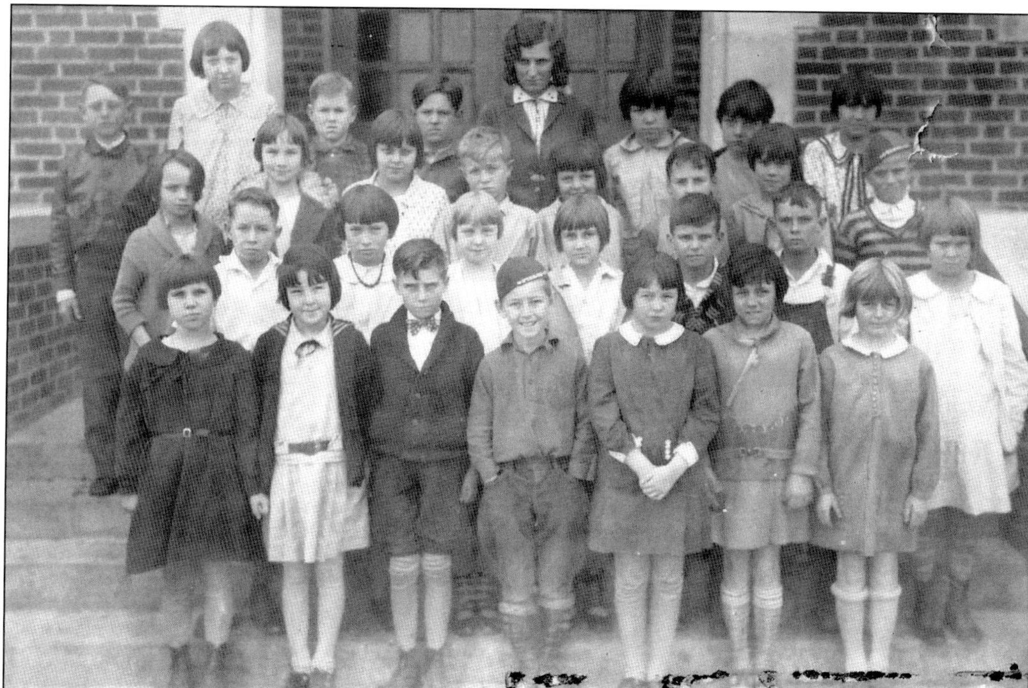

This is the Oakhurst Elementary School third-grade class about 1927. Mary Womack is in the first row, far right. The school went through the third grade, after which Oakhurst students attended Riverside Elementary. The school was built to accommodate children from Oakhurst and other surrounding Riverside neighborhoods. Wiley G. Clarkson designed the ochre-brick structure. (Delia Brelsford Shiflet.)

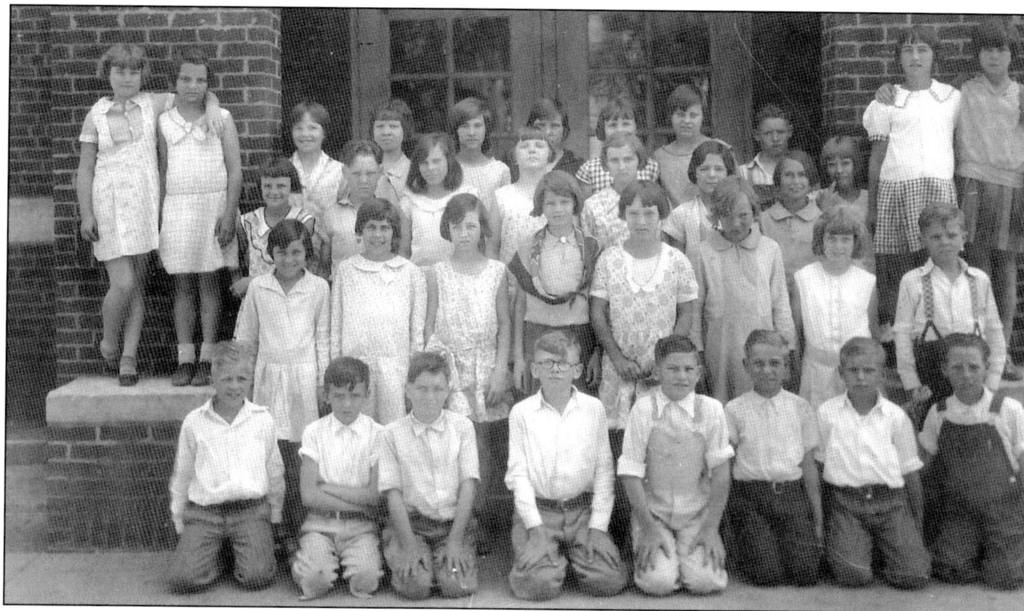

The fourth-grade class at Riverside Elementary School is seen here about 1928. Primrose Avenue resident Mary Womack is in the second row, second from right. She later attended Paschal High School and TCU on a scholarship, earning a degree in journalism. (Delia Brelsford Shiflet.)

Bill and Mary Womack pose for a photograph in 1933 before school. They both attended Oakhurst Elementary through third grade and then transferred to Riverside Elementary. This pattern continued for Oakhurst students until Oakhurst Elementary School received a major new addition in 1935. (Delia Brelsford Shiflet.)

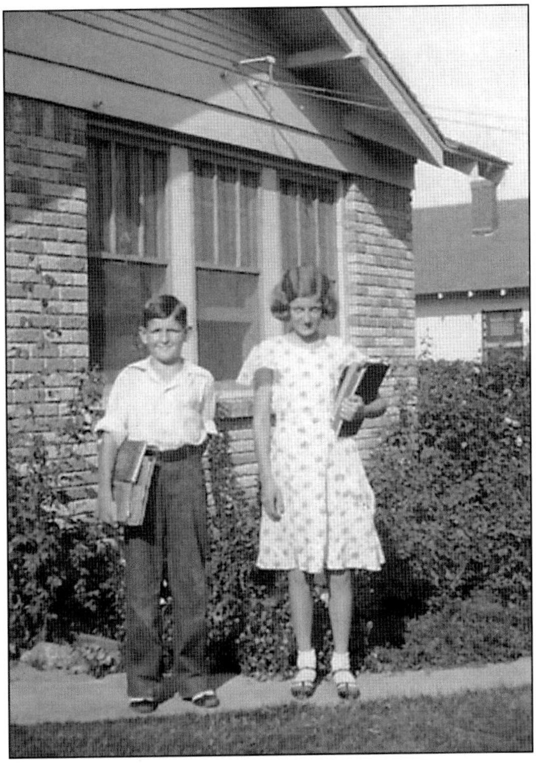

Oakhurst Elementary School, on Yucca Avenue, is seen below in 1935 as work progressed on the additions, which were made possible by federal funding and the Public Works Administration building program in Fort Worth. Note the lack of trees or houses west of the school. Riverside's Universal Mills is visible to the east, illustrating the sparseness of the surrounding area. (BWSCA/FWISD.)

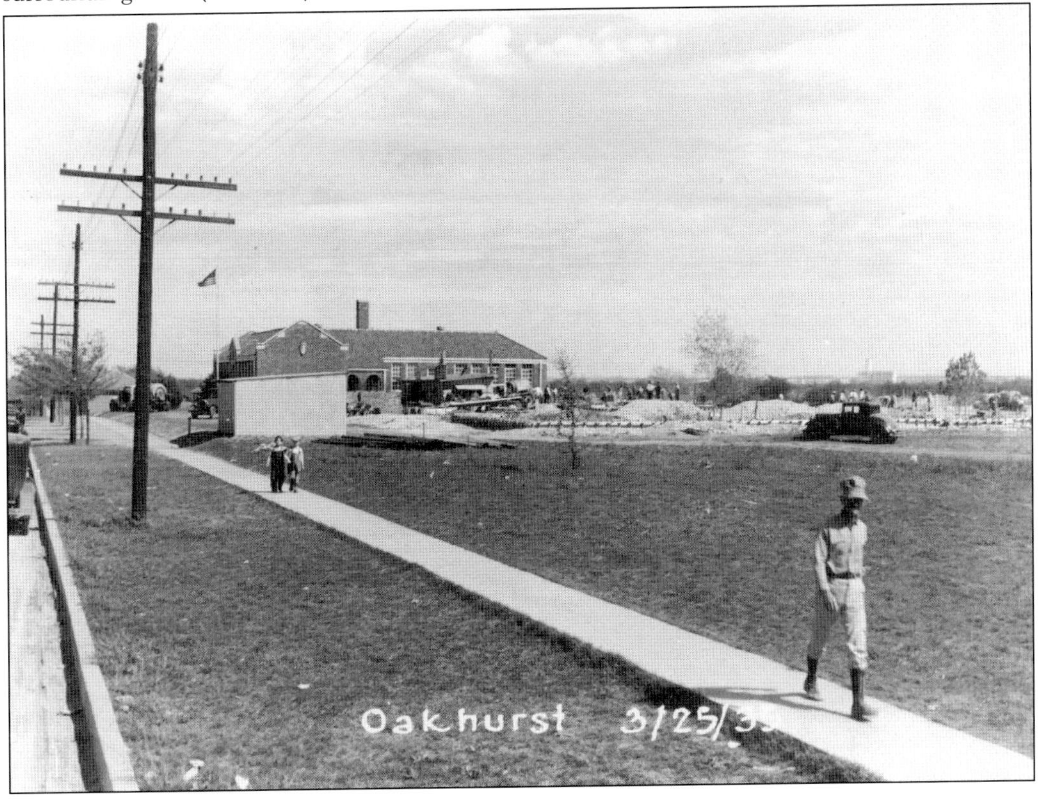

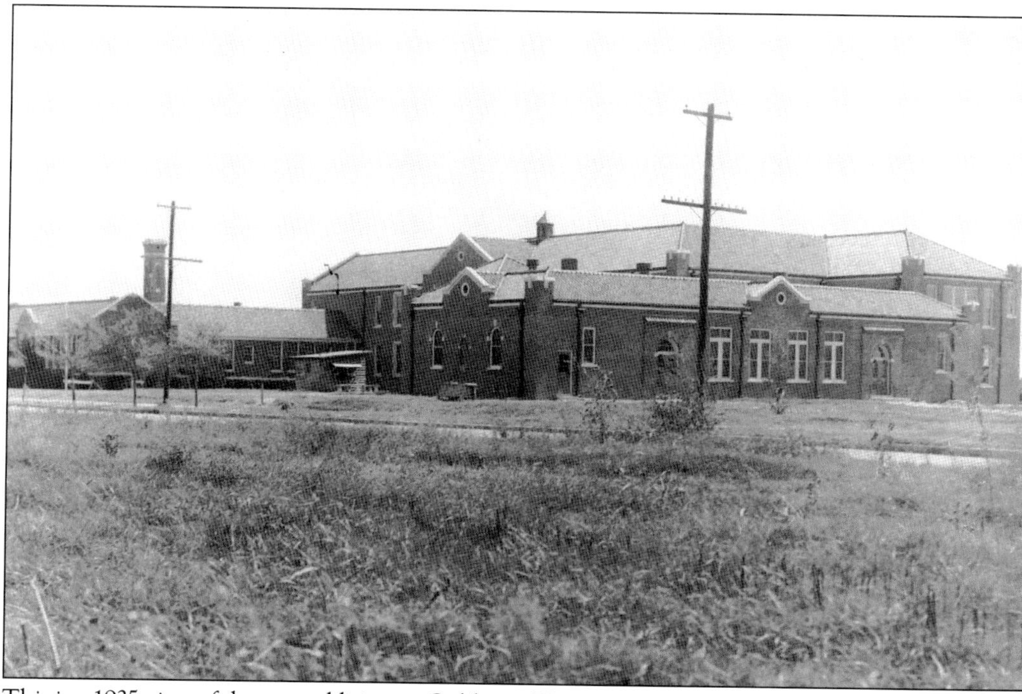

This is a 1935 view of the new addition to Oakhurst Elementary School. The original four-classroom structure, built in 1927–1928, is just to the left of the tile-roofed addition, which added 18 rooms. The addition was designed by J.B. Davies. The view is looking across Yucca Avenue before houses were built there. (BWSCA/FWISD.)

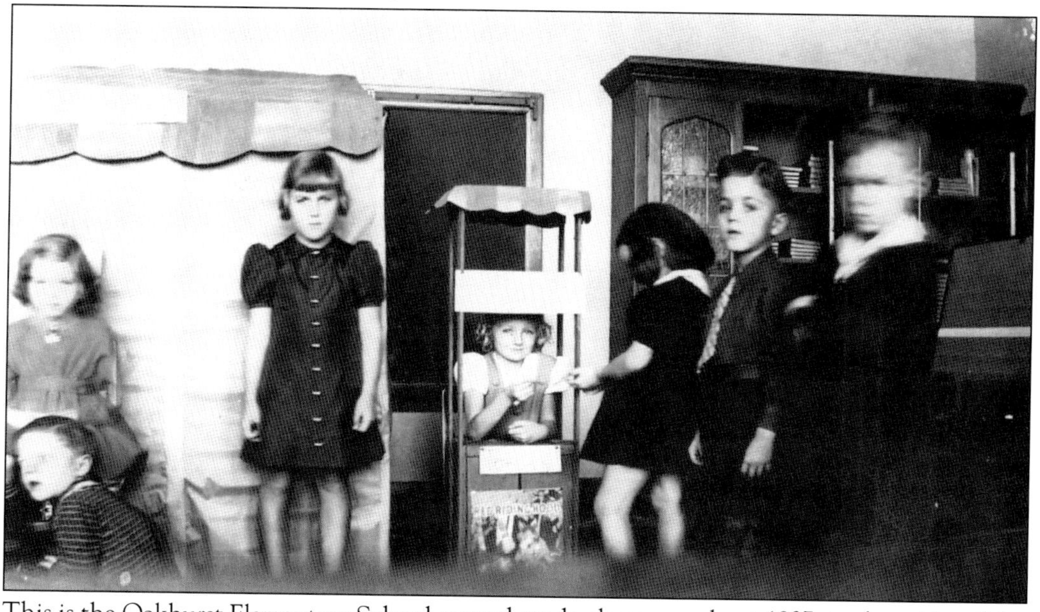

This is the Oakhurst Elementary School second-grade classroom about 1937, in the midst of the Great Depression. "There were a few families living in the gravel pit on the River Road," said Beverly Germany. "Others lived under the Belknap Bridge up until the war. The PTA made clothes available for the children. Principal Amelia Defenbal managed towels, soap, and shampoo with clean clothes for these children somehow." (Beverly Sharp Germany.)

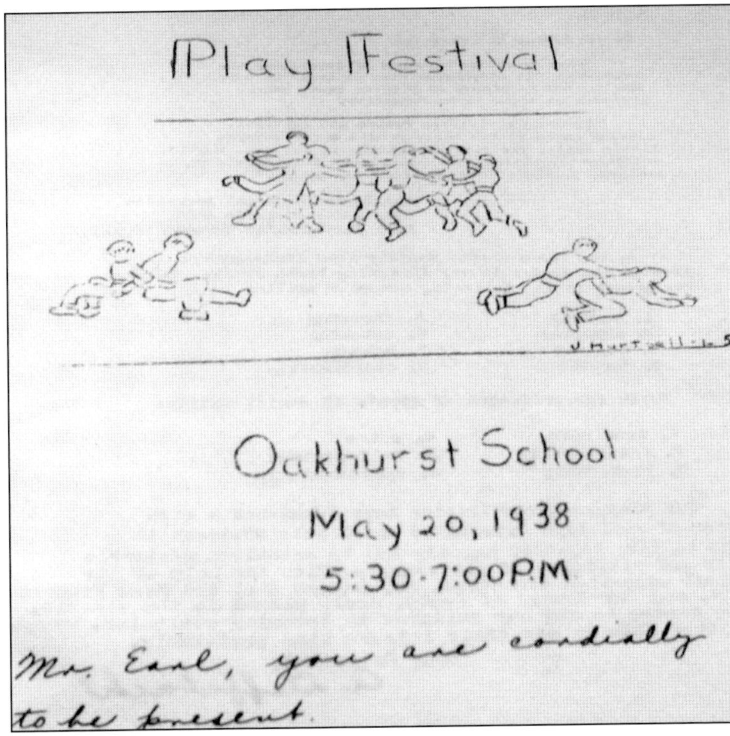
Play Festival

Oakhurst School

May 20, 1938

5:30-7:00PM

Mr. Earl, you are cordially to be present.

On May 20, 1938, the children of Oakhurst Elementary School performed in this play festival. (BWSCA/FWISD.)

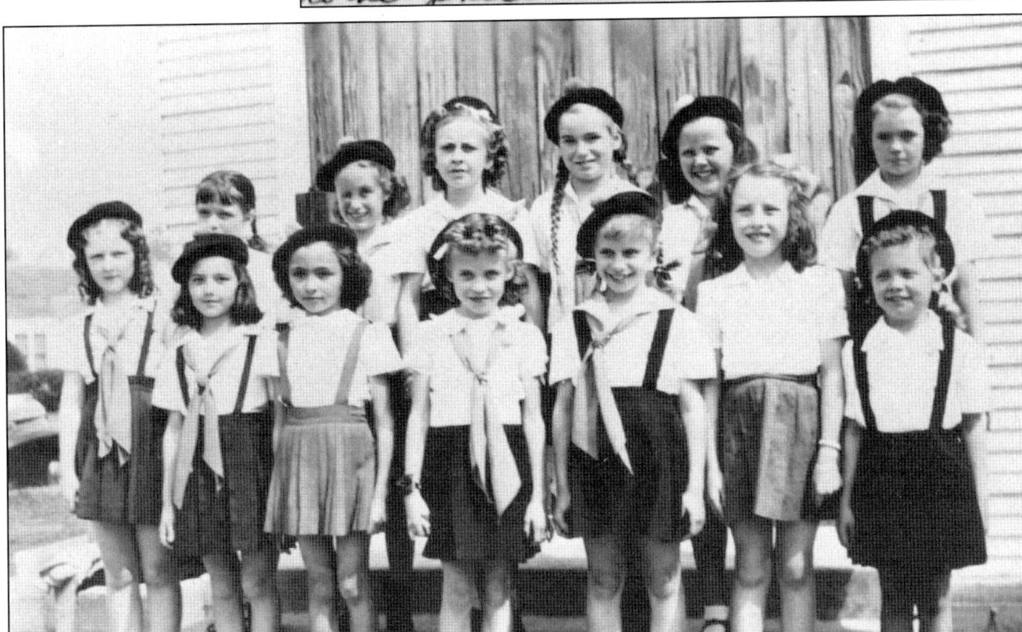

The Bluebirds from Oakhurst Elementary pose at Oakhurst Methodist Church in 1943. "The age requirement was 6 to 8 and then you were eligible for Camp Fire Girls," said Sue Shugart Drautz. The girls went on field trips to Mrs. Baird's Bakery and to the Swift and Armour plants. "We got to see how hot dogs were made," Drautz recalls. "I never wanted another one." (Sue Shugart Drautz.)

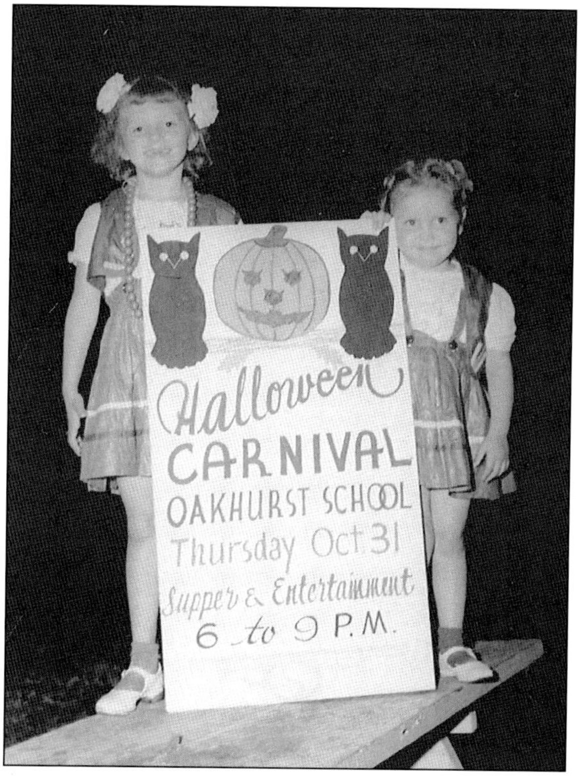

Gloria and Joyce Wakefield, of 2327 Marigold Avenue, advertised the Oakhurst Elementary School Halloween Carnival in 1946. The school served Oakhurst children until after 2000, when the attendance zone was changed. (Kathryn Dunson Wicker.)

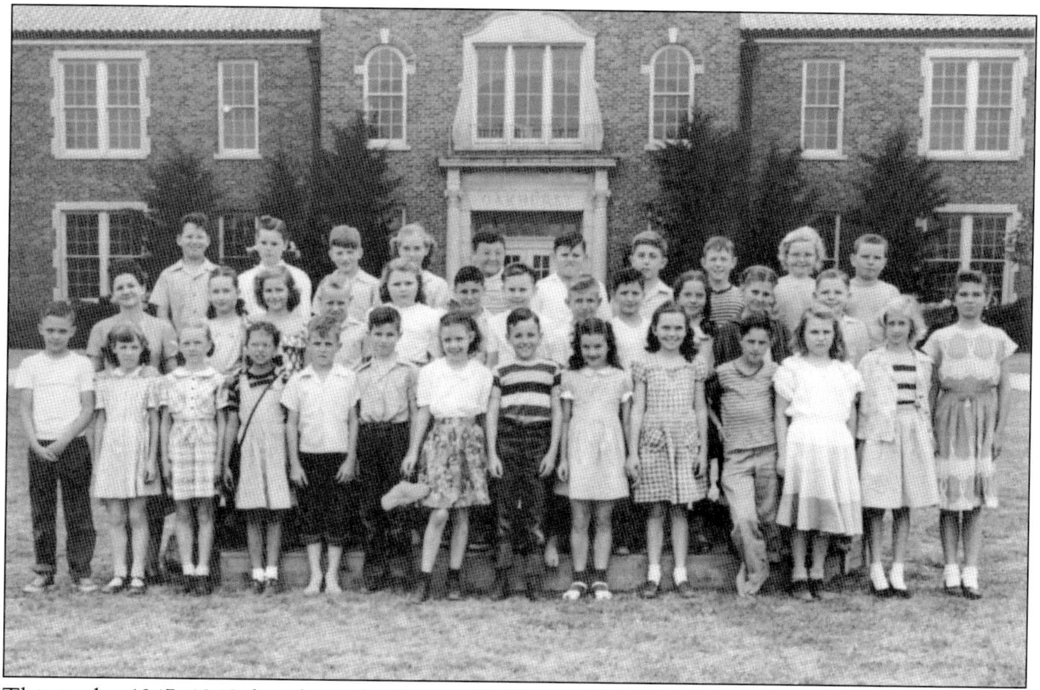

This is the 1947–1948 fourth-grade class at Oakhurst Elementary School. Louella Baker, third from left in the second row, was a member of the well-known Baker Brothers Nursery family of Riverside. (BWSCA/FWISD.)

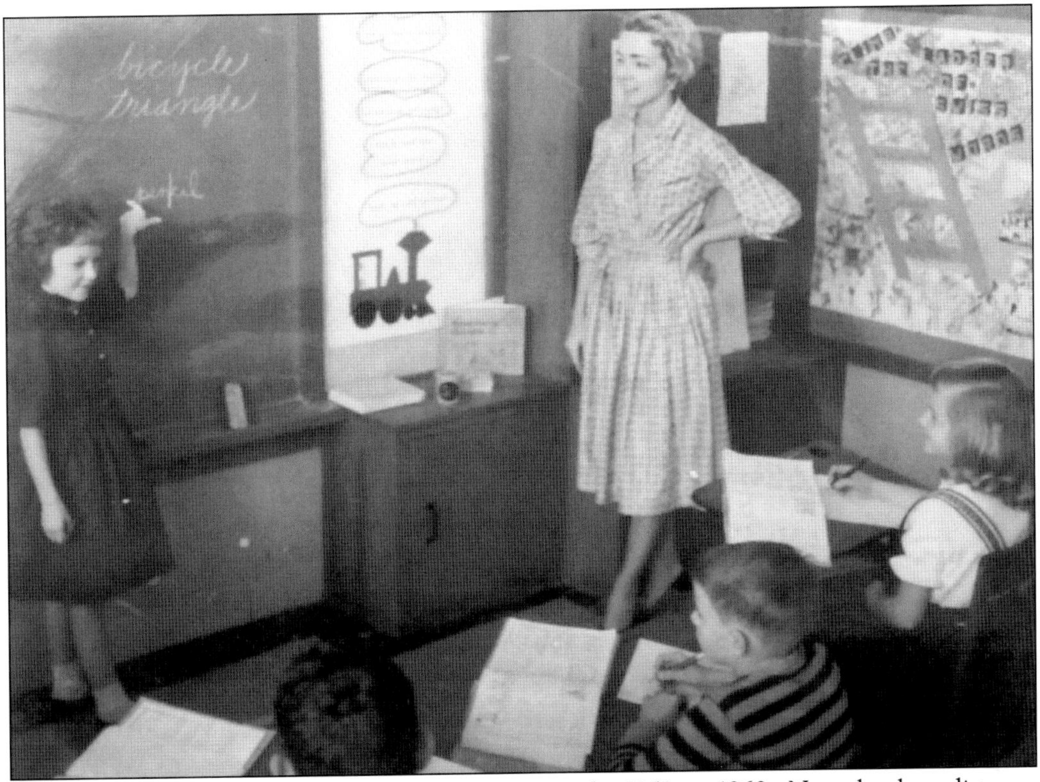

Here is an Oakhurst Elementary School classroom in the 1950s or 1960s. Note the short distance from the students' desks to the blackboard. (BWSCA/FWISD.)

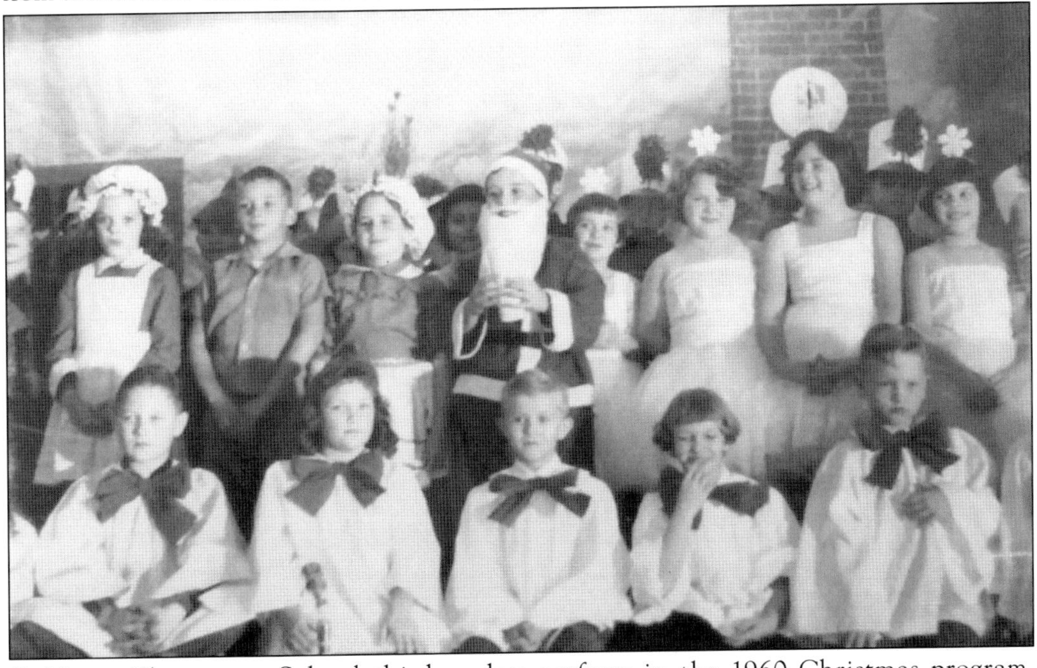

Oakhurst Elementary School third-graders perform in the 1960 Christmas program. (BWSCA/FWISD.)

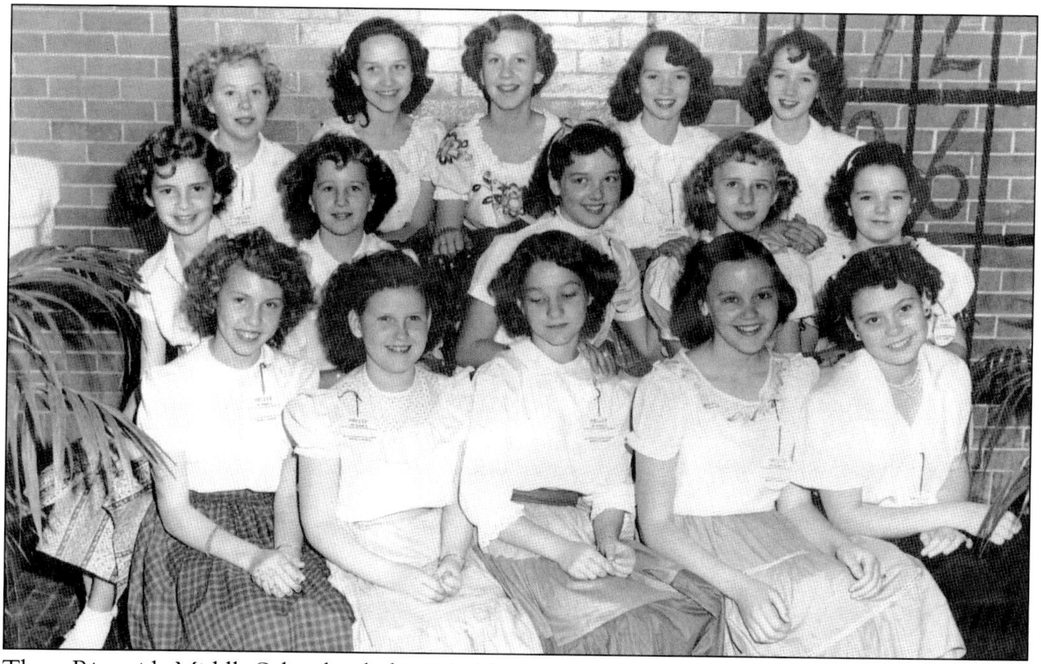

These Riverside Middle School girls from Oakhurst and other nearby neighborhoods participated in the 1949 Junior High Folk Dance Clinic at W.C. Stripling Middle School. They performed a Danish folk dance, "To Tur." Dance teams were sent from 11 other schools. Each team learned 10 dances and taught the other schools a dance. Among the participants were, in no particular order, Anna Keter, Sue Shugart, Vivian Blackwell, Mary Price, Janelle and Janet Bettes, Peggy Taylor, Christine Beck, Geron Simons, Martha Anderson, Beverly Stroup, Scotty Owen, Lavinia Jourdan, Shirley Ballew, and Sharon Rutledge. (Sue Shugart Drautz.)

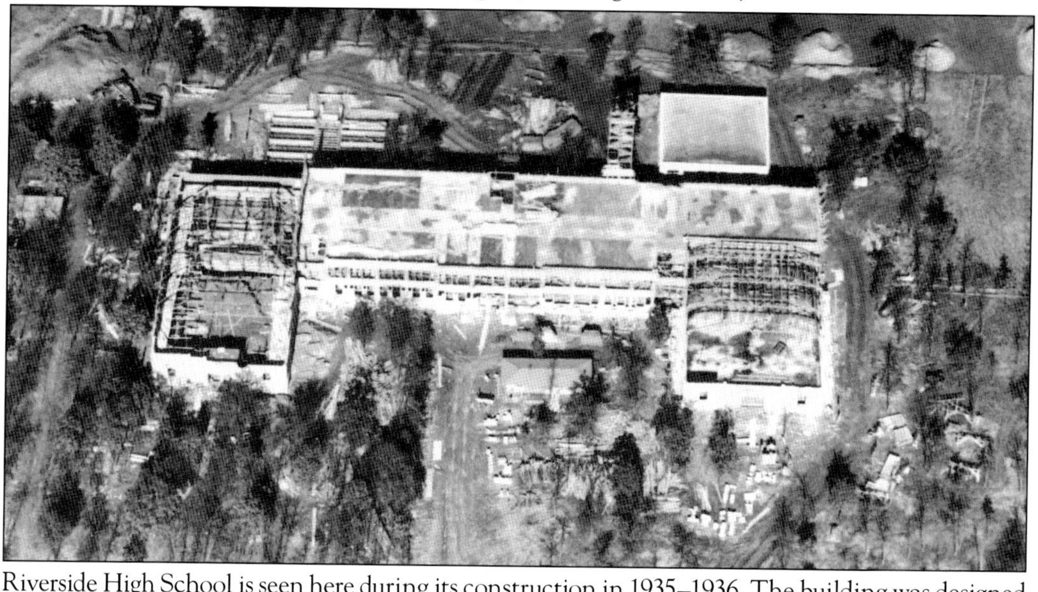

Riverside High School is seen here during its construction in 1935–1936. The building was designed by Wyatt C. Hedrick, an important Fort Worth architect who designed many other landmarks, including the Texas & Pacific Passenger Terminal. The high school building is designated a City of Fort Worth historic landmark. (BWSCA/FWISD.)

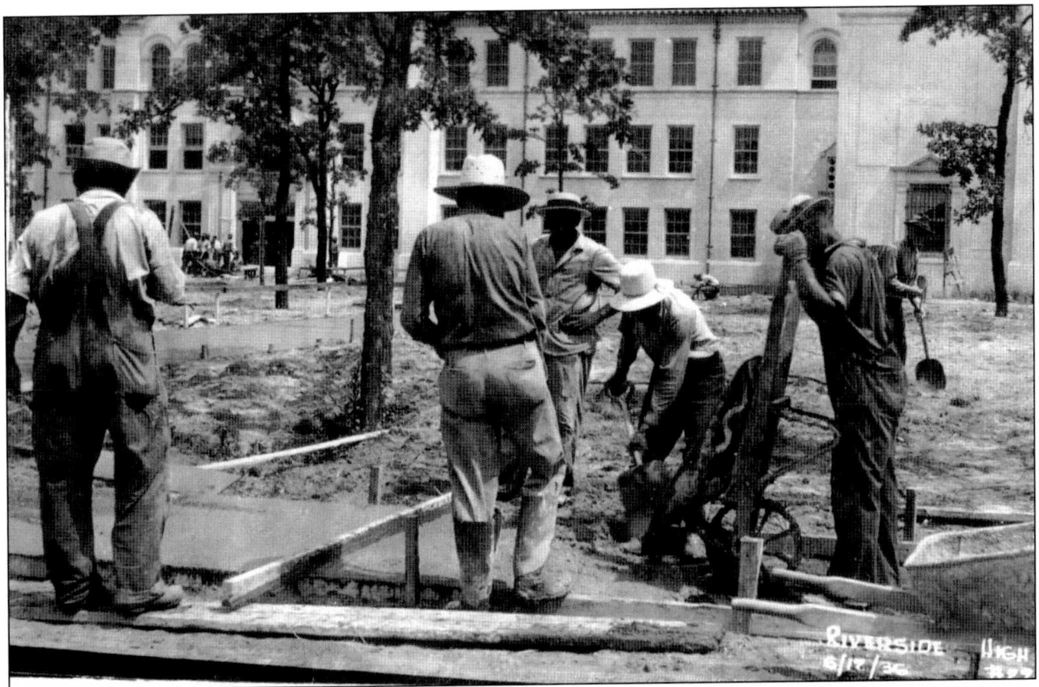

The new Riverside High School, constructed during the great Fort Worth building era of 1935–1936, was built with federal funds from the Public Works Administration. Oakhurst students now had a high school just six blocks away. Here, workers are putting in the landscaping designed by Hare & Hare for the 28-acre campus, at the corner of Riverside Drive and Yucca Avenue. It was the largest high school campus in the state at the state. (BWSCA/FWISD.)

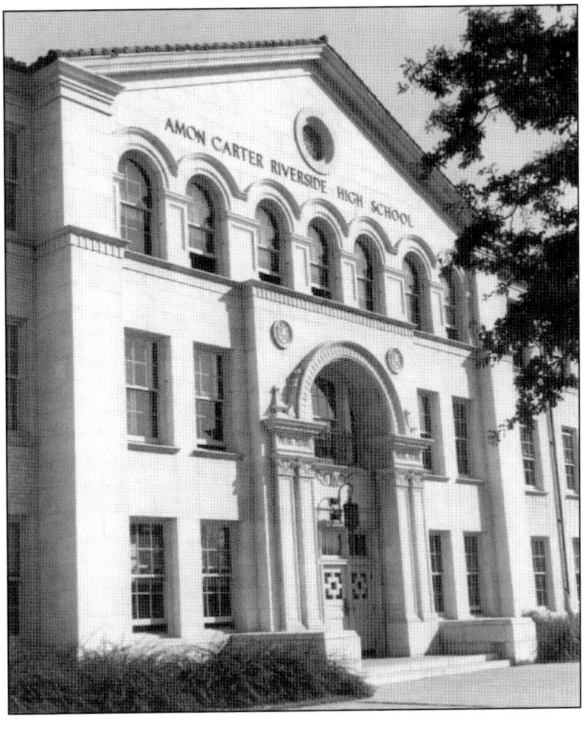

This is the facade of Riverside High School in 1941, after the Fort Worth Independent School District added *Star-Telegram* publisher Amon Carter's name. Carter personally asked the school board not to drop "Riverside" from the school name. He requested that the board adopt the name "Riverside Amon G. Carter High School." The board, however, insisted on putting his name first. (TCU Library Special Collections/SCUTA.)

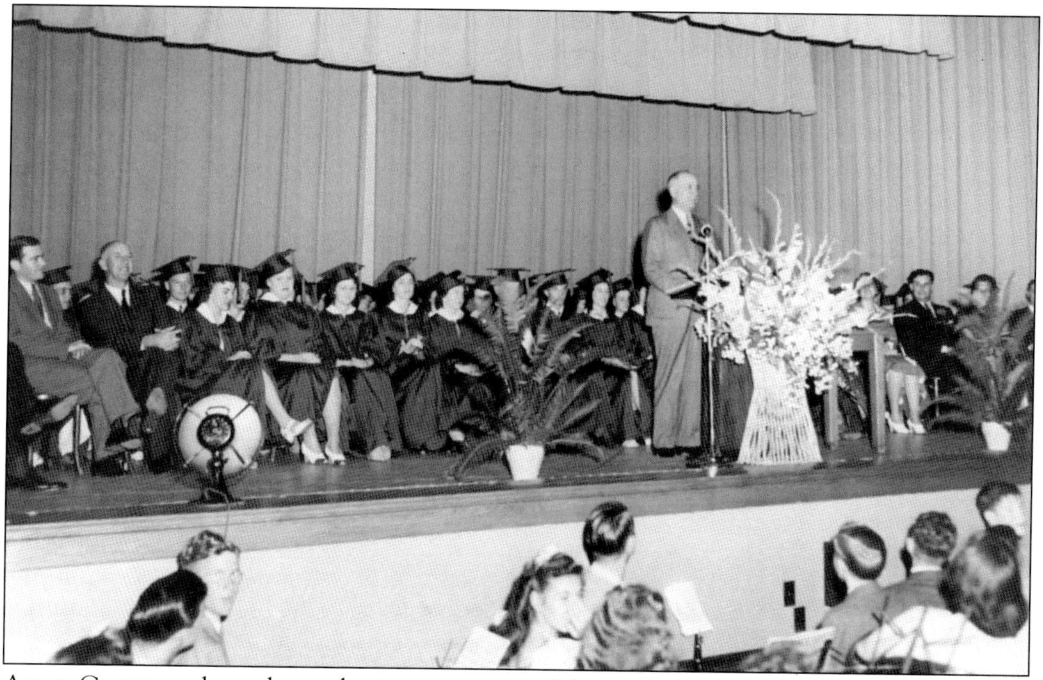

Amon Carter speaks at the graduation ceremony of the newly renamed Amon Carter Riverside High School in the early 1940s. Carter, who was not a high school graduate himself, was honored that the Fort Worth Independent School District named the school for him. Riverside boosters ensured the name change, although some on both sides of the Trinity River were unhappy about it. (TCU Library Special Collections/SCUTA.)

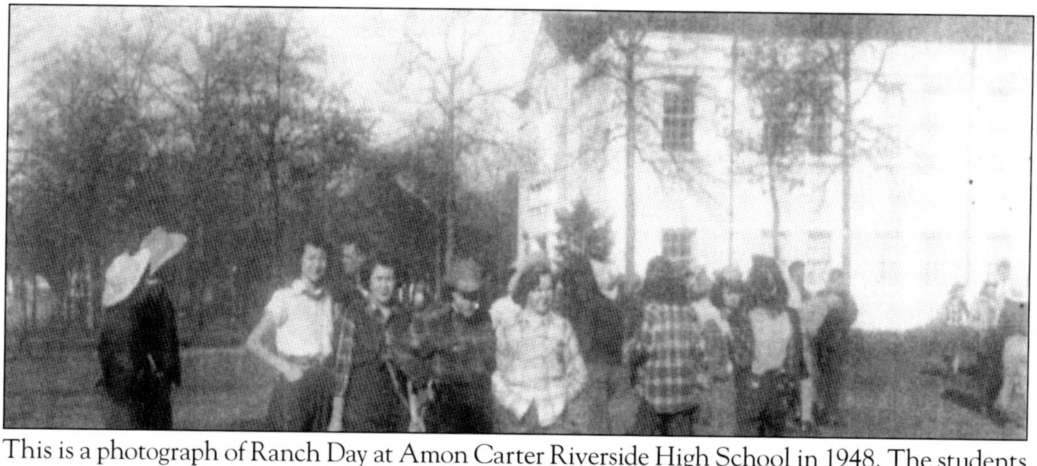

This is a photograph of Ranch Day at Amon Carter Riverside High School in 1948. The students are decked out in Western wear for their half-day off from classes to attend the Fort Worth Stock Show. (Beverly Sharp Germany.)

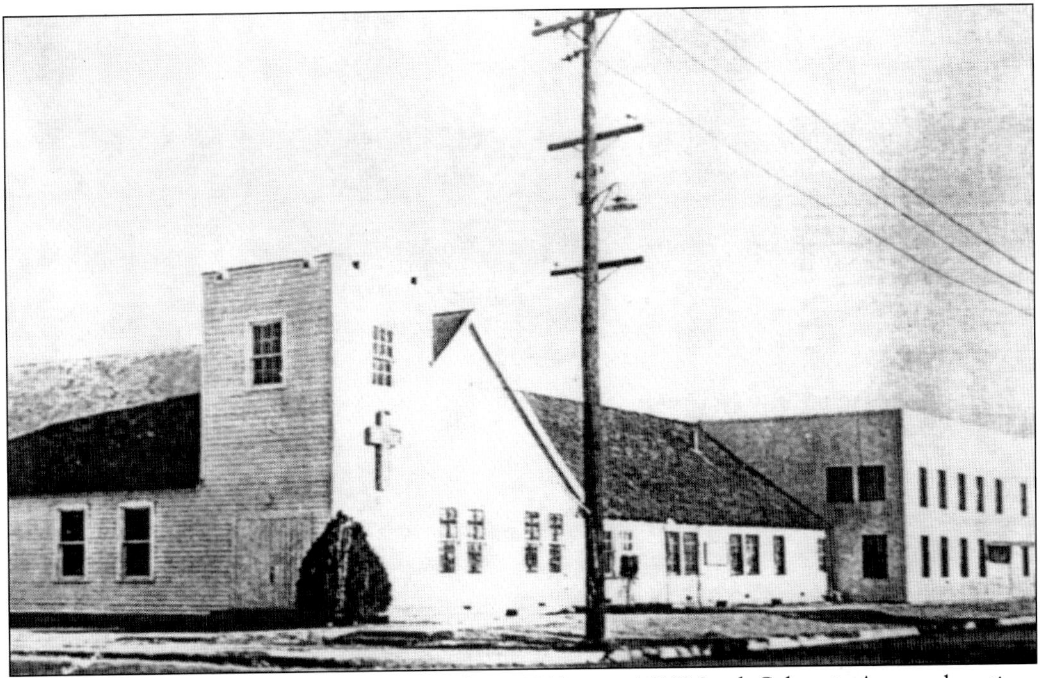

Oakhurst Methodist Church is seen here about 1942 at its 1516 North Sylvania Avenue location. (Faith UMC.)

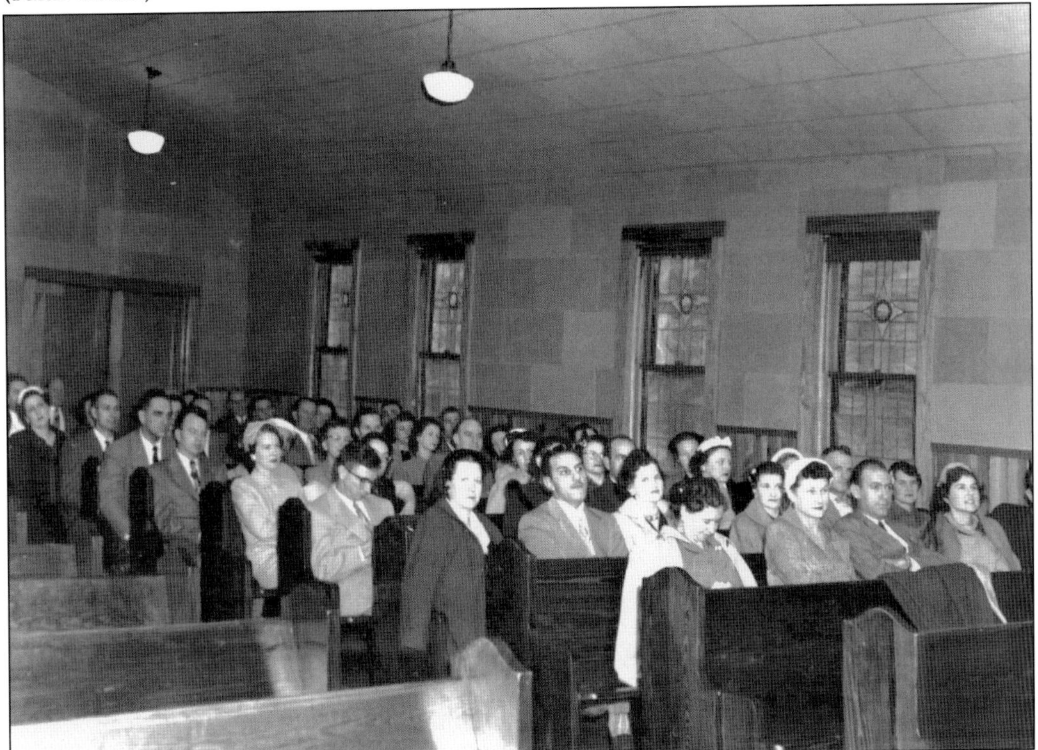

Oakhurst Methodist Church, Fidelis class of 1945, met in the church's sanctuary. Many Oakhurst residents were active members of the congregation. (Faith UMC.)

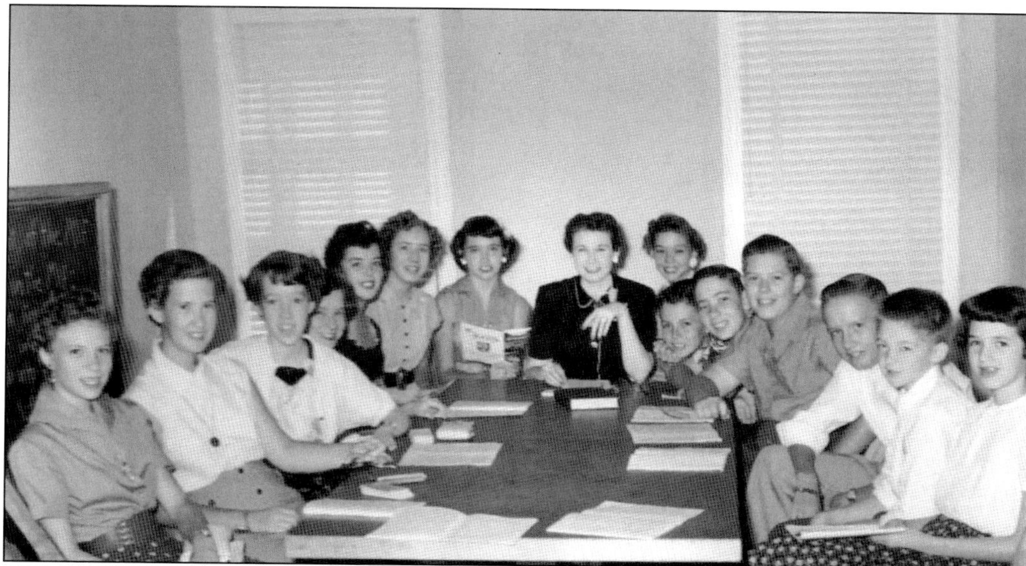

The Oakhurst Methodist Church Intermediate (eighth-grade) Sunday school class meets in 1954. Longtime Oakhurst resident Martha Stanton Lunday is third from left. (Faith UMC.)

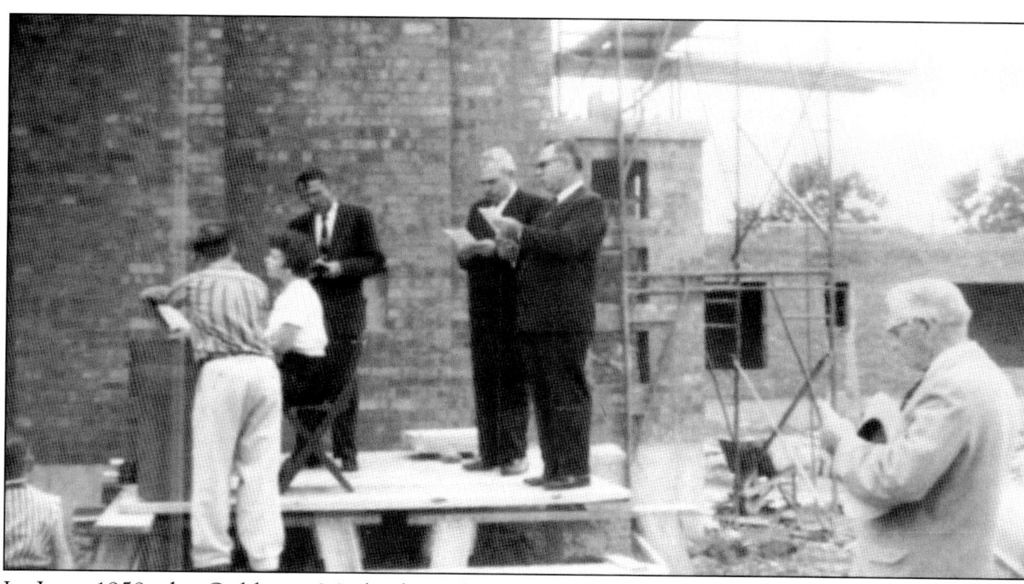

In June 1958, the Oakhurst Methodist Church congregation gathered for the laying of the cornerstone of its new building, at the corner of Springdale Road and Grace Avenue. Oakhurst's Marthe Frances Brown played the organ for the service. To the right of Brown are, from left to right, Rev. W.S. Fisher, Bishop W.C. Martin, Rev. Hayden Edwards, and W. Fisher (far right, foreground). (Faith UMC.)

This is the 1958 Oakhurst Methodist Church, at Springdale Road and Grace Avenue. The church was an early site of Oakhurst Neighborhood Association (ONA) meetings in the 1980s through the 2000s. The Police and Firefighter Appreciation Dinner, held to honor Oakhurst first responders, was sponsored by the Oakhurst Citizens on Patrol and the ONA. The dinner was held here for many years. (Doyle Willis Jr.)

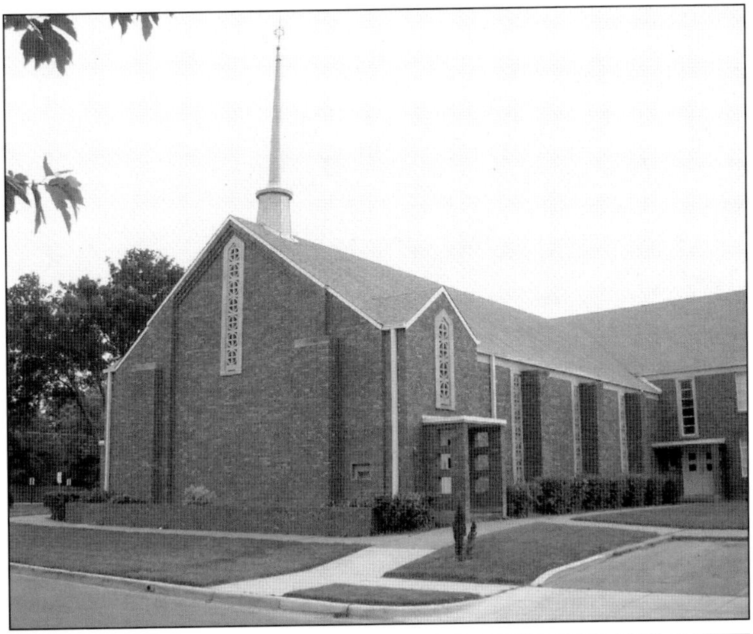

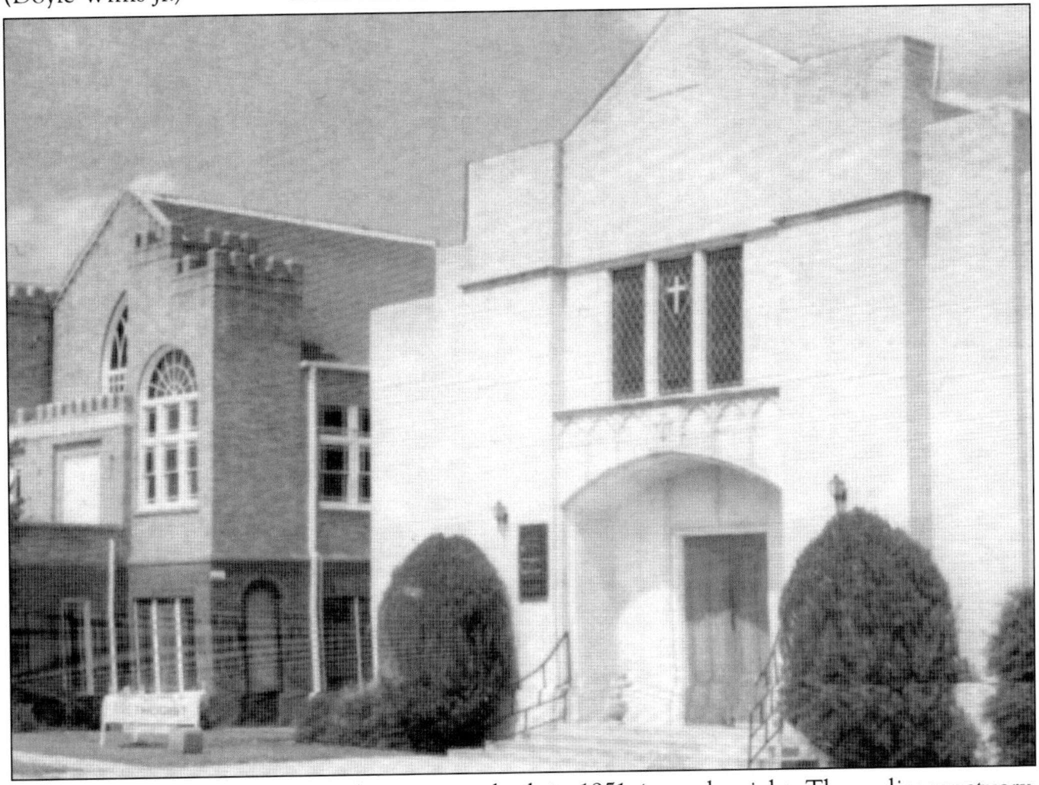

The Riverside Methodist Church sanctuary, built in 1951, is on the right. The earlier sanctuary, on the left, was converted into an educational building for the 1,000-member congregation. The church stood at 326 North Riverside Drive. The congregation later erected a building on Belknap Street. In the 2000s, the Riverside and Oakhurst United Methodist Church congregations merged to form the Faith United Methodist Church in the Belknap location. (Faith UMC.)

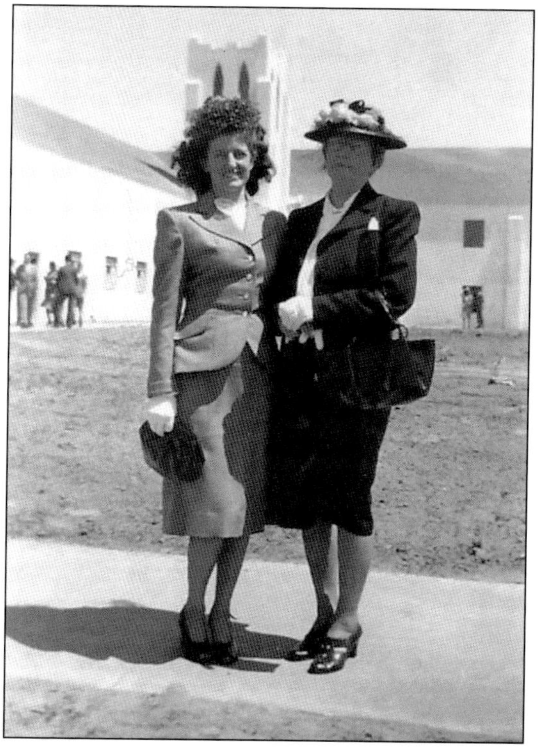

Mary Womack Brelsford and her mother, Bertha Womack, attended Riverside Christian Church, at 1000 Bonnie Brae Avenue, on Palm Sunday in 1947. The church's motto was, "When the Bible speaks, we speak; When the Bible is silent, we are silent." (Delia Brelsford Shiflet.)

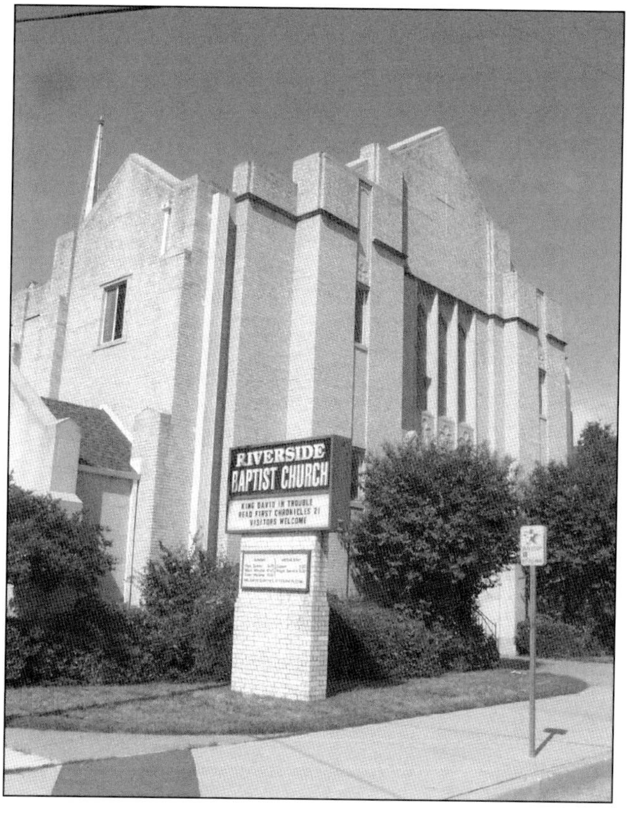

This is a photograph of Riverside Baptist Church, at Six Points. By 1954, a sanctuary had been constructed in addition to an earlier building. The church's large membership, which included many Oakhurst residents, stood at 2,938. (Doyle Willis Jr.)

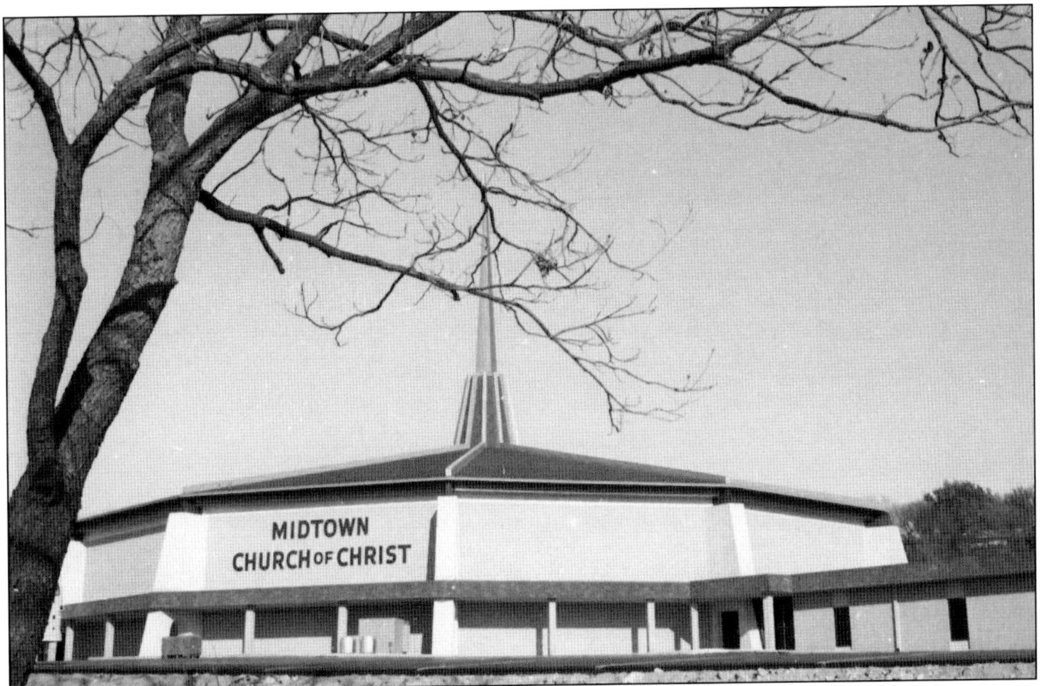

Midtown Church of Christ was established just west of Oakhurst in 1971 on land that was once owned by the Oakhurst Golf and Country Club. The congregation owned this building for approximately 30 years. (FWSTC/SCUTA.)

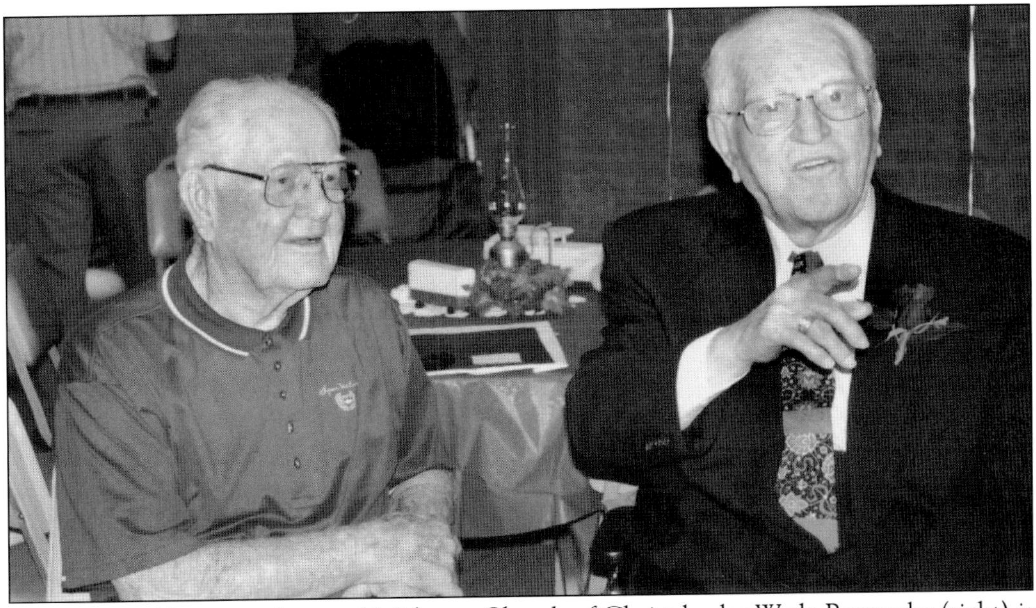

Longtime Oakhurst resident and Midtown Church of Christ leader Wade Banowsky (right) is seen at his 90th birthday party, held at the church. With him is his friend, professional golf legend Byron Nelson. Nelson knew Oakhurst from the 1930s, when he set an amateur record of 73 at the Oakhurst Golf Course. (Lazell Lambert Banowsky.)

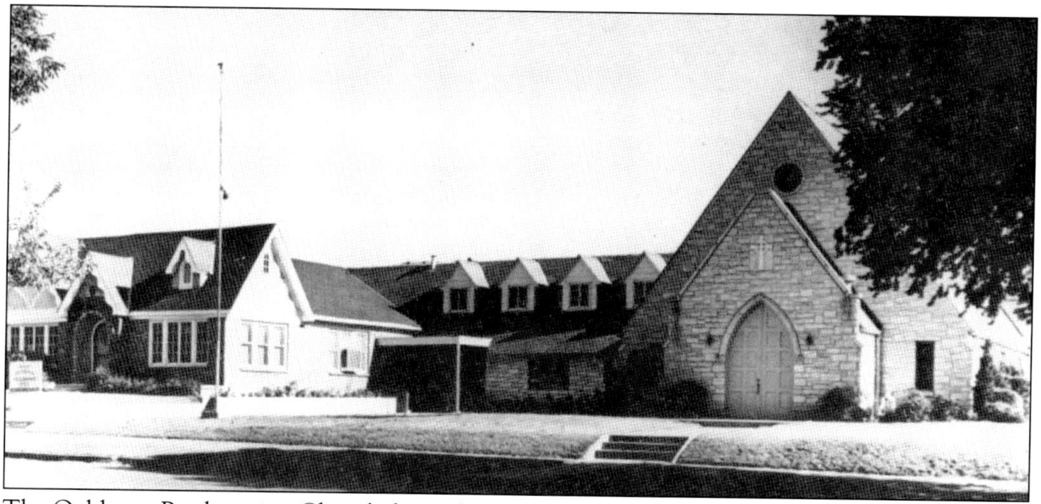

The Oakhurst Presbyterian Church formed in 1928. The sanctuary stood at the corner of Yucca Avenue and Chandler Street. The group's first structure was this Tudor-style house, intended as the preacher's "manse" and connected to the sanctuary. The congregation sold the site to the City of Fort Worth for construction of the Riverside Branch Library in the early 1960s and built a new sanctuary on Springdale Road. (Oakhurst Presbyterian Church.)

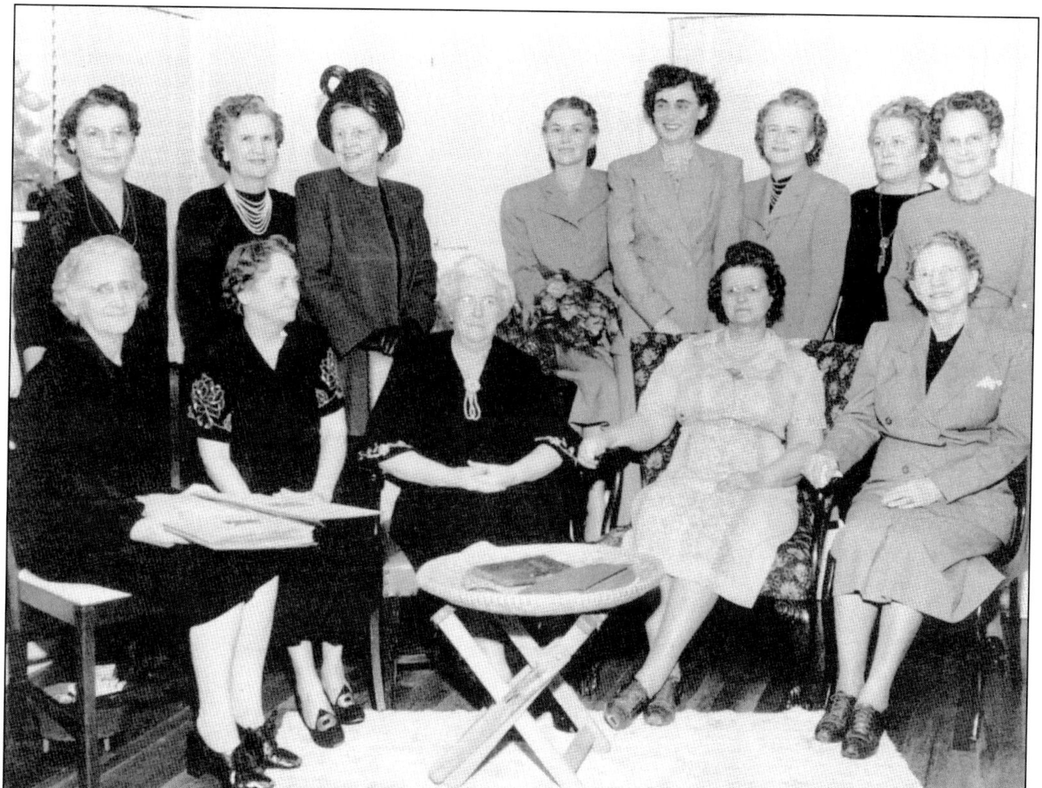

The Women's Council of Oakhurst Presbyterian Church is seen here in the mid-1940s. Many members of the congregation lived in Oakhurst, and the women's group often met in their homes. The congregation disbanded in 2012. (Oakhurst Presbyterian Church.)

Eight

The Suburban Becomes Urban

Oakhurst, 1960–2010

Oakhurst has had a remarkable journey, from being a purely agricultural area 150 years ago, to a suburban neighborhood barely inside the new city limits of Fort Worth in 1922, to today's central-city urban neighborhood in one of the fastest-growing cities in America.

Over the last 50 years, the neighborhood has experienced many of the same pressures and influences that other older, central-city areas have felt. Original buyers moved, the "middle-classness" of the neighborhood declined somewhat, demographics changed, and school populations grew. Retail centers in Riverside also often declined because of the advent of regional shopping malls.

One unusual advantage Oakhurst has had in the ongoing struggle to stay stable as a neighborhood is the presence of Mount Olivet Cemetery. The nature of its use meant it was never going anywhere, thus providing a kind of protective northern boundary for Oakhurst. The north-south Interstate 35, built in the early 1960s, provided another sort of barrier from the rest of the world. Many who find Oakhurst for the first time say it is the "best-kept secret" in Fort Worth.

Oakhurst has thrived on the organization of both its neighborhood association and its citizen-patrol group, the first of its kind in the city. The City of Fort Worth and the Fort Worth League of Neighborhoods have twice recognized Oakhurst as Fort Worth's Neighborhood of the Year, for 2006 and 2010. Oakhurst has also received national neighborhood awards. The 2010 listing of its entire 710-house collection in the National Register of Historic Places made it the largest historic neighborhood to be so designated in all of Tarrant County in more than 20 years.

Residents of Oakhurst cannot forget that it is fragile, even while it continues to accomplish goals of revitalization and stabilization. Future development will challenge the neighborhood to keep its identity. Ultimately, if it can keep its "country in the city" charm, the integrity of its architecture and plan, and its all-important trees, Oakhurst will prove to be Fort Worth's most livable neighborhood.

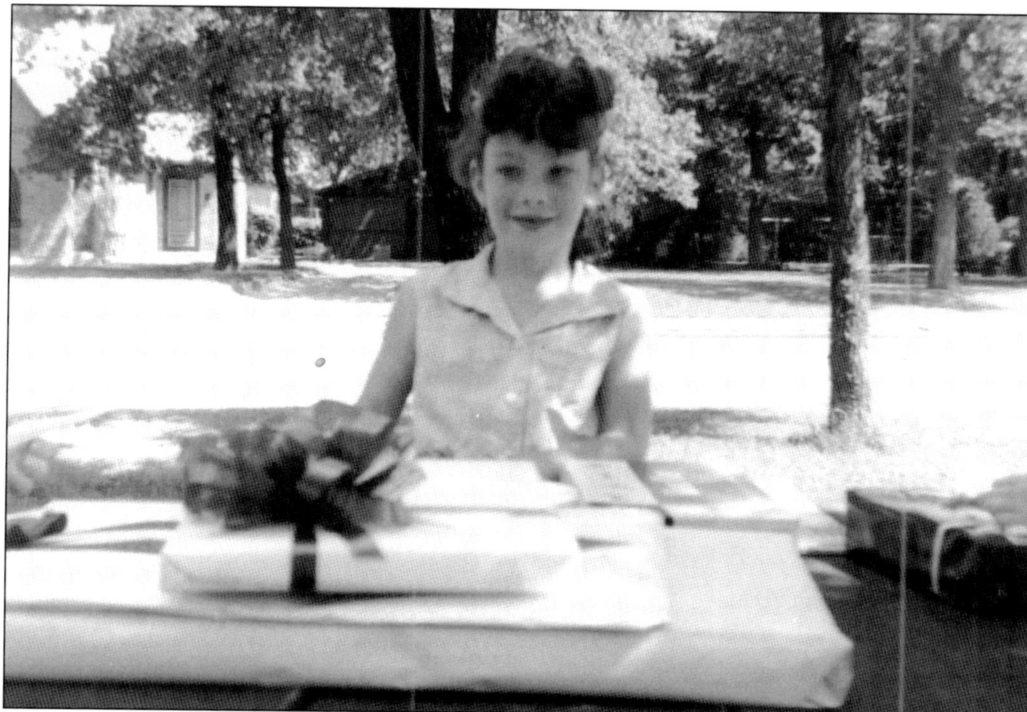

Janie Lambert is seen here on her birthday in September 1960 in Oakhurst Park. As an adult, she became a musician, once even singing backup for country music star Waylon Jennings when he performed at Billy Bob's Texas in the Fort Worth Stockyards. (Lazell Lambert Banowsky.)

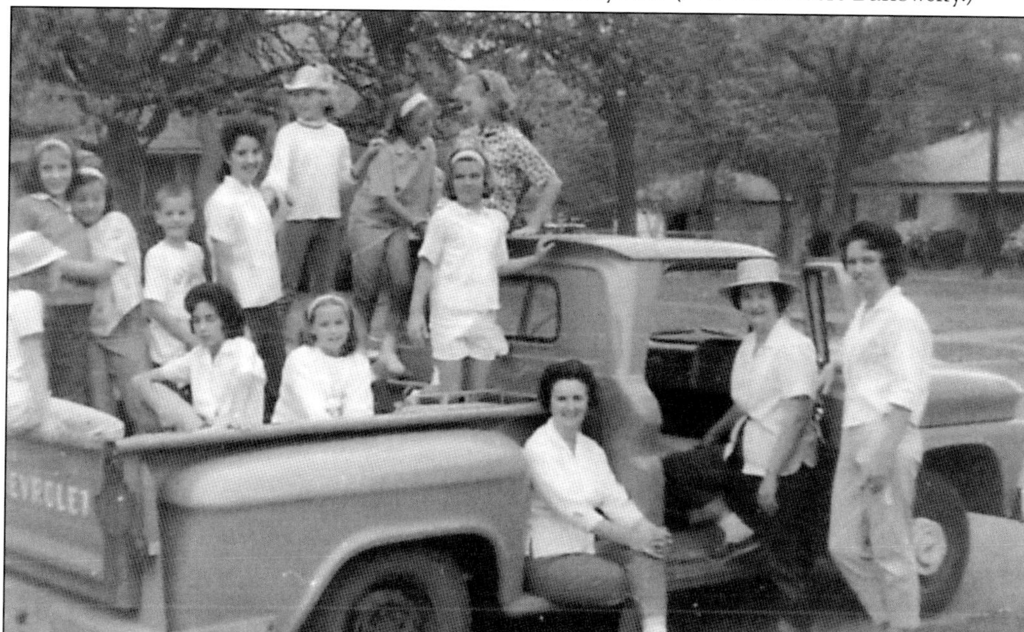

Beverly Mason (second from right) and other Oakhurst Camp Fire "mom" sponsors Martha Davis (seated on fender) and Peggy Barrow (far right) pose with Camp Fire Girls in the early 1960s. (Beverly Mason.)

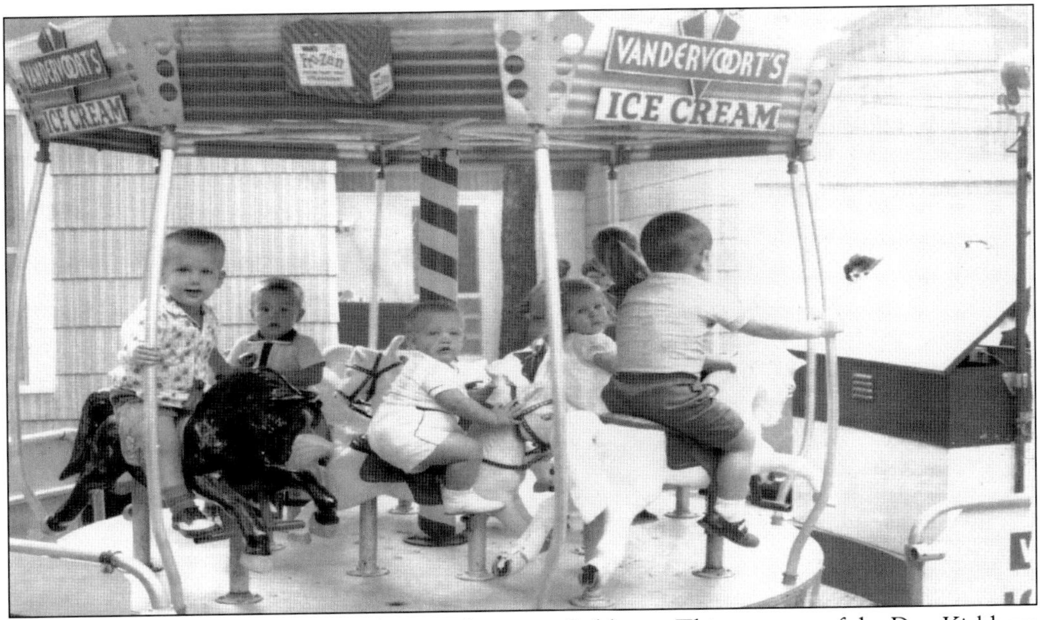

Many families have lived in more than one home in Oakhurst. This was true of the Don Kirkham family, who started their Oakhurst experience in a small cottage at 2305 Primrose Avenue. Here, in 1961, their son Ken (far left, on black horse) and his cousins enjoy his second birthday party on the Vandervoort's Ice Cream merry-go-round in their backyard on Primrose. Later, the family moved to a larger, Ranch-style home on Marigold Avenue. (Dr. Ken Kirkham.)

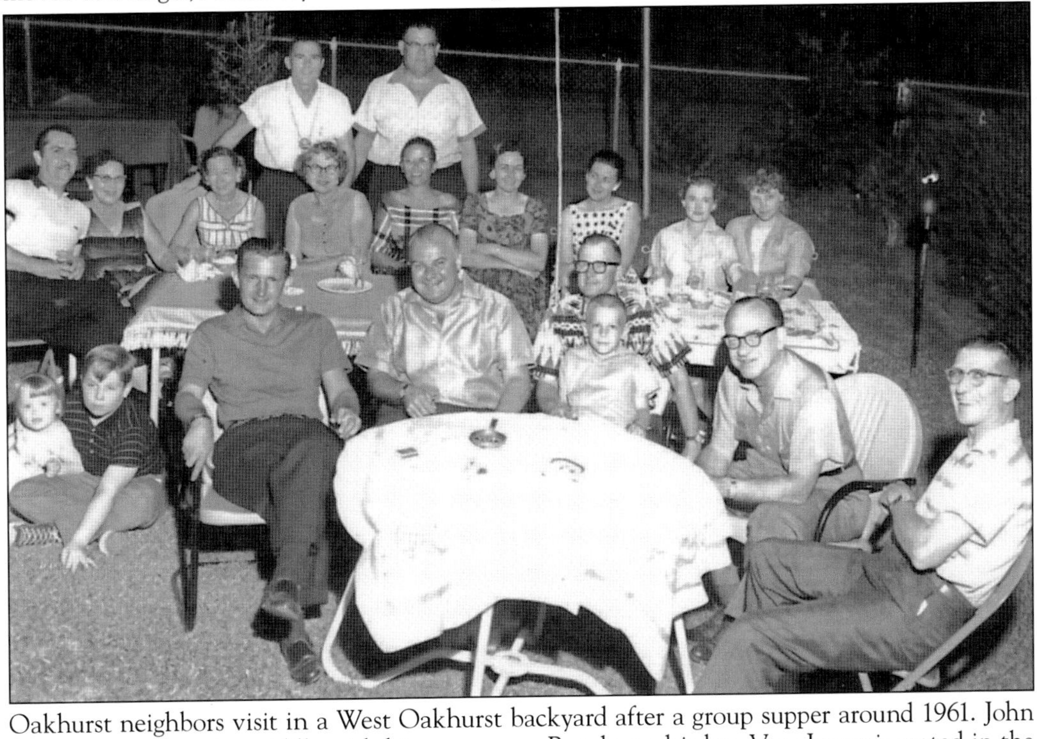

Oakhurst neighbors visit in a West Oakhurst backyard after a group supper around 1961. John James is seated in the middle with his young son, Randy, on his lap. Vera James is seated in the back, fifth from the right. (Leslie James.)

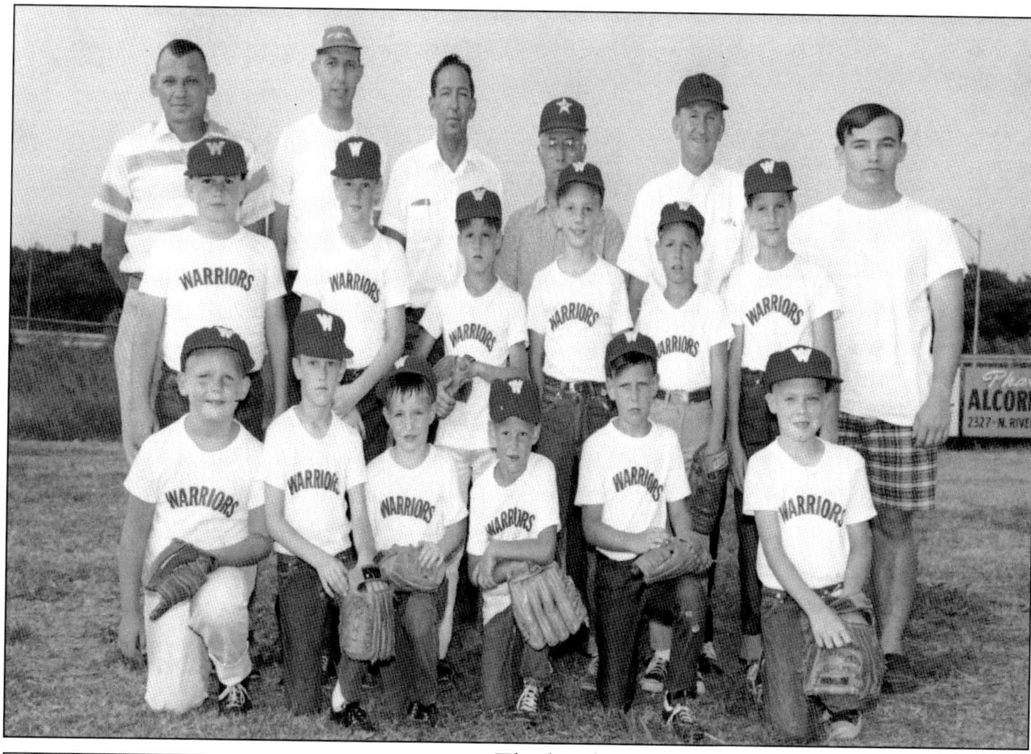

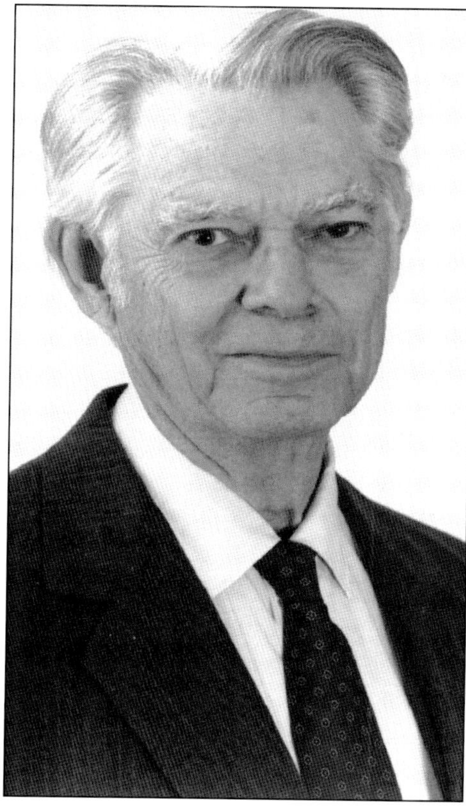

The local Little League team poses above in the 1960s at the Riverside field off of North Side Drive. Longtime Oakhurst resident Dwight Mason is second from left in the third row. D.E. Chipps Jr. (third row, fourth from left) was one of the coaches. Chipps's father, D.E. Chipps Sr., was shot and killed by J. Frank Norris, pastor of the First Baptist Church of Fort Worth, in the early 1920s. A sensational trial followed, in which the jury acquitted the minister. Chipps was a much-loved coach of this team. His wife, Mildred, was a favorite of neighborhood women because she always "had the coffee pot on" and invited them over for chats after dinner. (Beverly Mason.)

Poet William Barney grew up in Riverside. He often worked familiar Oakhurst places into his poetry. In his "A Birthdayful of Beard Tongues: Oakhurst Scenic Drive," published in 1999, he wrote about the limestone hills of the drive and their "seams of crumbling rock, the calcareous soil," which had not changed. Barney was a postal inspector for the Texas regional office. In 1982, Texas governor Mark White appointed him Poet Laureate of Texas. He also won the Robert Frost Award for best poetry, given by the American Institute of Letters. (Winston Barney/the Barney family.)

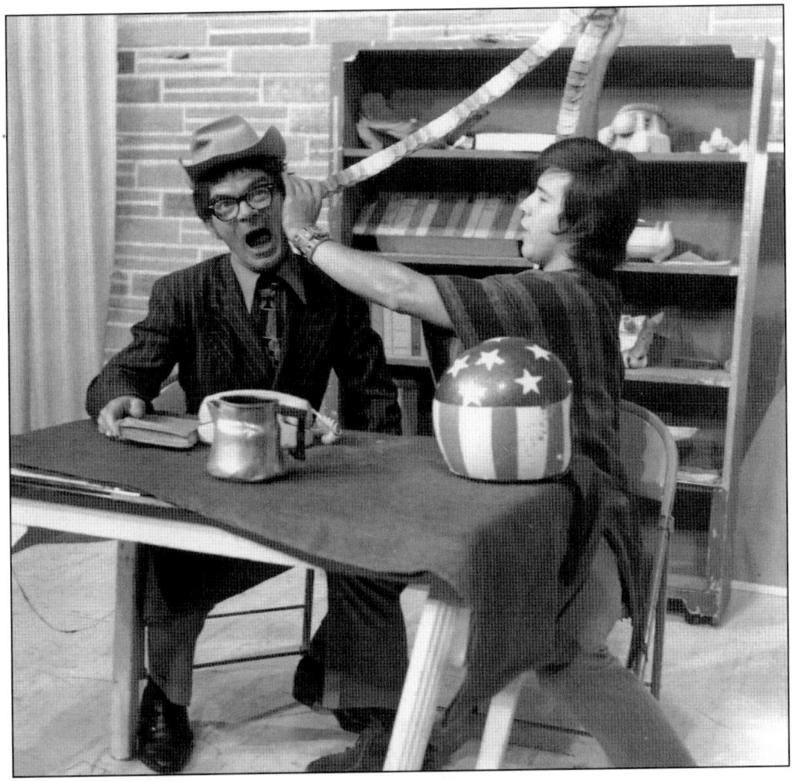

Cameraman Martin Rodriguez (right) clowns with KTVT Channel 11 legend Bill Camfield ("Icky Twerp") on the set of *Slam Bang Theater*, long a popular production of the station. Rodriguez and his family are Oakhurst residents. Camfield was a 1947 graduate of Amon Carter Riverside High School. "Camfield was an imp," Rodriguez said. "I never thought up a skit he couldn't do." (Martin Rodriguez.)

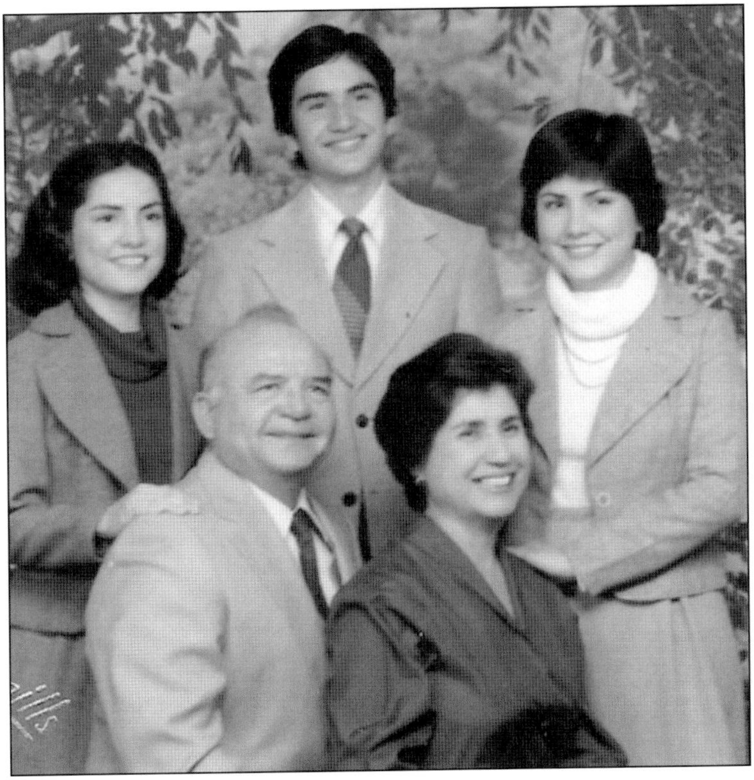

Louis and Yolanda Rodriguez pose with their children, Ruth (left), Louis Jr. (center), and Diana. The family moved to Oakhurst in 1979. They represent the passing of the generations in Oakhurst. Louis was a decorated World War II veteran and an engineer, and Yolanda was a teacher. Their children excelled at Amon Carter Riverside High School, and all of them graduated from prestigious colleges. Louis Jr. was a National Merit Scholar at Riverside High and earned two electrical engineering degrees at MIT. (Yolanda Rodriguez.)

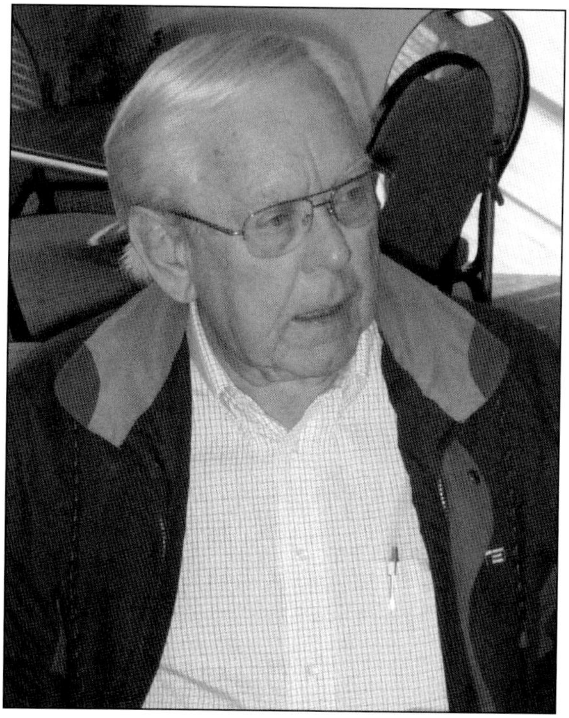

Dewayne Littlepage (correct spelling), an early president of the Oakhurst Neighborhood Association, attends a meeting of past presidents of the organization in the mid-2000s. (Author's collection.)

Below is an early edition of *The Oak Leaflet*, the newsletter of the Oakhurst Neighborhood Association. The publication, printed without interruption since 1981, is hand-delivered to each household. (AC.)

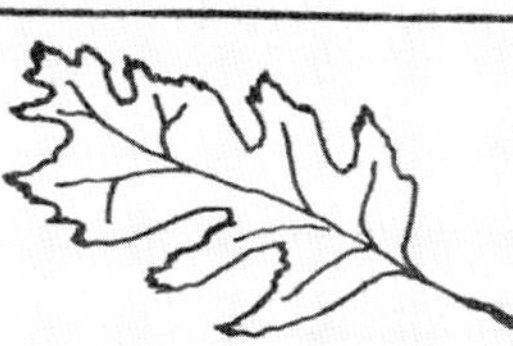

THE OAK LEAFLET

VOLUME 3 NUMBER 2

THE OAKHURST NEIGHBORHOOD ASSOCIATION NEWSLETTER

EDITOR: Margaret Bruce 838-2511

June 1983

REMINISCING by Suzanne Lowry Lasko

My family took me home to 1901 Marigold after I was born in 1939. We moved to the West side in 1951 so all my experiences in Oakhurst are those of a child. Being a child in Oakhurst in the forties is as near a utopia as I can imagine. My memories are happy ones.

I remember--with great enthusiasm--playing Tarzan with our neighborhood gang. The group included Minton and Gary Mahen, the Boatner boys, Elizabeth and Jack Hurley, Johnny Simon, Charldean Newell and David Gay. Later Johnny remembered our games in the *Tarzan* plays he wrote for Hip Pocket Theater. My father built us a tree house from which we could swing down a wonderful rope. I was a little miffed at having to be Jane but otherwise loved the hours and days we spent in "jungle" fantasy.

1949 was a bad year for the Lowry family. Our house burned and the Trinity River flood brought water over Scenic Drive and right up to the bottom of the hill at Marigold. Since we were the last house above the water everyone came there to marvel at the "new lake". A doctor on Smilax gave us all typhoid shots. In those days there were no polio shots and fear of polio was very real.

I remember walking to Oakhurst Elementary School. At the time I thought it was a great school and I know now from an adult perspective that it truly was a good school. Mr. Noble Norman was principal and Miss Jenkins, my sixth grade teacher, had to be one of the best in the system. It was in her class that I made the decision that I'd someday be a teacher "like Miss Jenkins".

Well, enough of my memories. I'm glad Oakhurst is still a vital neighborhood and that you gave me this opportunity to remember.

(Suzanne is now a member on the Fort Worth ISD Board. Her family lived where the Dwayne Littlepages now reside.)

Here is a list of the founding members of the Oakhurst Citizens on Patrol. The first of its kind in Fort Worth, the group formed to respond to an uptick in neighborhood crime in the early 1980s. The Fort Worth Police Department adopted the Oakhurst model, where citizens patrolled neighborhood streets and communicated with each other via radios, and fashioned its Citizens on Patrol (now called Code Blue) program after it. (AC.)

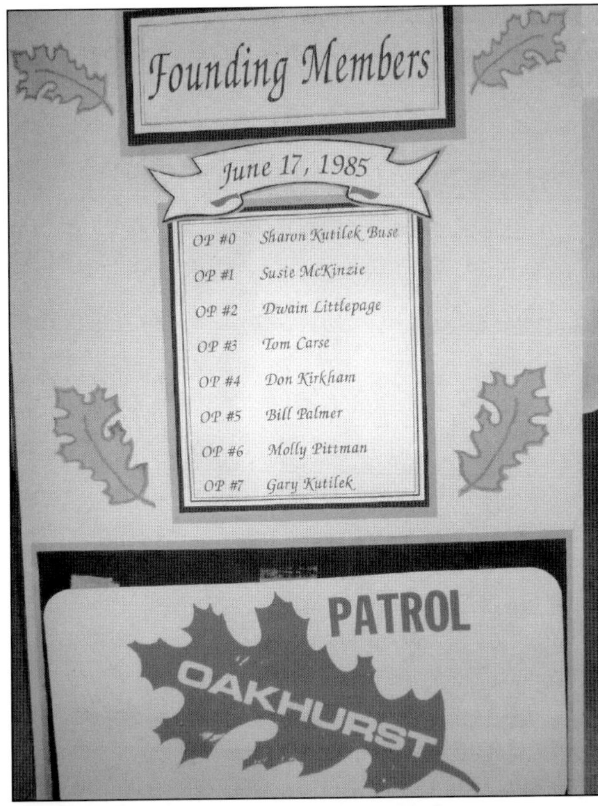

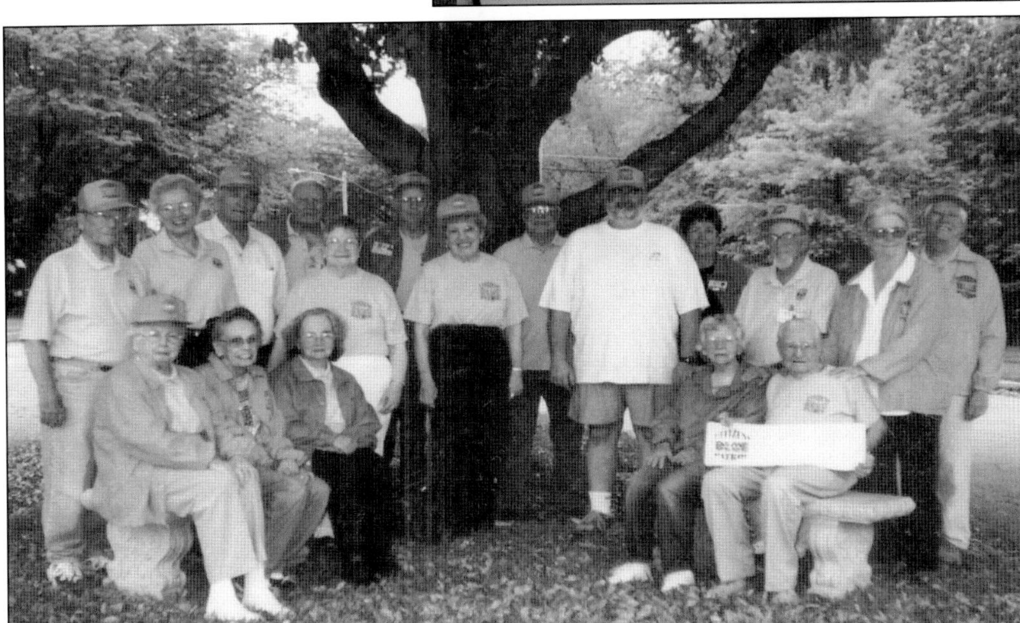

Oakhurst Neighborhood Association president and Oakhurst Citizens on Patrol member Margaret Bruce (standing, second from right) and other members of the Citizens on Patrol dedicated the flagpole at the Daisy Lane and North Sylvania Avenue entrance to the neighborhood in the 1990s. (Beverly Mason.)

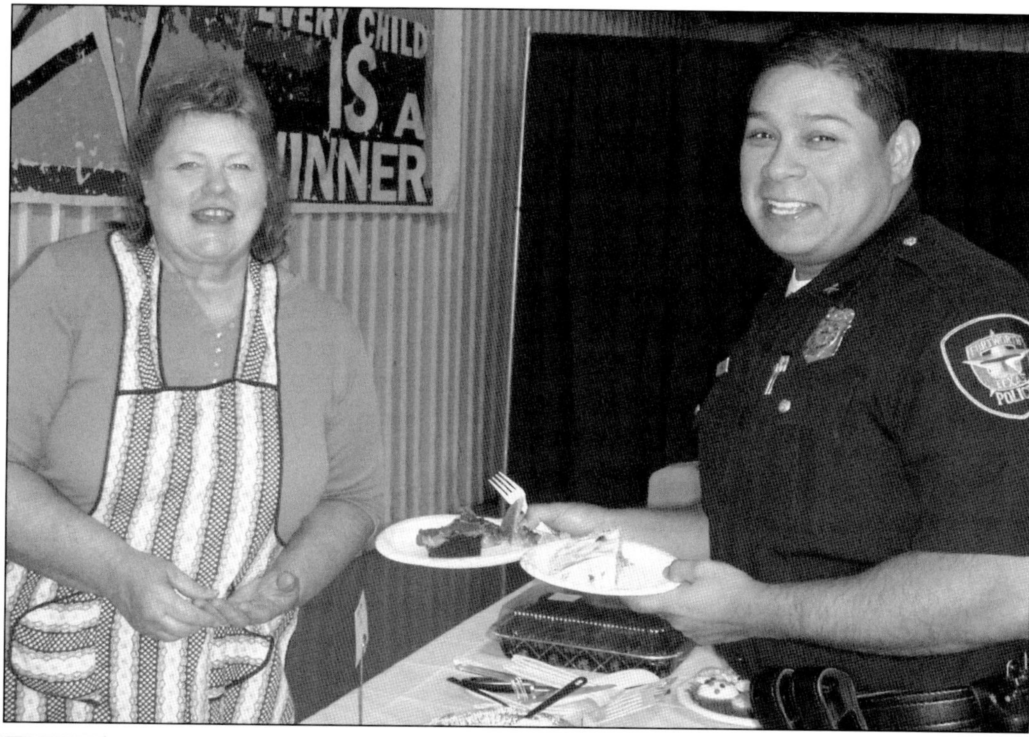

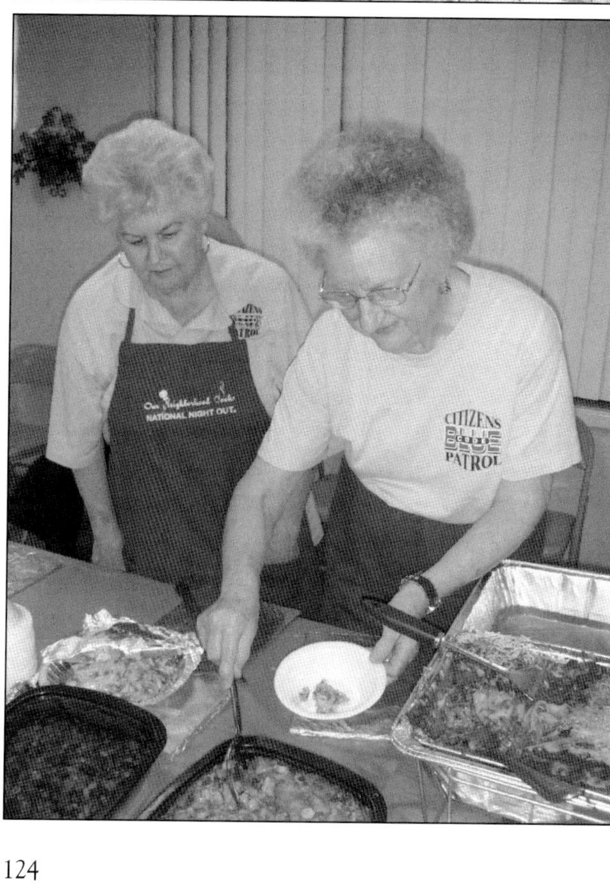

Above, Oakhurst Citizens on Patrol member Lynda Massey serves a Fort Worth patrol officer at the annual Oakhurst Citizens on Patrol Appreciation Dinner in the early 2000s. The Oakhurst patrol, with assistance from the Oakhurst Neighborhood Association (ONA), has feted firefighters and police officers with a homemade meal once a year for more than 25 years. In 2007, ONA and Citizens on Patrol won the Neighborhoods USA first-place award for best collaborative project for the dinner. (AC.)

Neighborhood and Oakhurst Citizens on Patrol stalwarts Duffy Lee (left) and Beverly Mason serve at the annual appreciation dinner in the early 2000s. Lee, the longtime chairman of ONA's welcoming committee, was legendary for taking homemade baked goods to new residents in Oakhurst. (AC.)

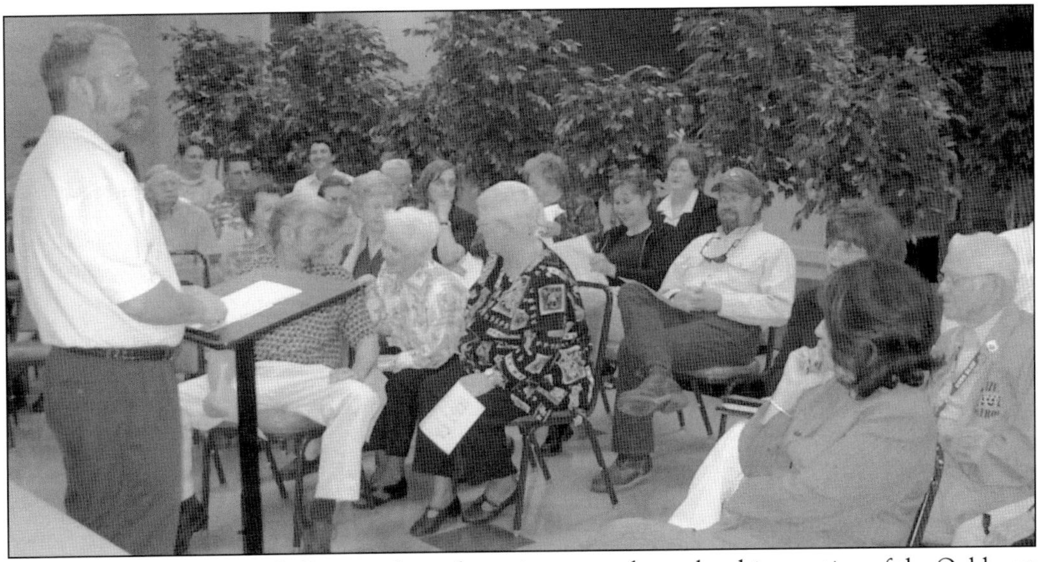

ONA president Preston Phillips speaks at the spring general membership meeting of the Oakhurst Neighborhood Association in 2004. ONA has consistently been one of the most active neighborhood associations in Fort Worth. *Fort Worth Weekly* dubbed it "most outstanding" as an organization advocating for neighborhood concerns. (Doyle Willis Jr.)

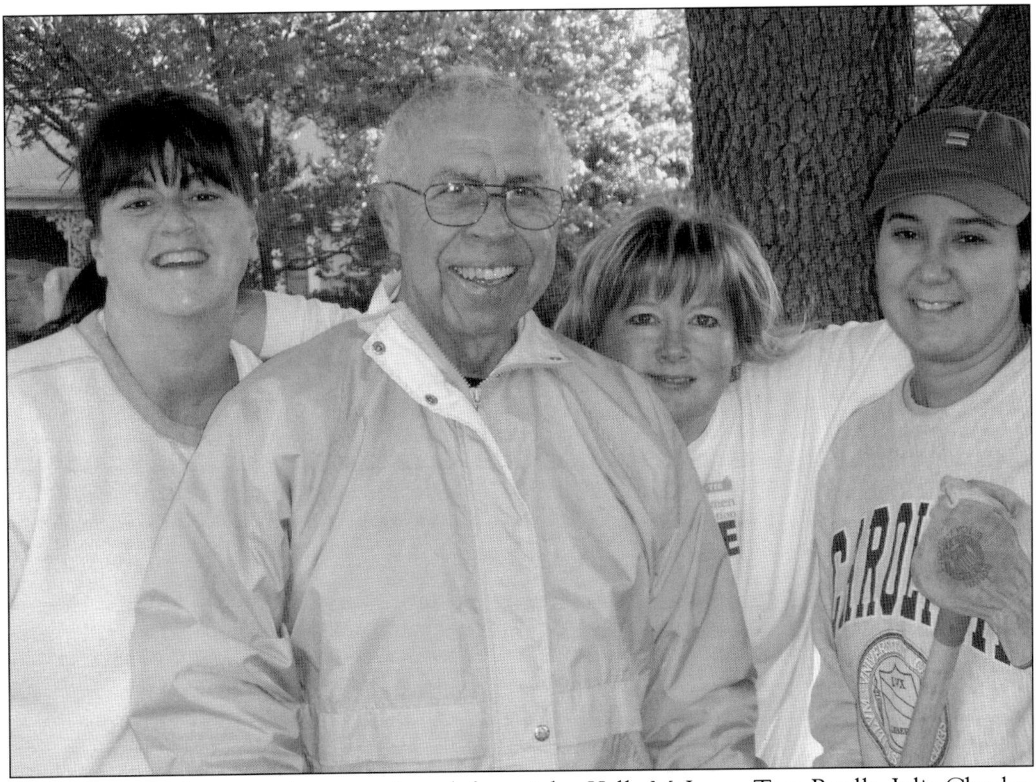

The ONA members seen here are, from left to right, Kelly McLean, Tom Boullt, Julie Charles, and Kathryn Omarkhail. They helped garden in the Oakhurst common area at Marigold Avenue and Bluebonnet Drive during the annual Cowtown Cleanup in the 2000s. (Doyle Willis Jr.)

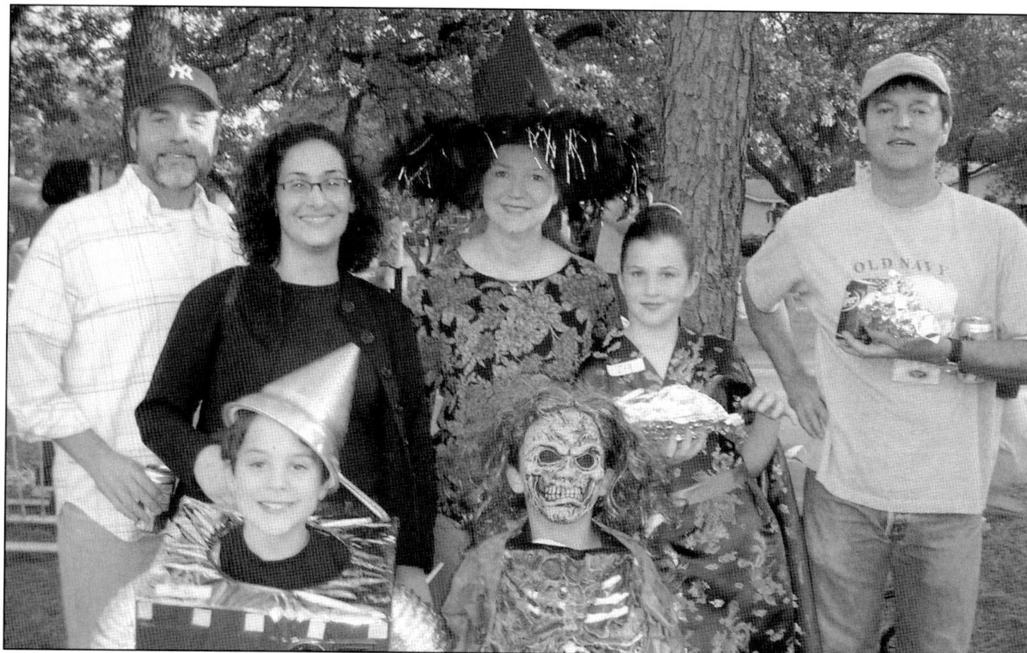

The Oakhurst Neighborhood Association's Halloween roast and costume contest for Oakhurst children is always held in Oakhurst Park. Attending the roast in 2006 are, from left to right, (first row) Josh Alford and Cameron Jensen; (second row) Brent and Michele Alford, Simianne and Muriel Hayden, and Fred Jensen. (AC.)

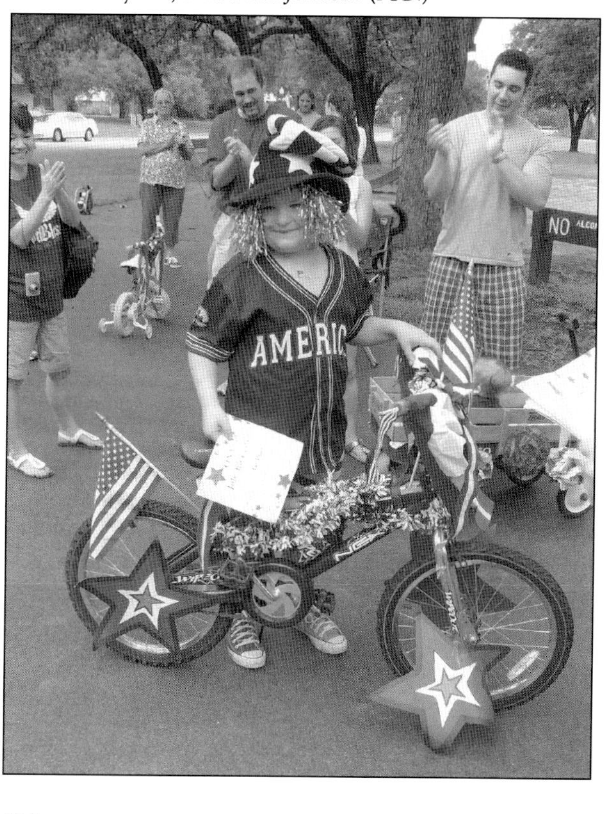

The Oakhurst Neighborhood Association hosts an annual Fourth of July picnic and parade. Here, Oakhurst resident Eliot Burk won the "Most Patriotic" award for his costume at the event, held in Oakhurst Park. (Doyle Willis Jr.)

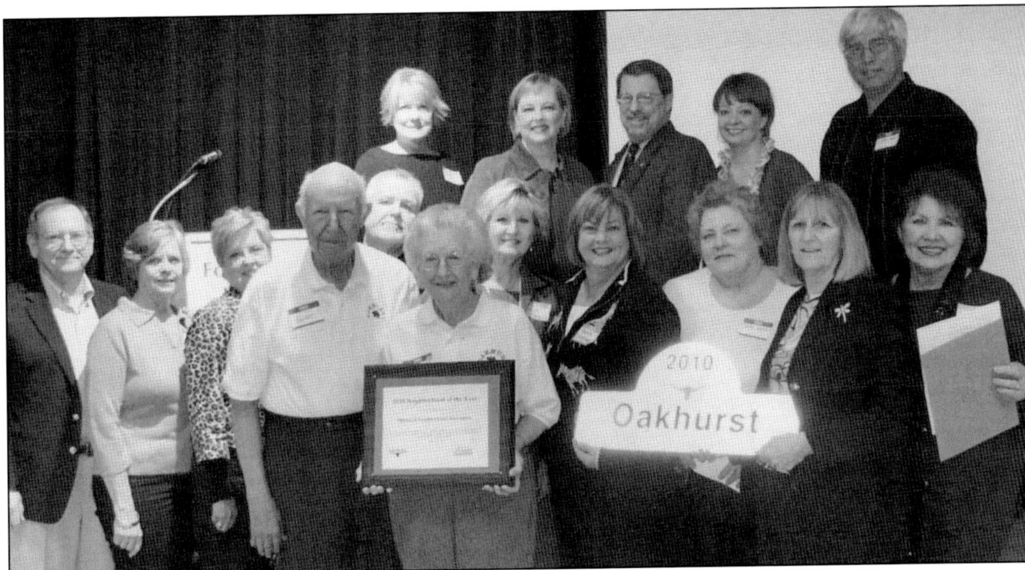

The Oakhurst Neighborhood Association is the only Fort Worth neighborhood organization to win the coveted Neighborhood of the Year Award twice. The first win was for 2006. Here, a large contingent of ONA members receives the award for the second time, for 2010. (Doyle Willis Jr.)

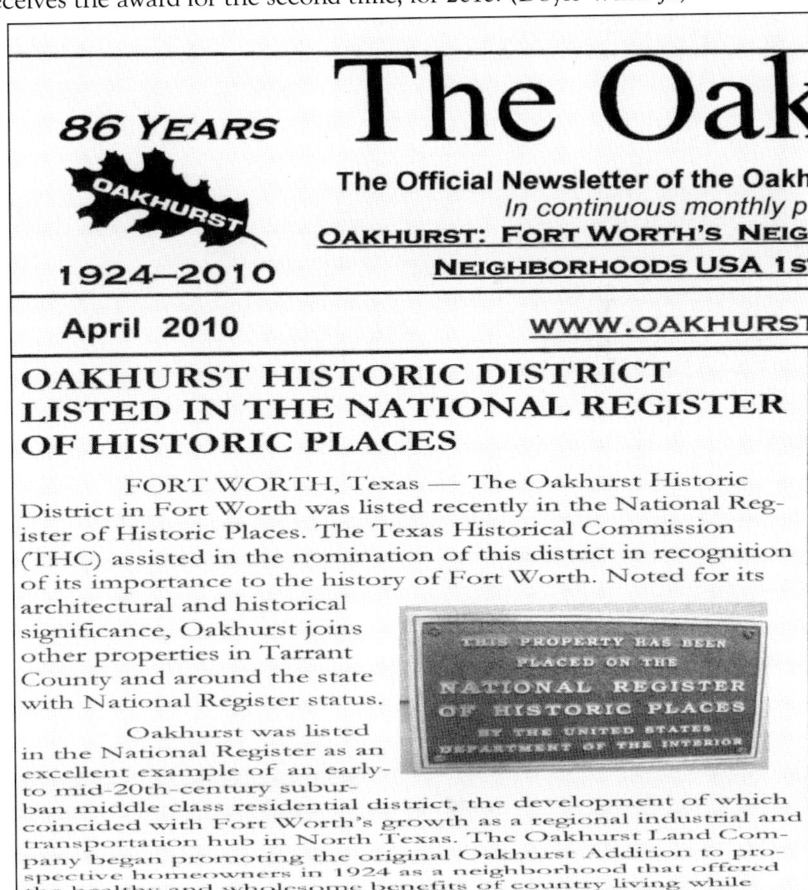

86 YEARS

OAKHURST

1924–2010

The Oak

The Official Newsletter of the Oakh

In continuous monthly p

OAKHURST: FORT WORTH'S NEIG

NEIGHBORHOODS USA 1S

April 2010

WWW.OAKHURST

OAKHURST HISTORIC DISTRICT LISTED IN THE NATIONAL REGISTER OF HISTORIC PLACES

FORT WORTH, Texas — The Oakhurst Historic District in Fort Worth was listed recently in the National Register of Historic Places. The Texas Historical Commission (THC) assisted in the nomination of this district in recognition of its importance to the history of Fort Worth. Noted for its architectural and historical significance, Oakhurst joins other properties in Tarrant County and around the state with National Register status.

Oakhurst was listed in the National Register as an excellent example of an early- to mid-20th-century suburban middle class residential district, the development of which coincided with Fort Worth's growth as a regional industrial and transportation hub in North Texas. The Oakhurst Land Company began promoting the original Oakhurst Addition to prospective homeowners in 1924 as a neighborhood that offered the healthy and wholesome benefits of country living while

The Oakhurst Historic District was officially listed in the National Register of Historic Places in February 2010. At the time of the listing, the district was the largest National Register residential district to be listed in Tarrant County in 20 years. (AC.)

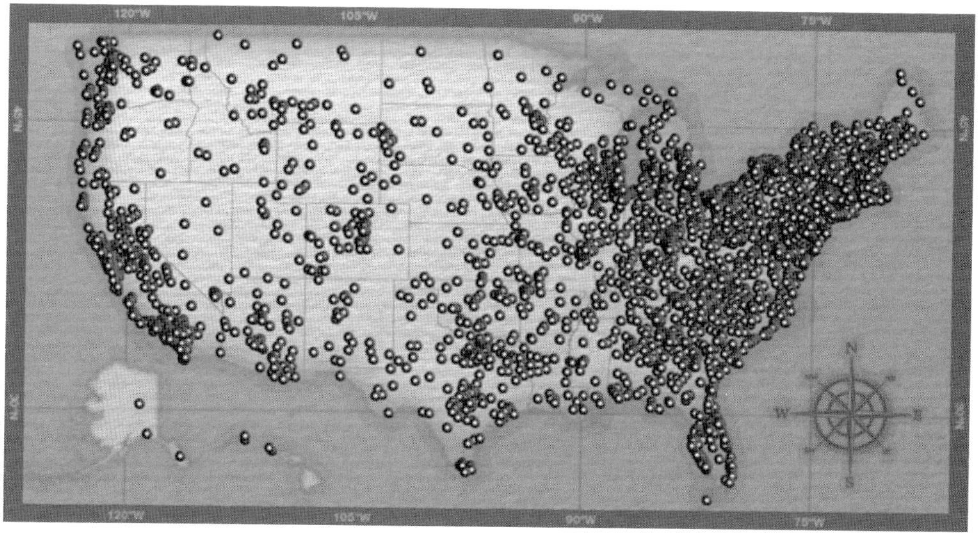